Better Homes and Gardens®

everymeal
easy

Meredith® Books
Des Moines, Iowa

Better Homes and Gardens® Every Meal Easy
Contributing Editor: Ellen Boeke
Contributing Designers: Angie Haupert Hoogensen,
    Rachael Thompson
Copy Chief: Doug Kouma
Copy Editor: Kevin Cox
Editorial Assistant: Sheri Cord
Book Production Manager: Mark Weaver
Contributing Proofreaders: Sarah Enticknap,
    Stephan Maras
Contributing Photographers: Marty Baldwin, Scott Little,
    Blaine Moats
Test Kitchen Director: Lynn Blanchard
Test Kitchen Product Supervisor: Jill Moberly
Test Kitchen Culinary Specialists: Marilyn Cornelius,
    Juliana Hale, Maryellyn Krantz, Colleen Weeden,
    Lori Wilson
Test Kitchen Nutrition Specialists: Elizabeth Burt, R.D.,
    L.D.; Laura Marzen, R.D., L.D.

Meredith® Books
Editorial Director: John Riha
Deputy Editor: Jennifer Darling
Managing Editor: Kathleen Armentrout
Brand Manager: Janell Pittman
Group Editor: Jan Miller
Associate Design Director: Erin Burns

Director, Marketing and Publicity: Amy Nichols
Executive Director, Sales: Ken Zagor
Director, Operations: George A. Susral
Director, Production: Douglas M. Johnston
Business Director: Janice Croat

Vice President and General Manager, SIM: Jeff Myers

Better Homes and Gardens® Magazine
Editor in Chief: Gayle Goodson Butler
Deputy Editor, Food and Entertaining: Nancy Wall Hopkins

Meredith Publishing Group
President: Jack Griffin
President, Better Homes and Gardens®: Andy Sareyan
Vice President, Corporate Sales: Michael Brownstein
Vice President, Manufacturing: Bruce Heston
Vice President, Consumer Marketing: David Ball
Director, Creative Services: Grover Kirkman
Consumer Product Marketing Director: Steve Swanson
Consumer Product Marketing Manager: Wendy Merical
Business Director: Jim Leonard

Meredith Corporation
Chairman of the Board: William T. Kerr
President and Chief Executive Officer: Stephen M. Lacy

In Memoriam: E.T. Meredith III (1933–2003)

All of us at Meredith® Books
are dedicated to providing you
with information and ideas to
enhance your life. We welcome
your comments and sugges-
tions. Write to us at: Meredith
Books Editorial Department,
1716 Locust St.,
Des Moines, IA 50309-3023.

Cover Photography:
Front cover: Chicken and
Sausage Gumbo (page 53)
Photographer:
Kritsada Panichgul

Our seal assures you that every
recipe in *Every Meal Easy* has
been tested in the Better Homes
and Gardens® Test Kitchen.
This means that each recipe
is practical and reliable, and
meets our high standards of
taste appeal. We guarantee
your satisfaction with this
book for as long as you own it.

We all know how important it is for our families to join together at mealtime, but the reality of our hectic lives makes that a challenge. We designed this collection of recipes— 332 of them—to help meet that challenge.

You'll find delicious ideas for everything from breakfast entrées to Sunday dinners that can involve the whole family. When you're on the run, put together crumb-free wraps or energy-packed snacks—perfect for those days when "dinner" must be eaten in the car or at a soccer game. Or breathe a sigh of relief when you come home on a weeknight to steaming slow cooker dishes that are ready to eat when you and the rest of the gang are. You'll even find hearty make-ahead recipes that you can refrigerate or freeze, then pop into the oven at the end of a frantic day.

At meal's end, surprise the people at your table with a yummy dessert. Our sweet treats will put a smile on everyone's face—yet will take only minutes to prepare.

With all the choices in *Every Meal Easy,* you'll find it simple to make satisfying meals that are easy, wholesome, and pleasing to even the pickiest eater in your family. Enjoy!

Autumn Vegetable Pilaf, page 152

{contents}

32

175

165

87

breakfast anytime

Strawberry-Stuffed French Toast
Prep: 20 min.   **Bake:** 15 min.

    Nonstick cooking spray
 4 purchased croissants, split
 1 8-ounce tub light cream cheese spread
    with strawberries
 2 eggs, lightly beaten
 ½ cup milk
 ½ teaspoon ground cinnamon
    Powdered sugar
    Fresh strawberries
    Maple syrup, warmed

1. Preheat oven to 375°F. Line a shallow baking pan with foil. Lightly coat the foil with cooking spray; set pan aside.

2. Spread cream cheese evenly over cut sides of the croissants. Place cut sides back together. In a shallow dish, whisk together the eggs, milk, and cinnamon. Dip each filled croissant in the egg mixture for 30 seconds, coating both sides. Place in prepared baking pan.

3. Bake about 15 minutes or until brown and heated through. Sprinkle with powdered sugar. Serve French toast warm with fresh strawberries and warm maple syrup. Makes 4 servings.

Per serving: 522 cal., 29 g fat (17 g sat. fat), 209 mg chol., 454 mg sodium, 53 g carbo., 3 g fiber, 13 g pro.

Breakfast isn't just for the a.m. anymore. Enjoy breakfast entrées for dinner or **try a muffin,** bread, or smoothie as a satisfying snack.

Granola French Toast

Start to Finish: 40 min.

  3   eggs, lightly beaten
  ¾   cup milk
  1   tablespoon sugar
1½ teaspoons finely shredded orange peel
  ½   teaspoon vanilla
  ¼   teaspoon ground cinnamon
 12 bias slices baguette-style French bread
      (½ inch thick)
  2   tablespoons butter
  1   cup granola, coarsely crushed
  1   recipe Cinnamon Yogurt Sauce
      Maple syrup (optional)

1. In a shallow dish, whisk together the eggs, milk, sugar, orange peel, vanilla, and cinnamon. Dip bread slices into egg mixture, coating both sides.

2. In a large skillet or on a griddle, melt 1 tablespoon of the butter over medium heat; add half of the dipped bread slices. Sprinkle some of the granola on top of each slice of bread in the skillet, pressing gently with spatula so the granola sticks. Cook for 2 to 3 minutes or until bottom is golden brown. Flip each slice, pressing lightly with the spatula. Cook about 2 minutes more or until golden brown. When removing from pan, flip each slice so the granola side is on top. Repeat with remaining butter, bread slices, and granola. Serve immediately with Cinnamon Yogurt Sauce and, if desired, maple syrup. Makes 4 servings.

Cinnamon Yogurt Sauce: In a small bowl, stir together one 6-ounce container plain nonfat yogurt; 1 tablespoon honey; ¼ teaspoon ground cinnamon, if desired; and ¼ teaspoon vanilla. Makes about ¾ cup.

Per serving: 501 cal., 16 g fat (7 g sat. fat), 183 mg chol., 516 mg sodium, 70 g carbo., 6 g fiber, 20 g pro.

No-Fry French Toast

Prep: 15 min.　**Bake:** 11 min.

　　Nonstick cooking spray
1　egg, lightly beaten
¾　cup fat-free milk
1　teaspoon vanilla
⅛　teaspoon ground cinnamon
8　slices Texas toast
¼　teaspoon finely shredded orange peel
½　cup orange juice
1　tablespoon honey
1　teaspoon cornstarch
⅛　teaspoon ground cinnamon
　　Powdered sugar (optional)

1. Preheat oven to 450°F. Coat a large baking sheet with cooking spray; set aside. In a shallow dish, whisk together the egg, milk, vanilla, and ⅛ teaspoon cinnamon. Cut each slice of Texas toast into 3 pieces. Soak the bread pieces in egg mixture about 1 minute per side. Place pieces on the prepared baking sheet.

2. Bake about 6 minutes or until pieces are light brown. Turn pieces over; bake for 5 to 8 minutes more or until golden brown.

3. Meanwhile, for orange syrup, in a small saucepan, stir together the orange peel, orange juice, honey, cornstarch, and ⅛ teaspoon cinnamon. Cook and stir over medium heat until thickened and bubbly. Reduce the heat. Cook and stir for 2 minutes more.

4. If desired, sprinkle the French toast with powdered sugar. Serve the toast with orange syrup for dipping. Makes 4 servings.

Per serving: 178 cal., 4 g fat (0 g sat. fat), 103 mg chol., 267 mg sodium, 29 g carbo., 0 g fiber, 9 g pro.

French Toast Casserole

Prep: 20 min.　**Chill:** 4 hr.　**Bake:** 40 min.
Stand: 15 min.

1　cup packed brown sugar
½　cup butter
2　tablespoons light-colored corn syrup
1　1-pound loaf unsliced cinnamon bread, sliced 1 inch thick
8　eggs, lightly beaten
3　cups half-and-half or light cream
2　teaspoons vanilla
½　teaspoon salt
1　tablespoon orange liqueur (optional)

1. In a medium saucepan, combine brown sugar, butter, and corn syrup; cook and stir over medium heat until mixture comes to a boil. Boil for 1 minute. Pour into a 3-quart rectangular baking dish.

2. Arrange bread slices on top of brown sugar mixture. In a large bowl, whisk together eggs, half-and-half, vanilla, and salt; pour over bread slices. Cover and chill for 4 to 24 hours.

3. Preheat oven to 350°F. Let baking dish stand at room temperature while oven preheats. Bake for 40 to 45 minutes or until top is brown and puffed and a knife inserted near the center comes out clean. Let stand for 15 minutes before serving. If desired, drizzle with orange liqueur. Makes 8 servings.

Per serving: 579 cal., 30 g fat (16 g sat. fat), 279 mg chol., 692 mg sodium, 65 g carbo., 1 g fiber, 14 g pro.

Waffle-wiches

Start to Finish: 5 min.

¼   cup peanut butter
2   frozen waffles, toasted
2   tablespoons honey
2   tablespoons raisins

1. Spread peanut butter on one of the toasted waffles. Drizzle with honey and sprinkle with raisins. Top with remaining waffle. If desired, cut into quarters. Makes 2 servings.

Per serving: 367 cal., 19 g fat (4 g sat. fat), 11 mg chol., 411 mg sodium, 44 g carbo., 3 g fiber, 10 g pro.

Sausage and Egg Sandwiches

Prep: 10 min. **Bake:** 12 min. **Cook:** 5 min.

4   low-fat, reduced-sodium sausage patties
2   tablespoons mayonnaise
1   tablespoon honey mustard
3   eggs
2   tablespoons water
⅛   teaspoon salt
   Dash ground black pepper
   Nonstick cooking spray
4   English muffins, split and toasted
4   slices Colby and Monterey Jack cheese

1. Preheat oven to 350°F. Place sausage patties in a shallow baking pan. Bake about 10 minutes or until heated through.

2. Meanwhile, in a small bowl, stir together mayonnaise and mustard; set aside In a small bowl, whisk together eggs, water, salt, and pepper. Coat an 8-inch nonstick skillet with cooking spray. Heat over medium-high heat until hot. Add egg mixture to skillet; reduce heat to medium. Immediately begin stirring egg mixture gently but continuously with a spatula until mixture resembles small pieces of cooked egg surrounded by liquid egg. Stop stirring; cook for 30 to 60 seconds more or until egg mixture is set but still moist.

3. Divide egg mixture into 4 portions. For each sandwich, spread bottom halves of muffins evenly with the mayonnaise mixture. Top each with egg portion, sausage patty, and cheese slice. Place muffin bottoms on baking sheet and return to oven for 2 to 3 minutes or until cheese melts. Add muffin tops. Makes 4 servings.

Per serving: 336 cal., 15 g fat (8 g sat. fat), 195 mg chol., 782 mg sodium, 29 g carbo., 2 g fiber, 18 g pro.

Breakfast Burritos

Start to Finish: 20 min.

4   strips turkey bacon* or bacon, chopped
¼   cup chopped, seeded green sweet pepper
⅛   teaspoon salt
⅛   teaspoon ground cumin
⅛   teaspoon crushed red pepper
8   eggs, lightly beaten
¼   cup milk
¼   cup chopped tomato
4   8-inch fat-free flour tortillas, warmed
½   cup shredded Monterey Jack cheese
   Light dairy sour cream and/or bottled salsa (optional)

1. In a large nonstick skillet, cook bacon and sweet pepper over medium heat until bacon is crisp, stirring occasionally; drain if necessary. Add salt, cumin, and crushed red pepper; cook and stir for 1 minute.

2. In a large bowl, whisk together eggs and milk. Add to skillet with bacon. Cook over medium heat, without stirring, until mixture begins to set on the bottom and around edge. With a spatula, lift and fold the egg mixture so the uncooked portion flows underneath. Cook for 2 to 3 minutes more or until egg mixture is cooked through but still moist. Remove from heat; stir in tomato.

3. Divide egg mixture among tortillas. Sprinkle with cheese. Roll up tortillas. If desired, serve with sour cream and salsa. Makes 4 servings.

*If using turkey bacon, coat skillet with nonstick cooking spray before cooking.

Per serving: 337 cal., 17 g fat (7 g sat. fat), 452 mg chol., 706 mg sodium, 26 g carbo., 8 g fiber, 23 g pro.

Sausage and Egg Sandwiches

{cracking the egg code}

- A nonstick skillet is best for cooking eggs.
- Make sure the skillet is good and hot before adding eggs. A drop of water should sizzle.
- Use a heat-resistant rubber scraper or spatula to stir and remove eggs.

Polenta with Sausage and Eggs

Start to Finish: 30 min.

½ of a 16-ounce tube refrigerated cooked polenta
Nonstick cooking spray
1 7-ounce package low-fat, reduced-sodium sausage links, halved crosswise
1 medium red sweet pepper, cut into bite-size strips
4 eggs
¼ cup purchased basil pesto

1. Slice or mash polenta and cook according to package directions. Keep warm.

2. Coat a large skillet with nonstick cooking spray. Add sausage and sweet pepper; cook and stir over medium-high heat about 4 minutes or until pepper is tender. Remove from skillet and keep warm.

3. Break eggs into skillet. Reduce heat to medium. When whites are set, add 1 to 2 teaspoons water to skillet. Cover skillet and cook eggs for 3 to 4 minutes or until yolks begin to thicken but are not hard. Transfer eggs to serving platter. Return sausage mixture to skillet. Stir in pesto and heat through. Serve eggs with sausage mixture and polenta. Makes 4 servings.

Per serving: 304 cal., 17 g fat (2 g sat. fat), 238 mg chol., 698 mg sodium, 16 g carbo., 2 g fiber, 17 g pro

Skillet Migas

Skillet Migas

Prep: 30 min. **Bake:** 30 min.

  8 ounces spicy bulk sausage or chorizo
  ½ cup chopped green sweet pepper (1 small)
  ¼ cup chopped red onion
  2 cloves garlic, minced
  5 large eggs, lightly beaten
  1½ cups lightly crushed corn tortilla chips
     (about 4 to 5 ounces)
  ½ cup bottled salsa
  1 small tomato, seeded and chopped (⅓ cup)
     (optional)
  1 4.5-ounce can diced green chile peppers,
     drained (optional)
  3 tablespoons snipped fresh cilantro
  1½ cups shredded cheddar cheese (6 ounces)
     Dairy sour cream
     Lime wedges

  1. Preheat oven to 350°F. In a 12-inch ovenproof skillet, combine sausage, sweet pepper, onion, and garlic. Cook over medium heat until sausage is brown and vegetables are tender, stirring to break up sausage. Drain off fat. Set aside.

  2. In a large bowl, stir together the eggs, crushed tortilla chips, salsa, tomato (if desired), green chiles (if desired), cilantro, and 1 cup of the cheese. Stir in the sausage mixture. Pour into skillet.

  3. Bake about 20 minutes or until egg mixture is almost set. Sprinkle with remaining ½ cup cheese; bake 10 minutes more or until cheese is golden and egg mixture is set and still shiny. Top each serving with sour cream. Serve with lime wedges. Makes 8 to 10 servings.

  Per serving: 212 cal., 25 g fat (10 g sat. fat), 156 mg chol., 317 mg sodium, 12 g carbo., 1 g fiber, 17 g pro.

Frittata with Cheese

Start to Finish: 25 min.

  8 eggs, lightly beaten
  ½ cup milk
  1 tablespoon snipped fresh herb* or
     1 teaspoon dried herb, crushed
  ¼ teaspoon salt
  ⅛ teaspoon ground black pepper
  2 tablespoons olive oil
  1 cup cut-up vegetables**
  ½ to 1 cup cut-up meat***
  ¼ to ½ cup shredded or crumbled cheese****
     (1 to 2 ounces)

  1. In a medium bowl, stir together eggs, milk, herb, salt, and pepper; set aside. In a large broiler-proof skillet, heat oil over medium heat; add vegetables. Cook and stir for time directed below or until vegetables are crisp-tender, stirring occasionally. Add meat to skillet.

  2. Pour egg mixture over vegetables and meat in skillet. Cook over medium heat. As mixture sets, run a spatula around edge of skillet, lifting egg mixture so uncooked portion flows underneath. Continue cooking and lifting edges until egg mixture is almost set (surface will be moist). Sprinkle with cheese.

  3. Place the skillet under broiler 4 to 5 inches from heat. Broil for 1 to 2 minutes or until top is just set and cheese melts. Makes 4 servings.

  *Herbs: basil, chives, cilantro, parsley

  **Vegetables: cook for 1 minute: cut-up marinated artichoke hearts. Cook for 2 to 4 minutes: shredded carrot, chopped asparagus, cooked cubed potato, chopped red or green sweet pepper, chopped green or red onion. Cook for 4 to 6 minutes: chopped zucchini or yellow squash, broccoli florets.

  ***Meats: ½ cup: crisp-cooked, drained, and crumbled bacon; chopped cooked ham or prosciutto; flaked smoked salmon; chopped pepperoni. 1 cup: cooked and drained bulk sausage (pork, Italian, chorizo); chopped smoked turkey; shredded deli-roasted chicken.

  ****Cheeses: ½ cup: shredded Swiss, shredded Gruyère, shredded cheddar (sharp or smoked), shredded American, shredded mozzarella (part-skim or smoked), shredded Gouda, shredded Edam, shredded Parmesan, shredded Colby-Jack. ¼ cup: crumbled feta, crumbled blue, shredded Monterey Jack with jalapeño peppers.

  Tip: You may use more than one vegetable or meat to equal the amount called for in the ingredient list.

  Per serving: 285 cal., 21 g fat (6 g sat. fat), 443 mg chol., 563 mg sodium, 4 g carbo., 1 g fiber, 19 g pro.

Hash Brown Omelet

Start to Finish: 15 min.

- 4 slices bacon, cut up
- 2 cups refrigerated shredded hash brown potatoes (about half of a 20-ounce package)
- ¼ cup chopped onion
- ¼ cup chopped green sweet pepper
- 4 eggs
- ¼ cup milk
- ½ teaspoon salt
  Dash ground black pepper
- 1 cup shredded cheddar cheese (4 ounces)
  Bias-sliced green onion (optional)

1. In a large skillet, cook bacon over medium-low heat until crisp. Using a slotted spoon, remove bacon from skillet and drain on paper towels; set aside. Drain skillet, reserving 2 tablespoons drippings in skillet.

2. In a large bowl, stir together potatoes, chopped onion, and sweet pepper. Pat potato mixture into the skillet. Cook, uncovered, over low heat about 7 minutes or until crisp and brown, turning once.

3. Meanwhile, in a small bowl, whisk together eggs, milk, salt, and black pepper. Pour egg mixture over potato mixture. Sprinkle with cheese and the reserved bacon. Cook, covered, over low heat for 5 to 7 minutes or until egg mixture is set. Run a spatula around edge of skillet to loosen omelet; fold omelet in half. Turn out of skillet onto plate. Cut into wedges. If desired, garnish with green onion. Makes 4 servings.

Per serving: 382 cal., 25 g fat (12 g sat. fat), 256 mg chol., 729 mg sodium, 20 g carbo., 1 g fiber, 19 g pro.

If you like, add sliced **ripe olives and mushrooms** with the sweet pepper.

Spicy Sicilian Strata

Prep: 35 min. **Chill:** 2 hr. **Bake:** 35 min. **Stand:** 10 min.

- **5** cups cubed French bread (1-inch cubes)
- **1** 3.5-ounce package sliced pepperoni, coarsely chopped
- **¼** cup pepperoncini salad peppers, drained, stemmed, and chopped
- **½** of a 10-ounce package frozen chopped spinach, thawed and well drained
- **¼** cup oil-packed dried tomatoes, drained and chopped
- **1** cup shredded Italian-blend cheese (4 ounces)
- **3** eggs, lightly beaten
- **1½** cups milk
- **1** teaspoon dried Italian seasoning, crushed
- **¼** teaspoon salt
- Dash cayenne pepper
- **¼** cup grated Parmesan cheese (1 ounce)

1. Preheat oven to 350°F. Spread bread cubes in a single layer in a 15×10×1-inch baking pan. Bake, uncovered, for 10 minutes, stirring once.

2. Place half of the bread cubes in a greased 2-quart square baking dish. Top with half of the pepperoni, half of the pepperoncini peppers, all of the spinach, and all of the tomatoes. Sprinkle with ½ cup of the Italian-blend cheese. Repeat layers with remaining bread, pepperoni, pepperoncini peppers, and Italian-blend cheese.

3. In a large bowl, whisk together eggs, milk, Italian seasoning, salt, and cayenne pepper. Slowly pour over layers in dish Press down lightly on top layer using the back of a large spoon. Sprinkle top with Parmesan cheese. Cover and chill for 2 to 24 hours.

4. Preheat oven to 350°F. Bake, uncovered, for 35 to 45 minutes or until a knife inserted near the center comes out clean (170°F). Let stand for 10 minutes before serving. Makes 6 servings.

Per serving: 316 cal., 18 g fat (8 g sat. fat), 146 mg chol., 1,006 mg sodium, 22 g carbo., 2 g fiber, 18 g pro.

Breakfast Pizza

Prep: 25 min. **Cook:** 20 min.

4	ounces plain or peppered bacon, diced
½	cup chopped green sweet pepper (1 small)
¼	cup sliced green onion (2)
1	12-inch Italian bread shell (Boboli®)
1	8-ounce tub cream cheese*
2	eggs
1	cup cubed cooked ham
1	cup shredded cheddar cheese (4 ounces)

1. Preheat oven to 400°F. In a large skillet, cook bacon over medium-low heat until crisp. Using a slotted spoon, remove bacon from skillet and drain on paper towels; set aside. Drain skillet, reserving about 1 tablespoon drippings in skillet. Add sweet pepper and green onion to reserved drippings; cook until tender. Drain and set aside.

2. Place pizza shell on a large baking sheet; set aside. In a small mixing bowl, beat cream cheese with an electric mixer just until smooth. Add eggs, one at a time, beating until combined. Spread cream cheese mixture over pizza shell. Sprinkle with bacon pieces, green pepper, and green onion. Top with ham.

3. Bake for 15 to 20 minutes or until cream cheese layer is set. Sprinkle with cheddar cheese. Bake for 3 to 4 minutes more or until cheese melts. Cut into wedges. Makes 6 to 8 servings.

*Note: If desired, use an herb-flavor cream cheese.

Tip: For quicker preparation, use precooked bacon; cook sweet pepper and onion in 1 tablespoon olive oil.

Shrimp Pizza: Prepare as above, except omit bacon. Substitute red sweet pepper for green sweet pepper and cook sweet pepper and onion in 1 tablespoon olive oil. Substitute 5 ounces cooked medium shrimp, peeled, deveined, and coarsely chopped (1 cup), or two 4-ounce cans small shrimp, drained, for ham, and shredded Mexican-blend cheese for the cheddar cheese. (If desired, use one 6-ounce can crab meat, drained, flaked, and cartilage removed for the shrimp.)

Mushroom-Artichoke Pizza: Omit bacon, sweet pepper, and green onion. In a large skillet, cook 2 cups fresh mushrooms, sliced, in 1 tablespoon olive oil over medium-high heat until golden. Continue as directed, substituting cooked mushrooms for ham and adding ½ cup marinated artichoke hearts, drained and coarsely chopped, and ½ cup slivered roasted red sweet pepper. Substitute shredded Italian-blend cheese for cheddar cheese.

Per serving: 410 cal., 27 g fat (13 g sat. fat), 126 mg chol., 635 mg sodium, 29 g carbo., 1 g fiber, 16 g pro.

As with any pizza, toy with the toppings to suit your taste.

Breakfast Pizza

Spicy Scrambled Eggs

Start to Finish: 10 min.

8	eggs
½	cup heavy cream or light cream
½	teaspoon salt
¼	teaspoon ground black pepper
1	tablespoon butter
½	cup shredded cheddar cheese (2 ounces)
¼	cup bottled hot salsa
2	teaspoons snipped fresh cilantro

1. In a medium bowl, whisk together eggs, cream, salt, and pepper. In a large skillet, melt butter over medium heat; pour in egg mixture. Cook over medium heat without stirring until mixture begins to set on the bottom and around edge.

3. Sprinkle cheese on egg mixture. With a spatula, lift and fold the partially cooked egg mixture so that the uncooked portion flows underneath. Continue cooking for 2 to 3 minutes or until egg mixture is cooked through but is still glossy and moist. Remove from heat.

4. In a small bowl, stir together salsa and cilantro. Serve eggs with salsa mixture. Makes 4 servings.

Per serving: 337 cal., 29 g fat (15 g sat. fat), 487 mg chol., 587 mg sodium, 2 g carbo., 0 g fiber, 17 g pro.

Hash Brown Casserole

Hash Brown Casserole

Prep: 20 min. **Bake:** 50 min. **Stand:** 10 min.

- 1   10.75-ounce can reduced-fat and reduced-sodium condensed cream of chicken soup
- 1   8-ounce carton light dairy sour cream
- ½   of a 30-ounce package frozen shredded hash brown potatoes (about 4 cups)
- 1   cup diced cooked ham (4 ounces)
- 1   cup cubed American cheese (4 ounces)
- ¼   cup chopped onion
- ⅛   teaspoon ground black pepper
- 1   cup cornflakes
- 3   tablespoons butter, melted

1. Preheat oven to 350°F. In a large bowl, stir together soup and sour cream. Stir in frozen potatoes, ham, cheese, onion, and pepper. Evenly spread the mixture in a 2-quart square baking dish. In a small bowl, combine cornflakes and butter. Sprinkle over potato mixture.

2. Bake for 50 to 55 minutes or until bubbly. Let stand for 10 minutes before serving. Makes 6 servings.

Per serving: 351 cal., 19 g fat (11 g sat. fat), 63 mg chol., 953 mg sodium, 35 g carbo., 2 g fiber, 13 g pro.

Sausage and Egg Alfredo Skillet

Start to Finish: 25 min.

 Nonstick cooking spray
- 1   7-ounce package low-fat, reduced-sodium sausage links
- ¼   cup sliced green onion (2)
- 6   eggs, lightly beaten
- ½   cup purchased reduced-fat Alfredo sauce
- 1½   teaspoons yellow mustard
- ½   cup shredded American cheese (2 ounces)

1. Coat a large skillet with nonstick cooking spray. Add sausage and green onion; cook and stir over medium heat until sausage is brown. Pour eggs over sausage mixture in skillet. Cook over medium heat, without stirring, until mixture begins to set on the bottom and around edge. With a spatula, lift and fold the egg mixture so the uncooked portion flows underneath. Cook for 2 to 3 minutes more or until egg mixture is cooked through but still moist. Remove from heat; cover and set aside.

2. In a small saucepan, stir together the Alfredo sauce and mustard. Heat over medium heat until bubbly. Stir in the cheese until melted. Cut egg mixture into wedges and serve with sauce. Makes 4 to 6 servings.

Per serving: 271 cal., 16 g fat (7 g sat. fat), 365 mg chol., 814 mg sodium, 5 g carbo., 0 g fiber, 23 g pro.

Egg dishes are so versatile. Use a different cheese, **try sausage instead of ham,** or toss in chopped veggies.

Buttermilk Pancakes

Prep: 15 min. **Cook:** 4 min. per batch

- $3\frac{1}{2}$ **cups all-purpose flour**
- $\frac{1}{4}$ **cup granulated sugar**
- 4 **teaspoons baking powder**
- 1 **teaspoon baking soda**
- $\frac{1}{2}$ **teaspoon salt**
- 2 **eggs, lightly beaten**
- 4 **cups buttermilk**
- $\frac{1}{3}$ **cup cooking oil**
  Desired fruit options (optional) (at right*)
  Desired syrup or pancake toppings (optional)

1. In a large bowl, stir together flour, sugar, baking powder, baking soda, and salt. In another large bowl, use a fork to combine eggs, buttermilk, and oil. Add egg mixture all at once to flour mixture. If desired, add fruit option. Stir just until moistened (batter should be slightly lumpy).

2. For standard-size pancakes, pour $\frac{1}{3}$ cup batter onto a hot, lightly greased griddle or heavy skillet. For dollar-size pancakes, use about 1 tablespoon batter. Cook over medium heat for 2 to 3 minutes on each side or until pancakes are golden brown, turning when tops of pancakes are bubbly and edges are slightly dry. Serve warm. If desired, top with syrup. Makes 20 to 24 standard-size pancakes or 120 dollar-size pancakes.

Tip: If you don't have buttermilk, place $\frac{1}{4}$ cup vinegar in a 4-cup glass measuring cup; add milk to equal 4 cups. Let stand for 5 minutes and proceed as above.

Per standard-size pancake: 141 cal., 5 g fat (1 g sat. fat), 23 mg chol., 228 mg sodium, 20 g carbo., 1 g fiber, 4 g pro.

Pancake Toppings

Simple Fruit Topping: In a microwave-safe medium bowl, stir together a 21-ounce can of cherry or blueberry pie filling and 2 tablespoons orange juice. If desired, microwave, covered, on 100 percent power (high) for 2 to $2\frac{1}{2}$ minutes or until heated through, stirring twice. Makes 2 cups.

Simple Sautéed Fruit: In a large skillet, melt 2 tablespoons butter over medium heat. Add 2 cups thinly sliced fresh fruit, such as apples, bananas, peaches, or pears (peeled, if desired) or frozen fruit and $\frac{1}{4}$ cup packed brown sugar to skillet. Cook and stir until sugar dissolves and fruit is tender. Makes about 2 cups.

{flapjack flips}

Whole Wheat Pancakes: Prepare Buttermilk Pancakes as directed, except substitute whole wheat flour for the all-purpose flour and packed brown sugar for the granulated sugar.

Cornmeal Pancakes: Prepare Buttermilk Pancakes as directed, except use $2\frac{1}{2}$ cups all-purpose flour and add 1 cup cornmeal.

Sausage Rolls: Prepare Buttermilk Pancakes. Roll finished pancakes around browned link sausages; secure with wooden toothpicks. Serve with a bowl of warm applesauce or syrup for dipping.

***Fruit Options:** Stir one of the following fruits into the pancake batter: 1 cup chopped fresh apple, apricot, peach, nectarine, or pear; 1 cup fresh or frozen blueberries; or $\frac{1}{2}$ cup chopped dried apple, pear, apricot, raisins, currants, dates, cranberries, blueberries, cherries, or mixed fruit.

Other Add-ins: Stir $\frac{1}{2}$ cup miniature milk chocolate baking pieces, chopped nuts, or granola into batter.

Easy Cinnamon Rolls

Start to Finish: 25 min.

- 1   8-ounce package refrigerated crescent roll dough (8)
- 1   tablespoon butter, melted
- 2   tablespoons granulated sugar
- 1   teaspoon ground cinnamon
- ½   cup powdered sugar
- ¼   teaspoon vanilla
- 1   to 2 teaspoons orange juice or milk

1. Preheat oven to 375°F. Grease an 8×1½- or 9×1½-inch round baking pan; set aside. Unroll dough (do not separate); press perforations to seal. Brush dough with melted butter. In a small bowl, stir together the granulated sugar and cinnamon; sprinkle over dough. Starting from a long side, roll up dough. Using a sharp knife, slice dough into eight 1½-inch pieces. Arrange pieces, cut sides up, in prepared pan, flattening each slightly.

2. Bake for 15 to 18 minutes or until golden. Remove and cool rolls slightly in pan on a wire rack. Remove from pan. In a small bowl, stir together powdered sugar, vanilla, and enough orange juice to make an icing of drizzling consistency. Drizzle over warm rolls. Serve warm. Makes 8 rolls.

Per roll: 155 cal., 7 g fat (2 g sat. fat), 4 mg chol., 241 mg sodium, 22 g carbo., 0 g fiber, 2 g pro.

If you think cinnamon rolls are **too much work**, think again. You can have these little gems on the table in half an hour.

Bagel Bites with Pumpkin Cream Cheese

Start to Finish: 15 min.

1   8-ounce package cream cheese, softened
½   cup canned pumpkin
2   tablespoons sugar
½   teaspoon pumpkin pie spice or
       ground cinnamon
       Bagels or English muffins, split and toasted
       Roasted sunflower seeds (optional)

1. In a medium bowl, beat cream cheese, pumpkin, sugar, and pumpkin pie spice with an electric mixer on medium speed until smooth. Cover and chill for up to 1 week.

2. To serve, quarter the bagel halves. Spread desired amount of the Pumpkin Cream Cheese on the cut sides of bagel pieces. If desired, sprinkle with sunflower seeds. Makes 1½ cups spread.

Per tablespoon: 39 cal., 3 g fat (2 g sat. fat), 10 mg chol., 28 mg sodium, 2 g carbo., 0 g fiber, 1 g pro.

Blueberry-Orange Scones

Prep: 20 min.   **Bake:** 12 min.

2¼   cups packaged biscuit mix
⅓   cup milk
1   egg, lightly beaten
1   teaspoon finely shredded orange peel
½   cup fresh blueberries
       Milk
       Sugar

1. Preheat oven to 400°F. In a large bowl, stir together biscuit mix, ⅓ cup milk, the egg, and orange peel until a soft dough forms. Carefully fold in the blueberries.

2. Turn dough out onto a lightly floured surface. Lightly knead 10 times or until nearly smooth. Pat dough into a 6-inch circle. Cut into 6 wedges. Arrange wedges on an ungreased baking sheet. Brush with additional milk and sprinkle lightly with sugar. Bake for 12 to 14 minutes or until golden. Serve warm. Makes 6 scones.

Per scone: 230 cal., 8 g fat (2 g sat. fat), 37 mg chol., 598 mg sodium, 33 g carbo., 1 g fiber, 5 g pro.

Fruit Salad Bowl

Prep: 30 min.

- 4 cups sliced fresh peaches, nectarines, plums, and/or apricots
- 1 to 2 cups assorted fresh berries, such as halved strawberries, blackberries, blueberries, and/or raspberries
- 1 to 2 cups 1-inch chunks honeydew melon or cantaloupe
- 1 to 2 tablespoons fresh lemon juice
- 1 to 2 tablespoons sugar (optional)
- 3 to 4 small cantaloupes, halved and seeded (optional)

1. Refrigerate a large glass serving bowl for 20 to 30 minutes. Add desired fruit to the bowl. Toss gently until fruits are just mixed. Sprinkle with lemon juice and sugar to taste. Toss gently until sugar is dissolved. To serve, if desired, spoon mixed fruits into cantaloupe halves. Makes 6 to 8 servings.

Per serving: 67 cal., 0 g fat (0 g sat. fat), 0 mg chol., 3 mg sodium, 17 g carbo., 3 g fiber, 1 g pro.

Down-to-Earth Granola

Prep: 15 min. **Bake:** 45 min.

- 4 cups regular rolled oats
- 1½ cups sliced almonds
- ½ cup packed brown sugar
- ½ teaspoon salt
- ½ teaspoon ground cinnamon
- ¼ cup cooking oil
- ¼ cup honey
- 1 teaspoon vanilla
- 1½ cups raisins or dried cranberries

1. Preheat oven to 300°F. In a large bowl, stir together oats, almonds, brown sugar, salt, and cinnamon. In a small saucepan, heat oil and honey just until warm. Stir in vanilla. Carefully pour honey mixture over oat mixture. Stir gently until combined.

2. Spread oats mixture evenly in a 15×10×1-inch baking pan. Bake for 45 minutes, stirring carefully every 15 minutes. Transfer pan to a wire rack; stir in raisins. Cool completely. Transfer granola to an airtight container or resealable plastic bags. Store at room temperature for 1 week or freeze for up to 3 months. Makes 24 servings (about ⅓ cup each).

Per serving: 174 cal., 8 g fat (1 g sat. fat), 0 mg chol., 51 mg sodium, 25 g carbo., 3 g fiber, 4 g pro.

Yam and Jam Muffins

Prep: 20 min. **Bake:** 18 min.

- 1¾ cups all-purpose flour
- ⅓ cup packed brown sugar
- 1½ teaspoons baking powder
- ½ teaspoon baking soda
- 1 teaspoon apple pie spice or ground cinnamon
- ¼ teaspoon salt
- ½ of a 17-ounce can sweet potatoes, drained
- 1 egg, lightly beaten
- ½ cup milk
- ⅓ cup fruit jam or preserves
- ¼ cup cooking oil

1. Preheat oven to 400°F. Lightly grease twelve 2½-inch muffin cups or line with paper bake cups; set aside. In a large bowl, stir together flour, brown sugar, baking powder, baking soda, apple pie spice, and salt. Make a well in center of the flour mixture; set aside.

2. In another bowl, mash the drained sweet potatoes with a fork. Stir in egg, milk, jam, and oil. Add sweet potato mixture all at once to flour mixture. Stir just until moistened (batter will be lumpy). Spoon batter into prepared muffin cups, filling each about three-fourths full.

3. Bake for 18 to 20 minutes or until golden and a wooden toothpick inserted in centers comes out clean. Cool in muffin cups on a wire rack for 5 minutes. Remove from muffin cups. Cool slightly. If desired, top with additional jam or preserves. Makes 12 muffins.

Per muffin: 215 cal., 6 g fat (1 g sat. fat), 19 mg chol., 174 mg sodium, 39 g carbo., 1 g fiber, 3 g pro.

Fruit Muesli

Start to Finish: 10 min.

- 4 cups multigrain cereal with rolled rye, oats, barley, and wheat
- 1 cup regular rolled oats
- ¾ cup chopped almonds or pecans, toasted
- 1 cup toasted wheat germ
- 1 6-ounce package dried cranberries
- ½ cup roasted sunflower seeds
- ½ cup dried banana chips, coarsely crushed

1. In a large airtight container, stir together all ingredients. Cover and refrigerate for up to 4 weeks. If desired, serve muesli with yogurt. Makes 12 servings (⅔ cup each).

Per serving: 346 cal., 12 g fat (3 g sat. fat), 1 mg chol., 48 mg sodium, 48 g carbo., 4 g fiber, 14 g pro.

Banana Oat Muffins

Prep: 20 min.   **Bake:** 14 min.   **Cool:** 5 min.

Nonstick cooking spray
1½   cups oat bran*
1   cup all-purpose flour
2   teaspoons baking powder
½   teaspoon salt
¼   teaspoon baking soda
1   egg, lightly beaten
¾   cup mashed ripe banana
½   cup fat-free milk
¼   cup honey
2   tablespoons cooking oil
½   cup semisweet chocolate pieces or raisins

1. Preheat oven to 400°F. Lightly coat the bottoms of twelve 2½-inch muffin cups with cooking spray; set aside. In a medium bowl, stir together oat bran, flour, baking powder, salt, and baking soda. Make a well in the center of the flour mixture; set aside.

2. In another bowl, stir together the egg, banana, milk, honey, and oil. Add banana mixture all at once to flour mixture. Stir just until moistened (batter will be lumpy). Fold in chocolate pieces. Spoon batter into prepared muffin cups, filling each about two-thirds full.

3. Bake for 14 to 16 minutes or until golden and a wooden toothpick inserted in centers comes out clean. Cool in muffin cups on a wire rack for 5 minutes. Remove from muffin cups; serve warm. Makes 12 muffins.

*If you don't have oat bran, place 2 cups regular rolled oats in a food processor. Process until finely ground.

Per muffin: 167 cal., 6 g fat (2 g sat. fat), 18 mg chol., 175 mg sodium, 30 g carbo., 3 g fiber, 4 g pro.

Buttermilk Coffee Cake

Buttermilk Coffee Cake

Prep: 15 min.　**Bake:** 25 min.

1½	cups all-purpose flour
1	cup packed brown sugar
⅓	cup butter
1	teaspoon baking powder
¼	teaspoon baking soda
¼	teaspoon ground cinnamon
¼	teaspoon ground nutmeg
½	cup buttermilk or sour milk*
1	egg, lightly beaten

1. Preheat oven to 375°F. Grease an 8×8×2-inch baking pan; set aside. In a medium bowl, stir together flour and brown sugar. Using a pastry blender, cut in butter until mixture resembles fine crumbs; set aside ½ cup of the crumb mixture. To remaining crumb mixture, stir in baking powder, baking soda, cinnamon, and nutmeg. Stir in buttermilk and egg.

2. Pour into prepared baking pan; spread evenly. Sprinkle with the reserved crumb mixture. Bake about 25 minutes or until a wooden toothpick inserted near the center comes out clean. Serve warm. Makes 9 servings.

Nutty Topping: Stir ⅓ cup chopped nuts into reserved crumb mixture.

*Tip: To make ½ cup sour milk, place 1½ teaspoons lemon juice or vinegar in a glass measuring cup. Add enough milk to make ½ cup total liquid; stir. Let mixture stand for 5 minutes before using.

Per serving: 246 cal., 8 g fat (5 g sat. fat), 43 mg chol., 184 mg sodium, 41 g carbo., 1 g fiber, 3 g pro.

Caramel Bubble Ring

Prep: 25 min.　**Bake:** 35 min.　**Stand:** 1 min.

⅓	cup chopped pecans
¾	cup sugar
4	teaspoons ground cinnamon
2	11-ounce packages (12 each) refrigerated breadsticks
⅓	cup butter, melted
½	cup caramel ice-cream topping
2	tablespoons maple-flavor syrup

1. Preheat oven to 350°F. Generously grease a 10-inch fluted tube pan. Sprinkle half of the pecans in the bottom of the prepared pan; set aside. In a small bowl, stir together sugar and cinnamon; set aside.

2. Separate each package of breadstick dough on the perforated lines into 6 spiral pieces, making 12 pieces total. Do not unroll. Cut the pieces in half crosswise. Dip each piece of dough into melted butter; roll in sugar mixture to coat. Arrange dough pieces in the prepared pan.

3. Sprinkle with remaining pecans. In a measuring cup, stir together caramel topping and syrup; drizzle over dough pieces in pan.

4. Bake about 35 minutes or until light brown, covering ring with foil for the last 10 minutes to prevent overbrowning.

5. Let stand for 1 minute. (If it stands for more than 1 minute, the ring will be difficult to remove from pan.) Invert onto a serving platter. Spoon any topping and nuts remaining in the pan onto rolls. Serve warm. Makes 10 to 12 servings.

Per serving: 367 cal., 13 g fat (4 g sat. fat), 17 mg chol. 567 mg sodium, 58 g carbo., 2 g fiber, 5 g pro.

{coffee cake stir-ins}

Stir one of the following into Buttermilk Coffee Cake batter:

❋ ¼ cup dried cherries and ¼ cup miniature semisweet baking pieces
❋ ½ cup raisins or other chopped dried fruit
❋ ¼ cup shredded coconut and ¼ cup chopped macadamia nuts
❋ ½ cup toffee bits
❋ ¼ cup chopped peanuts and ¼ cup miniature semisweet baking pieces
❋ 1 cup fresh blueberries or raspberries

Refrigerated breadsticks, biscuits, or cinnamon rolls help **jump start** quick breakfast breads.

Orange Biscuit Coffee Rolls

Prep: 15 min. **Bake:** 30 min. **Cool:** 30 min.

- 1¼ cups sugar
- 1 tablespoon finely shredded orange peel
- ⅓ cup orange juice
- ¼ cup butter, melted
- 2 10-ounce packages refrigerated biscuits (10 biscuits each)

1. Preheat oven to 375°F. Grease a 10-inch fluted tube pan. Set aside.

2. In a small bowl, stir together sugar and orange peel. In another small bowl, stir together orange juice and melted butter.

3. Separate biscuits. Dip each into the orange juice mixture, then roll in the sugar mixture.

4. Arrange the biscuits upright with flat sides together in the prepared pan. Pour any remaining orange juice mixture over biscuits.

5. Bake for 30 minutes. Cool in pan on a wire rack for 1 minute. (If they stand for more than 1 minute, the rolls will be difficult to remove.) Invert pan onto a serving platter; remove pan. Cool for 30 minutes. Serve warm. Makes 10 servings (20 biscuits).

Per serving: 240 cal., 6 g fat (2 g sat. fat), 13 mg chol., 395 mg sodium, 44 g carbo., 0 g fiber, 3 g pro.

Blueberry Breakfast Rolls

Prep: 15 min. **Bake:** 12 min. **Cool:** 5 min.

- 1 12.4-ounce package (8) refrigerated cinnamon rolls with icing
- 1 cup frozen blueberries, thawed and well-drained
- ⅓ cup blueberry preserves
- 1 teaspoon finely shredded lemon peel
- ¼ cup chopped pecans, toasted if desired
  Milk (optional)

1. Preheat oven to 375°F. Lightly grease sixteen 2½-inch muffin cups. Remove cinnamon rolls from package; set icing aside. Cut each cinnamon roll in half crosswise. Press a roll half in bottom and about ½ inch up side of each muffin cup.

2. In a small bowl, stir together blueberries, preserves, and lemon peel. Spoon filling into muffin cups. Sprinkle with pecans.

3. Bake about 12 minutes or until golden. Cool in muffin cups on a wire rack for 5 minutes. Remove from muffin cups and place on a wire rack.

4. Place icing from package in a small bowl. If necessary, stir in a little milk to make icing drizzling consistency. Drizzle icing over rolls. Serve warm. Makes 16 rolls.

Per roll: 110 cal., 4 g fat (1 g sat. fat), 0 mg chol., 172 mg sodium, 18 g carbo., 0 g fiber, 1 g pro.

Lemon Bread

Prep: 20 min.   **Bake:** 45 min.   **Cool:** 10 min.

1⅓	cups all-purpose flour
½	cup sugar
1½	teaspoons baking powder
¼	teaspoon salt
1	egg, lightly beaten
⅔	cup milk
3	tablespoons cooking oil, or butter or margarine, melted
2	teaspoons finely shredded lemon peel
1	tablespoon lemon juice
⅓	cup chopped, toasted almonds or walnuts
2	tablespoons lemon juice (optional)
1	tablespoon sugar (optional)

1. Preheat oven to 350°F. Grease the bottom and ½ inch up sides of a 7×4-inch loaf pan; set aside. In a medium bowl, stir together flour, the ½ cup sugar, the baking powder, and salt. Make a well in the center of the flour mixture; set aside.

2. In another bowl, stir together egg, milk, oil, lemon peel, and the 1 tablespoon lemon juice. Add egg mixture all at once to flour mixture. Stir just until moistened (batter will be lumpy). Fold in nuts. Spoon batter into prepared pan.

3. Bake for 45 to 50 minutes or until a wooden toothpick inserted near the center comes out clean. If desired, stir together the 2 tablespoons lemon juice and the 1 tablespoon sugar. Brush top of warm loaf with lemon-sugar mixture. Cool in pan on a wire rack for 10 minutes. Remove from pan; cool completely on wire rack. Wrap and store overnight before serving. Makes 1 loaf (12 slices).

Per slice: 141 cal., 6 g fat (1 g sat. fat), 19 mg chol., 106 mg sodium, 20 g carbo., 1 g fiber, 2 g pro.

Cinnamon-Sugar Biscuits

Prep: 25 min.   **Bake:** 10 min.

2¼   cups packaged biscuit mix
⅔   cup milk
2   tablespoons sugar
1   teaspoon ground cinnamon

1. Preheat oven to 400°F. Lightly coat eight 2½-inch muffin cups with nonstick cooking spray; set aside. In a medium bowl, stir together biscuit mix and milk until a soft dough forms.

2. Turn dough out onto a lightly floured surface. Lightly knead 10 times or until nearly smooth. Roll or pat dough into an 8-inch square. Sprinkle with sugar and cinnamon. Cut into sixteen 2-inch squares. Gently press 2 squares together, sugar sides up. Place in prepared muffin cups, sugar sides up.

3. Bake for 10 to 12 minutes or until golden. Remove from muffin cups; serve warm. Makes 8 biscuits.

Per biscuit: 159 cal., 6 g fat (2 g sat. fat), 2 mg chol., 426 mg sodium, 26 g carbo., 0 g fiber, 3 g pro.

Cinnamon Granola Loaf

Prep: 20 min.   **Rise:** 45 min.   **Bake:** 25 min.

3   tablespoons sugar
1   teaspoon ground cinnamon
1   1-pound loaf frozen sweet or white bread dough, thawed
2   tablespoons butter, softened
½   cup granola cereal, crushed
½   cup chopped almonds or pecans, toasted

1. Grease an 8×4×2-inch loaf pan; set aside. In a small bowl, combine sugar and cinnamon; set aside.

2. On a lightly floured surface, roll the thawed bread dough into a 10×8-inch rectangle. Spread 1 tablespoon of the softened butter over dough. Sprinkle with 2 tablespoons of the sugar mixture. Sprinkle with crushed granola and the nuts to within ½ inch of the edges. Starting from a short side, roll up tightly. Pinch seam to seal. Place, seam side down, in prepared pan.

3. Cover and let rise in a warm place until nearly double in size (45 to 60 minutes).

4. Preheat oven to 350°F. Bake about 25 minutes or until bread sounds hollow when tapped. Transfer from pan to a wire rack. Spread remaining 1 tablespoon butter over top and sprinkle with the remaining sugar mixture. Makes 1 loaf (12 slices).

Per slice: 172 cal., 6 g fat (2 g sat. fat), 5 mg chol., 208 mg sodium, 25 g carbo., 1 g fiber, 4 g pro.

Cinnamon gives its spicy bite to mixes and frozen dough for a sweet breakfast treat.

Cinnamon-Sugar Biscuits

Cinnamon Granola Loaf

Banana-Apple Butter Bread

Orange-Berry Smoothie

Start to Finish: 15 min.

- 3 medium oranges, peeled, seeded, and cut up
- 2 6-ounce containers vanilla low-fat yogurt
- 1 cup fresh strawberries, stems removed
- 1 medium banana, cut up
- 2 cups ice cubes

1. In a blender, combine oranges, yogurt, strawberries, and banana. Cover and blend until smooth, scraping down sides of blender as necessary. With blender running, gradually add ice cubes through hole in the top and blend until frothy. Pour into glasses. Makes 4 servings.

Per serving: 156 cal., 1 g fat (1 g sat. fat), 4 mg chol., 58 mg sodium, 33 g carbo., 4 g fiber, 6 g pro.

Fruit and Yogurt Smoothies

Start to Finish: 10 min.

- 1½ cups cut-up fresh fruit, such as strawberries or raspberries; cantaloupe or honeydew melon; papaya or kiwifruit
- 1 medium banana, cut up
- 1 6-ounce carton vanilla low-fat yogurt
- ¾ cup milk
  Honey (optional)
  Fruit slices (optional)

1. In a blender, combine cut-up fruit, banana, yogurt, and milk. Cover and blend until smooth, scraping down sides of blender as necessary. Pour into tall glasses. If desired, stir in some honey and garnish with additional fruit slices. Makes 4 servings.

Per serving: 103 cal., 2 g fat (1 g sat. fat), 6 mg chol., 48 mg sodium, 19 g carbo., 2 g fiber, 4 g pro.

Banana-Apple Butter Bread

Prep: 25 min.   **Bake:** 45 min.   **Cool:** 10 min.

- 1½ cups all-purpose flour
- 1½ teaspoons baking powder
- ½ teaspoon ground cinnamon
- ¼ teaspoon baking soda
- ¼ teaspoon salt
- ⅛ teaspoon ground nutmeg
- 2 eggs, lightly beaten
- ¾ cup sugar
- ½ cup mashed ripe banana
- ½ cup apple butter
- ¼ cup cooking oil

1. Preheat oven to 350°F. Grease and flour the bottom and ½ inch up sides of a 9×5-inch loaf pan; set aside. In a large bowl, stir together flour, baking powder, cinnamon, baking soda, salt, and nutmeg. Make a well in the center of the flour mixture; set aside.

2. In another bowl, stir together the eggs, sugar, banana, apple butter, and oil. Add egg mixture all at once to flour mixture. Stir just until moistened. Spoon batter into prepared pan.

3. Bake about 45 minutes or until a wooden toothpick inserted near the center comes out clean. Cool in pan on a wire rack for 10 minutes. Remove from pan; cool completely on a wire rack. Wrap and store overnight before serving. Makes 1 loaf (16 slices).

Per slice: 168 cal., 4 g fat (1 g sat. fat), 26 mg chol., 92 mg sodium, 31 g carbo., 1 g fiber, 2 g pro.

Blend 'n' Go

Start to Finish: 10 min.

- 1 cup sliced fresh or frozen fruit, such as peaches, berries, bananas, and/or orange sections
- 1 6- to 8-ounce carton vanilla low-fat yogurt
- ½ cup reduced-fat milk
- 1 tablespoon honey

1. In a blender, combine fruit, yogurt, milk, and honey. Cover and blend until smooth, scraping down sides of blender as necessary. Makes 1 serving.

Per serving: 342 cal., 5 g fat (3 g sat. fat), 18 mg chol., 163 mg sodium, 66 g carbo., 3 g fiber, 13 g pro.

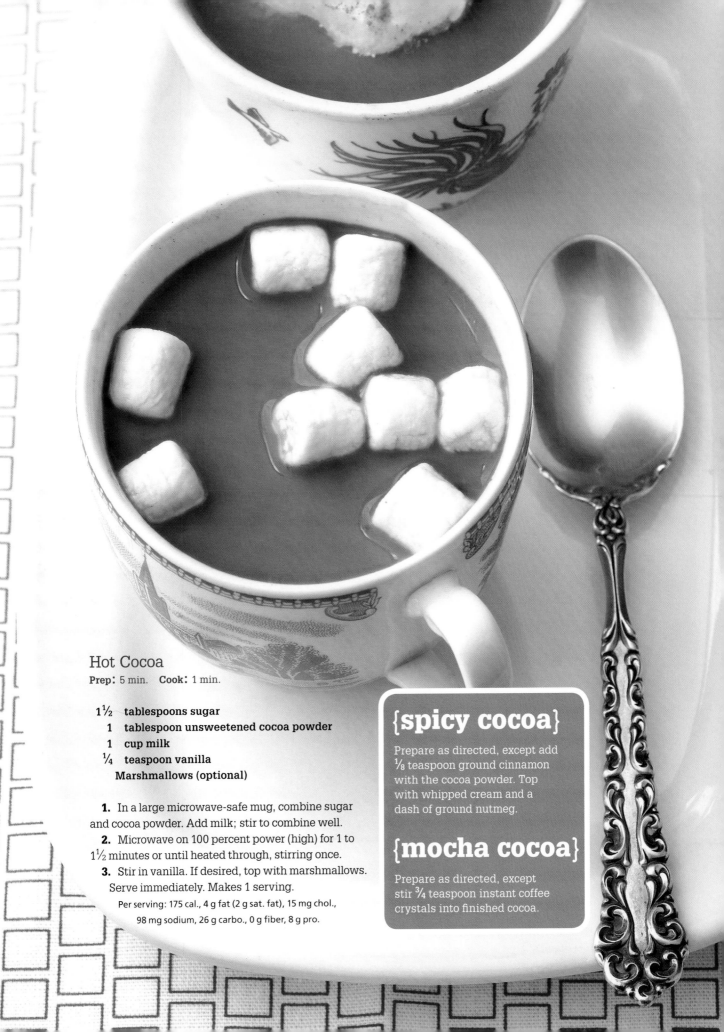

Hot Cocoa

Prep: 5 min.   **Cook:** 1 min.

1½	tablespoons sugar
1	tablespoon unsweetened cocoa powder
1	cup milk
¼	teaspoon vanilla
	Marshmallows (optional)

1. In a large microwave-safe mug, combine sugar and cocoa powder. Add milk; stir to combine well.

2. Microwave on 100 percent power (high) for 1 to 1½ minutes or until heated through, stirring once.

3. Stir in vanilla. If desired, top with marshmallows. Serve immediately. Makes 1 serving.

Per serving: 175 cal., 4 g fat (2 g sat. fat), 15 mg chol., 98 mg sodium, 26 g carbo., 0 g fiber, 8 g pro.

{spicy cocoa}

Prepare as directed, except add ⅛ teaspoon ground cinnamon with the cocoa powder. Top with whipped cream and a dash of ground nutmeg.

{mocha cocoa}

Prepare as directed, except stir ¾ teaspoon instant coffee crystals into finished cocoa.

snappy
sand

Deli-Style Submarines

wiches

Whether for lunch, dinner, or a snack, sandwiches are **mealtime workhorses**. They are filling, portable when you're on the go, and can suit any taste.

Deli-Style Submarines

Start to Finish: 20 min.

- 1 16-ounce loaf French bread
- ½ of an 8-ounce carton dairy sour cream ranch dip
- 1 cup shredded lettuce
- ¾ cup shredded carrot (1 large)
- 8 ounces thinly sliced cooked roast beef, ham, or turkey
- ½ of a medium cucumber, seeded and shredded
- 4 ounces thinly sliced mozzarella or provolone cheese

1. Cut the bread in half horizontally. Spread dip on cut sides of bread. On the bottom half of the bread, layer lettuce, carrot, roast beef, cucumber, and cheese. Replace top half of bread. Cut sandwich into 8 portions. Secure portions with toothpicks. Makes 8 servings.

To Make Ahead: Prepare as directed, except do not cut into portions. Wrap sandwich in plastic wrap and chill for up to 4 hours. Cut and serve as directed.

Tip: For for a lower-fat sandwich, substitute light dairy sour cream ranch dip for the regular sour cream dip.

Per serving: 250 cal., 6 g fat (3 g sat. fat), 24 mg chol., 743 mg sodium, 34 g carbo., 2 g fiber, 14 g pro.

Ham Focaccia Sandwiches

Start to Finish: 10 min.

- 1 individual Italian flatbread (focaccia) or ciabatta roll
- 1 tablespoon bottled creamy garlic or ranch salad dressing
- 1 slice deli-sliced cooked ham
- 2 cherry tomatoes, thinly sliced
- 1 slice provolone cheese
- 1 tablespoon chopped roasted red sweet peppers
- 1 leaf romaine lettuce

1. Slice the bread in half horizontally. Spread salad dressing on the cut side of the bottom half. On the bottom half, layer ham, tomatoes, provolone, sweet peppers, and romaine. Cover with top half of roll. Wrap and chill for up to 24 hours. Makes 1 sandwich.

Per sandwich: 461 cal., 19 g fat (7 g sat. fat), 45 mg chol., 1,235 mg sodium, 54 g carbo., 4 g fiber, 22 g pro.

New Orleans-Style Muffuletta

Prep: 10 min.   **Chill:** 4 hr.

½   cup coarsely chopped pitted ripe olives
½   cup chopped pimiento-stuffed green olives
1   tablespoon snipped fresh parsley
2   teaspoons lemon juice
½   teaspoon dried oregano, crushed
1   tablespoon olive oil
1   clove garlic, minced
1   16-ounce loaf ciabatta or unsliced French bread
6   lettuce leaves
3   ounces thinly sliced salami, pepperoni, or summer sausage
3   ounces thinly sliced cooked ham or turkey
6   ounces thinly sliced provolone, Swiss, or mozzarella cheese
1   or 2 medium tomatoes, thinly sliced
⅛   teaspoon coarsely ground black pepper

1. In a small bowl, stir together ripe olives, green olives, parsley, lemon juice, and oregano. Cover and chill for 4 to 24 hours.

2. Stir together olive oil and garlic. Horizontally split loaf of bread and hollow out inside of the top half, leaving a ¾-inch-thick shell.

3. Brush the bottom half of the bread with olive oil mixture. Top with lettuce, meats, cheese, and tomato slices. Sprinkle tomato slices with pepper. Stir olive mixture. Mound over tomato slices. Add top of bread. To serve, cut into six portions. Makes 6 sandwiches.

Italian-style Muffuletta: Prepare as above, except omit the olives, parsley, lemon juice, and oregano; omit step 1. Drain a 16-ounce jar of pickled mixed vegetables, reserving the liquid. Chop the vegetables, removing any stems if present. In a medium bowl, combine chopped vegetables; 2 tablespoons of the reserved liquid; ¼ cup chopped pimiento-stuffed green olives and/or pitted ripe olives; 1 clove garlic, minced; and 1 tablespoon olive oil. Assemble sandwich as above, spooning the pickled vegetable mixture over the tomato slices.

Per sandwich: 435 cal., 21 g fat (8 g sat. fat), 41 mg chol., 1,512 mg sodium, 43 g carbo., 3 g fiber, 20 g pro.

Ham Salad Sandwiches

Prep: 20 min.

- 2 cups finely chopped cooked ham
- 1 stalk celery, finely chopped (½ cup)
- ½ cup mayonnaise or salad dressing
- ¼ cup thinly sliced green onion (2)
- 1 tablespoon Dijon-style mustard
- ¼ teaspoon dried basil, crushed
- 6 croissants or 12 slices bread
- 1 4-ounce round Brie or Camembert cheese, sliced

1. In a medium bowl, stir together ham, celery, mayonnaise, green onion, mustard, and basil.

2. Cut croissants in half horizontally. Place a scant ½ cup ham salad on each croissant bottom. Divide cheese slices among sandwiches. Add croissant tops. Serve immediately. Makes 6 sandwiches.

Per sandwich: 526 cal., 37 g fat (14 g sat. fat), 96 mg chol., 1,451 mg sodium, 29 g carbo., 2 g fiber, 19 g pro.

Easy Fish Sandwiches

Start to Finish: 25 min.

- 4 frozen battered or breaded fish fillets
- 3 tablespoons mayonnaise or salad dressing
- 1 teaspoon finely shredded lime peel
- 2 teaspoons lime juice
- 1 cup packaged shredded cabbage with carrot (coleslaw mix) or shredded cabbage
- 4 3½- to 4-inch French-style or club rolls, split
- ½ cup bottled salsa
- ½ cup sliced pitted kalamata olives
- 2 tablespoons capers, drained

1. Cook fish according to package directions. Meanwhile, in a medium bowl, stir together mayonnaise, lime peel, and lime juice. Add cabbage; stir until combined. Set aside. Hollow out top halves of each roll, leaving a ½-inch-thick shell. Place a fish fillet on the bottom half of each roll. Top with cabbage mixture and salsa. Sprinkle with olives and capers. Add roll tops. Makes 4 sandwiches.

Per sandwich: 383 cal., 22 g fat (3 g sat. fat), 26 mg chol., 1,165 mg sodium, 37 g carbo., 3 g fiber, 12 g pro.

Shrimp Pinwheels

Shrimp Pinwheels

Prep: 30 min.   **Chill:** 1 hr.

- 1 ripe avocado, halved, seeded, and peeled
- ½ of an 8-ounce package cream cheese, softened
- ¼ cup ketchup
- 1 tablespoon prepared horseradish
- 1 teaspoon finely shredded lemon peel
- 2 tablespoons lemon juice
- ½ teaspoon chili powder
- 6 9- to 10-inch red, green, and/or plain flour tortillas
- 3 cups shredded spinach leaves
- ⅔ cup smoked almonds, chopped
- 10 ounces peeled and deveined cooked shrimp, chopped
  Party picks (optional)

1. In a medium bowl, mash avocado with a fork. Add cheese; stir until smooth. Stir in ketchup, horseradish, lemon peel, lemon juice, and chili powder.

2. On one tortilla, spread ¼ cup of the avocado mixture, leaving 1-inch border around the edges. Top with a layer of spinach. Sprinkle with a scant 2 tablespoons almonds and about ¼ cup shrimp. Roll up tightly. Secure with a party pick, if necessary, to prevent unrolling. Repeat with remaining tortillas, avocado mixture, spinach, almonds, and shrimp.

3. Place rolled tortillas on a tray or platter. Cover and chill for up to 4 hours before serving. To serve, cut each rolled tortilla into 1-inch slices, discarding ends. Secure with party picks, if necessary. Arrange slices on a serving platter. Makes about 36 slices.

Per serving: 82 cal., 4 g fat (1 g sat. fat), 19 mg chol., 137 mg sodium, 8 g carbo., 1 g fiber, 4 g pro.

Focaccia Turkey Sandwiches

Start to Finish: 15 min.

- 1 8- to 9-inch Italian flatbread (focaccia)
- ¼ to ½ cup reduced-calorie Thousand Island salad dressing
- 4 ounces sliced cooked turkey breast
- ¼ cup thinly sliced red onion
- 1 small tomato, sliced
- 4 leaves romaine lettuce

1. Cut focaccia into four wedges. Slice each wedge in half horizontally. Spread cut sides of bread with dressing. Layer bottom half of each focaccia wedge with turkey, onion, tomato, and lettuce. Add top half of each focaccia wedge. Makes 4 servings.

Per serving: 355 cal., 10 g fat (3 g sat. fat), 14 mg chol., 472 mg sodium, 53 g carbo., 5 g fiber, 16 g pro.

Carrot-Raisin PB Sandwiches

Start to Finish: 15 min.

- 8 slices white, whole wheat, or cinnamon bread
- ½ to ⅔ cup peanut butter
- ¼ cup raisins
- ¼ cup shredded carrot

1. Preheat broiler. Spread peanut butter over half of the bread slices; top with raisins, carrot, and remaining bread slices. Broil 4 inches from heat for 1 to 2 minutes.

Turn sandwiches over. Broil for 1 to 2 minutes more or until toasted. Cut sandwiches into triangles or squares. Makes 4 servings.

Per serving: 354 cal., 18 g fat (4 g sat. fat), 1 mg chol., 422 mg sodium, 39 g carbo., 4 g fiber, 13 g pro.

Triple-Decker Chicken Clubs

Start to Finish: 20 min.

- ⅔ cup light mayonnaise or salad dressing
- ¼ teaspoon ground black pepper
- 2 6-ounce packages refrigerated cooked chicken breast strips, chopped
- 1 cup chopped cored apple
- 8 leaves lettuce
- 12 slices whole wheat bread, toasted*
- 1 large tomato, sliced
- 8 slices packaged ready-to-serve cooked bacon

1. In a large bowl, combine mayonnaise and pepper. Stir in chicken and apple. Place a lettuce leaf on 4 of the toasted bread slices. Top lettuce with tomato slices and bacon, then another slice of bread. Top with remaining lettuce; spoon chicken mixture on lettuce. Top with remaining bread slices. Makes 4 sandwiches.

*For smaller sandwiches, use 8 slices bread and 4 leaves lettuce. Assemble sandwiches as directed, omitting the middle layer of bread and lettuce.

Per sandwich: 504 cal., 24 g fat (5 g sat. fat), 84 mg chol., 1,349 mg sodium, 44 g carbo., 6 g fiber, 32 g pro.

Carrot-Raisin PB Sandwiches

Triple-Decker Chicken Clubs

Parmesan Chicken Salad Sandwiches

Start to Finish: 10 min.

½   cup light mayonnaise or salad dressing
1   tablespoon lemon juice
2   teaspoons snipped fresh basil
2½   cups chopped cooked chicken or turkey
¼   cup grated Parmesan cheese
¼   cup thinly sliced green onion (2)
3   tablespoons finely chopped celery
    Salt and ground black pepper
12   slices whole wheat bread, toasted

1. For dressing, in a small bowl, stir together mayonnaise, lemon juice, and basil. Set aside.

2. For salad, in a medium bowl, combine chicken, Parmesan cheese, green onion, and celery. Pour dressing over chicken mixture; toss to coat. Season to taste with salt and pepper. Serve immediately or cover and chill in the refrigerator for 1 to 4 hours. Serve chicken salad on toasted wheat bread. Makes 6 sandwiches.

Per sandwich: 194 cal., 12 g fat (3 g sat. fat), 61 mg chol., 366 mg sodium, 2 g carbo., 0 g fiber, 18 g pro.

{sandwich salads}

❈ Add crunch to chicken salad with chopped celery, shredded carrots, sliced or slivered almonds, chopped apple, or even water chestnuts.

❈ Sweeten a sandwich salad with dried cherries, raisins, or other dried fruit. Or try sliced grapes or whole berries.

❈ Sandwich salads don't have to go between slices of bread. Wrap them in a lettuce leaf, spoon them over fresh greens, or fill an avocado or small cantaloupe half.

Basil Chicken Wraps

Start to Finish: 15 min.

- 4   8- or 9-inch plain flour tortillas or tomato- or spinach-flavor flour tortillas
- 1   recipe Basil Mayonnaise
      Fresh basil leaves
- 12 ounces thinly sliced cooked chicken or turkey, cut into thin strips
- $\frac{1}{2}$ cup roasted red sweet peppers, cut into thin strips

1. Place the stack of tortillas on foil; wrap tightly. Heat in a 350°F oven about 10 minutes or until warm.

2. Spread Basil Mayonnaise evenly over warm tortillas. Arrange basil leaves, chicken, and sweet peppers on tortillas. Roll up tortillas, folding in one side. Makes 4 wraps.

Basil Mayonnaise: Stir together $\frac{1}{2}$ cup light mayonnaise or salad dressing, 1 tablespoon snipped fresh basil, and 1 small clove garlic, minced. If desired, stir in $\frac{1}{8}$ teaspoon cayenne pepper. Makes about $\frac{1}{2}$ cup.

Per wrap: 366 cal., 15 g fat (3 g sat. fat), 44 mg chol., 1,330 mg sodium, 37 g carbo., 2 g fiber, 21 g pro.

Chicken and Hummus Wraps

Prep: 15 min.

- 1 7-ounce carton desired-flavor hummus or one 8-ounce tub cream cheese spread with garden vegetables
- 4 10-inch flour tortillas
- ⅓ cup plain low-fat yogurt or dairy sour cream
- 1 6-ounce package refrigerated cooked chicken breast strips
- ¾ cup coarsely chopped roma tomatoes (2 large)
- ¾ cup thinly sliced cucumber

1. Spread hummus evenly over tortillas; spread yogurt over hummus. Top with chicken, tomatoes, and cucumber. Roll up tortillas. Makes 4 wraps.

Per wrap: 288 cal., 9 g fat (2 g sat. fat), 31 mg chol., 713 mg sodium, 36 g carbo., 3 g fiber, 16 g pro.

Turkey and Tomato Wraps

Start to Finish: 15 min.

- 4 leaves butterhead lettuce (Bibb or Boston)
- 4 ounces very thinly sliced cooked turkey breast
- 2 teaspoons honey mustard or light mayonnaise or salad dressing
- 1 small roma tomato, halved and very thinly sliced

1. Place lettuce leaves on a flat surface. Cut leaves in half lengthwise and remove center vein.

2. Place ½ ounce of the turkey on each leaf just below the center. Spread honey mustard over turkey. Top with tomato slices. Roll up, starting from a short side. Secure with wooden toothpicks. Makes 8 wraps.

Per 2 wraps: 35 cal., 1 g fat (0 g sat. fat), 11 mg chol., 338 mg sodium, 3 g carbo., 0 g fiber, 5 g pro.

Roasted Turkey, Bacon, and Avocado Wraps

Start to Finish: 20 min.

- 1 ripe avocado
- 2 tablespoons freshly squeezed lime juice
   Salt and ground black pepper
- 10 ounces cooked turkey breast, cut into bite-size strips
- 6 tablespoons light mayonnaise or salad dressing
- 4 flour tortillas (9 to 10 inches in diameter)
- 8 slices packaged ready-to-serve cooked bacon

1. Halve avocado lengthwise; remove and discard seed. Peel and slice halves lengthwise. Place slices in a small bowl; drizzle with 1 tablespoon of the lime juice and sprinkle with salt and pepper to taste.

2. In a medium bowl, toss turkey with the remaining 1 tablespoon lime juice and salt and pepper to taste.

3. Spread mayonnaise on one side of each tortilla, leaving a 1-inch border. Top mayonnaise with avocado, turkey, and bacon. Roll up tortillas while folding in the sides to completely enclose filling. Halve filled tortillas crosswise to serve. Makes 4 wraps.

Per wrap: 400 cal., 22 g fat (5 g sat. fat), 49 mg chol., 1,430 mg sodium, 31 g carbo., 4 g fiber, 20 g pro.

Roasted Turkey, Bacon, and Avocado Wraps

Crunchy Beef Wraps

Start to Finish: 20 min.

- 8 8-inch flour tortillas
- ¾ pound lean ground beef
- ½ cup chopped red or green onion
- 2 cups packaged shredded cabbage with carrot (coleslaw mix)
- 1 cup frozen whole kernel corn
- ¼ cup bottled barbecue sauce
- 1 teaspoon toasted sesame oil
   Barbecue sauce (optional)

1. Preheat oven to 350°F. Stack tortillas and wrap in foil. Heat in oven for 10 minutes to soften. Meanwhile, for filling, in a large skillet, cook ground beef and onion until meat is brown; drain well. Stir in cabbage mix and corn. Cover and cook about 4 minutes or until vegetables are tender, stirring once. Stir in barbecue sauce and sesame oil. Cook and stir until heated through.

2. Spoon ½ cup filling onto each tortilla below center. Fold bottom edge up and over filling. Fold opposite sides in, just until they meet. Roll up from bottom. If desired, serve with additional sauce. Makes 4 servings

Per serving: 388 cal., 14 g fat (5 g sat. fat), 54 mg chol., 409 mg sodium, 44 g carbo., 4 g fiber, 21 g pro.

Southwest Chicken Wraps

Start to Finish: 20 min.

- ½ of a 28-ounce package frozen cooked breaded chicken strips (about 24 strips)
- ½ of an 8-ounce tub light cream cheese
- 1 green onion, thinly sliced
- 1 tablespoon snipped fresh cilantro
- 6 7- to 8-inch flour tortillas
- 1 red sweet pepper, seeded and cut into bite-size strips
- ½ cup shredded reduced-fat or regular Monterey Jack cheese (2 ounces)
   Bottled salsa (optional)

1. Bake the chicken strips according to package directions.

2. Meanwhile, in a small bowl, stir together the cream cheese, green onion, and cilantro. Spread over tortillas. Top with pepper strips and cheese. Top with hot chicken strips. Roll up tortillas around filling. Cut in half to serve. Secure tortillas shut with toothpicks. If desired, serve with salsa. Makes 6 servings.

Per serving: 356 cal., 20 g fat (6 g sat. fat), 54 mg chol., 610 mg sodium, 27 g carbo., 1 g fiber, 18 g pro.

{burger bites}

❋ Buy the freshest ground meat you can. Always check the "sell by" date on the package.

❋ Store ground meat in the coldest part of the refrigerator for no more than two days.

❋ Freeze ground meat for longer storage but use it within four months for the best quality.

❋ Cook beef burgers to a doneness of 160°F and ground poultry to 165°F. Test doneness by sticking an instant-read thermometer into the side of the burger.

French Onion Burgers

Prep: 20 min.   **Broil:** 14 min.

1	tablespoon olive oil
3	cups sliced onion
¼	teaspoon salt
¾	teaspoon coarsely ground black pepper
1½	pounds lean ground beef
2	tablespoons Worcestershire sauce
2	cloves garlic, minced
¾	cup shredded regular or reduced-fat Swiss cheese (3 ounces)
4	¾-inch-thick slices French or Italian bread

1. In a large skillet, heat oil over medium heat. Add onion; cook about 10 minutes or until golden, stirring occasionally. Stir in salt and ¼ teaspoon of the pepper. Cover; keep warm.

2. Meanwhile, in a large bowl, combine beef, Worcestershire sauce, the remaining ½ teaspoon pepper, and the garlic; mix well. Shape the beef mixture into eight 4-inch-diameter patties. Top four of the patties evenly with the cheese. Top with remaining patties, pressing down lightly and sealing edges to enclose cheese.

3. Place burgers on the unheated rack of a broiler pan. Broil 4 inches from the heat for 14 to 18 minutes or until an instant-read thermometer inserted into the thickest part of the burger registers 160°F, turning once halfway through broiling.

4. Add bread slices to pan for the last 1 to 2 minutes of broiling or until toasted, turning once. Serve patties on toasted bread slices topped with onion mixture. Makes 4 burgers.

Per burger: 535 cal., 27 g fat (11 g sat. fat), 127 mg chol., 576 mg sodium, 32 g carbo., 2 g fiber, 40 g pro.

Chicken Dinner Burgers
Prep: 15 min. Cook: 12 min.

- 1 egg, lightly beaten
- ½ teaspoon salt
- ¼ teaspoon ground black pepper
- 1 pound uncooked lean ground chicken or turkey
- ¼ cup fine dry bread crumbs
- 1 tablespoon olive oil
- ¼ cup barbecue sauce
- 4 slices Texas toast or other thick-sliced bread
  Prepared coleslaw (optional)
  Pickle slices (optional)

1. In a medium bowl, combine egg, salt, and pepper. Add chicken and bread crumbs; mix well. Shape the chicken mixture into four ¾-inch-thick patties.

2. In a large nonstick skillet, cook patties over medium heat in hot oil about 10 minutes or until an instant-read thermometer inserted into the thickest part of the burger registers 165°F, turning once halfway through cooking. Brush patties on each side with barbecue sauce. Cook for 1 minute more on each side to glaze.

3. Place burgers on slices of Texas toast. If desired, top with a spoonful of coleslaw and a few pickle slices. Makes 4 burgers.

Per burger: 371 cal., 17 g fat (1 g sat. fat), 103 mg chol., 912 mg sodium, 27 g carbo., 0 g fiber, 28 g pro.

Meatball Hoagies
Start to Finish: 30 min.

- 1 medium onion, thinly sliced
- 1 medium red or green sweet pepper, seeded and cut into thin strips
- 1 tablespoon olive oil
- 16 ounces frozen cooked Italian meatballs
- 2 cups refrigerated marinara sauce
- ¼ teaspoon crushed red pepper
- 6 hoagie buns or ciabatta rolls, split
- 6 slices provolone cheese (6 ounces)

1. In a large saucepan, cook onion and sweet pepper in hot oil over medium heat for 4 to 5 minutes or until crisp-tender. Add meatballs, marinara sauce, and crushed red pepper. Bring to boiling; reduce heat. Simmer, covered, about 15 minutes or until the meatballs are heated through.

2. To serve, place provolone cheese on bottom halves of buns. Spoon meatball mixture over cheese. If desired, broil sandwiches 4 to 5 inches from heat for 1 to 2 minutes or until cheese melts. Makes 6 hoagies.

Per hoagie: 696 cal., 29 g fat (11 g sat. fat), 44 mg chol., 1,642 mg sodium, 84 g carbo., 7 g fiber, 26 g pro.

Great Grilled Burgers
Prep: 20 min. Grill: 15 min.

- 1½ pounds lean ground beef
- 1 teaspoon dried Italian seasoning, crushed
- ½ teaspoon salt
- ½ teaspoon ground black pepper
- ¼ cup finely chopped onion
- 2 slices Edam, cheddar, or Monterey Jack cheese (2 ounces)
- 2 hamburger buns, split and toasted
  Desired toppers, such as lettuce leaves, tomato slices, onion slices, and/or pickles
  Ketchup and/or yellow mustard

1. In a large bowl, combine beef, Italian seasoning, salt, and pepper; mix well. Transfer half of the mixture to another bowl to use for the Mini Cheddar Burgers (recipe opposite). Add finely chopped onion to the remaining beef mixture in the bowl; mix well. Lightly shape beef mixture into two ¾-inch-thick patties.

2. For a charcoal grill, grill patties on the rack of an uncovered grill directly over medium heat for 14 to 18 minutes or until an instant-read thermometer inserted into the thickest part of the burger registers 160°F, turning once halfway through grilling. Top each burger with a slice of cheese; grill about 1 minute more or until cheese melts. (For a gas grill, preheat grill. Reduce heat to medium. Place patties on grill rack over heat. Cover and grill as above.) To serve, place patties on buns with desired toppers. Serve with ketchup and/or mustard. Makes 2 burgers.

Per burger: 540 cal., 25 g fat (11 g sat. fat), 131 mg chol., 945 mg sodium, 31 g carbo., 2 g fiber, 44 g pro.

{freezer fare}

Frozen meatballs are an easy-to-find convenience food that puts meal preparation in the express lane. Float them in soup, stuff them in a bun, or simmer them in sauce to go over pasta. For easier eating for kids or in sandwiches, choose the smaller ½-ounce meatballs.

Mini Cheddar Burgers

Make this recipe for the kids when you make Great Grilled Burgers (recipe opposite).

Prep: 20 min.   **Grill:** 11 min.

- ½   recipe Great Grilled Burgers (opposite)
- 4   slices cheddar cheese (4 ounces)
- 8   ½-inch-thick slices baguette-style French bread, toasted, or 4 small round dinner rolls (such as potato rolls or dollar rolls), split
- Pimiento-stuffed olives, small pickles, and/or cherry tomatoes (optional)
- Ketchup and/or yellow mustard

1. Using reserved beef mixture from Great Grilled Burgers, shape mixture into four ¾-inch-thick patties.

2. For a charcoal grill, grill patties on the rack of an uncovered grill directly over medium heat for 10 to 12 minutes or until an instant-read thermometer inserted into the thickest part of the burger registers 160°F, turning once halfway through grilling. Top each burger with a slice of cheese, trimming cheese to cover burger. Grill about 1 minute more or until cheese melts. (For a gas grill, preheat grill. Reduce heat to medium. Place patties on grill rack over heat. Cover and grill as above.) To serve, place burger between slices of French bread. If desired, garnish with olives, pickles, and/or tomatoes. Serve with ketchup and/or mustard. Makes 4 burgers.

Per burger: 376 cal., 16 g fat (8 g sat. fat), 76 mg chol., 732 mg sodium, 28 g carbo., 2 g fiber, 27 g pro.

Meatball Sandwiches with Spicy Mayo

Start to Finish: 30 min.

24   1-ounce frozen cooked Italian-style meatballs, thawed

¾   cup light mayonnaise or salad dressing

2   to 3 tablespoons snipped fresh cilantro

1   to 1½ teaspoons chili powder

6   ciabatta or other hearty buns, split

1   cup shredded Monterey Jack cheese with jalapeño peppers or Monterey Jack cheese (4 ounces)

⅓   cup shredded carrot (1 small)

⅓   cup shredded, peeled jicama

1   to 2 jalapeño peppers, seeded and thinly sliced (optional)

1. Heat meatballs according to package directions. In a small bowl, stir together mayonnaise, cilantro, and chili powder; set aside.

2. Place ciabatta, split sides up, on a large baking sheet. Divide and sprinkle cheese on ciabatta bottoms. Broil 4 inches from heat about 1 minute or until ciabatta bottoms are toasted and cheese is melted. Spread cut side of ciabatta tops with mayonnaise mixture. Place hot meatballs on ciabatta bottoms and top with carrot, jicama, and jalapeno slices. Top with the ciabatta tops, pressing down gently but firmly. Serve immediately. Makes 6 servings.

Per serving: 537 cal., 24 g fat (9 g sat. fat), 106 mg chol., 1,010 mg sodium, 53 g carbo., 3 g fiber, 28 g pro.

Corny Egg and Ham Sandwiches

Start to Finish: 30 min.

Nonstick cooking spray
4 eggs, lightly beaten
¼ cup milk
¼ teaspoon salt
⅛ teaspoon ground black pepper
½ cup chopped cooked ham
⅓ cup frozen whole kernel corn, thawed
4 English muffins, halved and toasted
4 slices reduced-fat American cheese, halved

1. Lightly coat a medium skillet with cooking spray. Heat skillet over medium heat. In a small bowl, beat together eggs, milk, salt, and pepper. Add to skillet. Cook, without stirring, until egg mixture begins to set on the bottom and around the edge. Using a spatula, lift and fold the partially cooked egg mixture so uncooked portion flows underneath. Continue cooking and folding until egg mixture is cooked through, but still glossy and moist. Remove from heat. Stir in the ham and corn.

2. Place 4 English muffin halves on a baking sheet. Top each with a half slice of cheese, then top with some of the egg mixture. Add remaining cheese slices. Broil 4 to 5 inches from the heat for 1 to 2 minutes or until the cheese melts. Top with remaining muffin halves. Serve immediately. Makes 4 servings.

Per serving: 297 cal., 11 g fat (4 g sat. fat), 233 mg chol., 951 mg sodium, 31 g carbo., 2 g fiber, 18 g pro.

Roasted Veggie Sandwiches

Prep: 25 min. **Bake:** 8 min.

1 small zucchini (6 ounces), thinly sliced lengthwise
1 small yellow summer squash (6 ounces), thinly sliced lengthwise
1 medium onion, thinly sliced (½ cup)
½ cup sliced fresh mushrooms
½ of a red sweet pepper, cut into thin strips (½ cup)
2 tablespoons olive oil
½ teaspoon salt
¼ teaspoon ground black pepper
2 large pita bread rounds, halved
4 teaspoons bottled vinaigrette or Italian salad dressing
3 ounces smoked provolone or mozzarella cheese, shredded (¾ cup)

1. Preheat oven to 450°F. Place zucchini, summer squash, onion, mushrooms, and sweet pepper in a large bowl. Add oil, salt, and pepper; toss to coat. Spread mixture evenly in a 15×10×1-inch baking pan. Roast for 8 to 10 minutes or until vegetables are tender.

2. Divide roasted vegetables among pita bread halves; drizzle with salad dressing. Top with shredded cheese. If desired, place the filled pitas on a baking sheet and bake in the 450°F. oven for 2 to 3 minutes or until cheese melts. Makes 4 servings.

Per serving: 270 cal., 16 g fat (5 g sat. fat), 15 mg chol., 669 mg sodium, 24 g carbo., 2 g fiber, 10 g pro.

Smashed Veggie-Cheese Sandwiches

Start to Finish: 23 min.

- **8** ½-inch-thick slices country French white or wheat bread
- **4** teaspoons olive oil or cooking oil
- **2** tablespoons honey mustard or bottled ranch salad dressing
- **4** ounces thinly sliced cheddar or farmer cheese
- **½** cup thinly sliced cucumber or roma tomatoes
- **½** cup fresh spinach leaves or broccoli slaw mix
- **¼** cup thinly sliced red onion or red sweet pepper strips
- **1** 32-ounce can or bottle ready-to-serve tomato soup* (4 cups)
- **1** cup chopped roma tomatoes (about 3)
- **1** tablespoon balsamic vinegar

1. Brush one side of bread slices lightly with oil. Brush other side of bread slices with honey mustard. Top the mustard sides of four of the bread slices with cheese. Top cheese with cucumber, spinach, and red onion. Top with remaining bread slices, mustard sides down.

2. Preheat an indoor electric grill or a large skillet over medium heat. Place the sandwiches on the grill rack. If using a covered grill, close lid. Grill sandwiches until bread is golden and cheese is melted. (For a covered grill, allow 3 to 5 minutes. For an uncovered grill or skillet, allow 6 to 8 minutes, turning once halfway through grilling.) With a long serrated knife, cut sandwiches in half.

3. Meanwhile, in a medium saucepan, stir together soup, tomatoes, and vinegar; heat through. Serve soup with sandwiches. Makes 4 servings.

*Or prepare two 10.75-ounce cans condensed tomato soup according to directions on the can.

Per serving: 413 cal., 13 g fat (3 g sat. fat), 9 mg chol., 1,380 mg sodium, 60 g carbo., 4 g fiber, 11 g pro.

Easy Tuna Melts

Start to Finish: 26 min.

- 1 10.2-ounce package refrigerated large flaky biscuits (5)
- 1 pint deli tuna salad (2 cups)
- 1 cup shredded cheddar and/or Swiss cheese (4 ounces)

1. Bake biscuits according to package directions; cool. Use a fork to split each biscuit in half. Spread the tuna salad evenly on biscuit halves. Sprinkle with the cheese. Arrange biscuits on a baking sheet.

2. Preheat broiler. Broil sandwiches 4 to 5 inches from heat for 2 to 3 minutes or until cheese melts and browns slightly. Makes 10 tuna melts.

Tip: For a more adult sandwich, stir a little Cajun seasoning and a few chopped pimiento-stuffed olives into the tuna salad before spreading on biscuits.

Per tuna melt: 217 cal., 12 g fat (4 g sat. fat), 17 mg chol., 509 mg sodium, 15 g carbo., 0 g fiber, 11 g pro.

Classic Grilled Cheese Sandwich

Start to Finish: 9 min.

- 1 tablespoon butter, softened
- 2 slices white or whole wheat bread
- 2 slices process American or Swiss cheese
- 1 ounce thinly sliced cooked ham

1. Spread butter on one side of each slice of bread. Place one slice, buttered side down, in a skillet. Place cheese slices on top of bread, cutting cheese to fit so all bread is covered (overlap as necessary); top with ham. Place remaining slice of bread on sandwich, buttered side up.

2. Cook sandwich over medium heat for 3 to 5 minutes or until bottom slice of bread is toasted and cheese begins to melt; turn sandwich. Cook for 1 to 2 minutes more or until bottom slice of bread is toasted and cheese is melted. Makes 1 sandwich.

Grilled Cheddar and Salami Sandwich: Prepare as above, except substitute cheddar or Colby and Monterey Jack cheese for the American cheese and thinly sliced salami for the ham.

Note: If you are making an additional sandwich, carefully add it to the hot skillet with the first one. Cooking times may be slightly less.

Per sandwich: 494 cal., 33 g fat (20 g sat. fat), 100 mg chol., 1,636 mg sodium, 27 g carbo., 2 g fiber, 21 g pro.

Try this recipe with chicken salad or different cheeses.

Easy Tuna Melts

Classic Grilled Cheese Sandwich

Crescent-Wrapped Hot Dogs

Crescent-Wrapped Hot Dogs

Prep: 20 min.   **Bake:** 13 min.

- 1   8-ounce package refrigerated crescent rolls (8)
- 8   hot dogs
- ½   cup shredded cheddar cheese (2 ounces)

1. Preheat oven to 375°F. Unroll dough and separate at perforations. Roll each portion into a 12-inch rope. Roll dough in a spiral around each hot dog. Arrange on a foil-lined baking sheet.

2. Bake for 12 to 15 minutes or until rolls are golden. Sprinkle each with cheese. Bake about 1 minute more or until cheese is melted. Makes 8 servings.

Per serving: 205 cal., 12 g fat (4 g sat. fat), 22 mg chol., 493 mg sodium, 18 g carbo., 0 g fiber, 7 g pro.

Grilled Swiss and Corned Beef Sandwich

Prep: 5 min.   **Cook:** 4 min.

- 1   tablespoon butter, softened
- 2   slices white or whole wheat bread
- 2   slices process Swiss cheese
- 1   tablespoon low-calorie Thousand Island salad dressing
- 2   tablespoons sauerkraut, drained
- 1   ounce thinly sliced corned beef

1. Spread butter on one side of each slice of bread. Place one slice, buttered side down, in a skillet. Place cheese slices on top, cutting cheese to fit so bread is covered (overlap as necessary). Spread dressing over cheese; top with sauerkraut and corned beef. Place remaining slice of bread on sandwich, buttered side up.

2. Cook sandwich over medium heat for 3 to 5 minutes or until bottom slice of bread is toasted and cheese begins to melt; turn sandwich. Cook for 1 to 2 minutes more or until bottom slice of bread is toasted and cheese is melted. Makes 1 sandwich.

Grilled Provolone and Pepperoni Sandwich: Prepare as above, except substitute provolone cheese for the Swiss cheese, 1 tablespoon pizza sauce for the salad dressing, and 5 to 6 slices (½ ounce) thinly sliced pepperoni for the corned beef. Omit sauerkraut.

Note: If you are making an additional sandwich, carefully add it to the hot skillet with the first one. Cooking times may be slightly less.

Per sandwich: 500 cal., 35 g fat (18 g sat. fat), 98 mg chol., 1,051 mg sodium, 29 g carbo., 2 g fiber, 21 g pro.

Greek-Style Pita Pockets

Start to Finish: 30 min.

- 1   pound ground beef
- 1   14.5-ounce can no-salt-added stewed tomatoes
- ½   teaspoon ground allspice or cinnamon
- ¼   teaspoon garlic salt
- ¼   teaspoon ground black pepper
- 2   pita bread rounds, halved crosswise, or four 6-inch flour tortillas
- ½   cup plain nonfat yogurt
- 2   tablespoons thinly sliced green onion (1)

1. For filling, in a large saucepan, cook beef until no longer pink; drain off fat. Stir in undrained tomatoes, allspice, garlic salt, and pepper. Bring to boiling; reduce heat. Cover and simmer for 10 minutes, stirring often. Uncover and simmer for 5 to 10 minutes more or until most of the liquid has evaporated, stirring often.

2. To serve, spoon filling into each pita half or onto each tortilla. Top with yogurt and green onion. If using tortillas, roll up tortillas, folding in the sides to enclose filling. Makes 4 pockets.

Per pocket: 430 cal., 24 g fat (10 g sat. fat), 86 mg chol., 365 mg sodium, 27 g carbo., 2 g fiber, 25 g pro.

Shape Sandwiches
Start to Finish: 5 min.

- 2 slices whole-wheat bread
- ¼ cup spreadable cream cheese
  Toppers (halved strawberries, apple slices, banana slices, or raspberries)

1. Using small cutters, cut out desired shapes (square, circle, triangle, or rectangle) from bread. Spread cream cheese evenly on shapes. Let children add fruit toppers to the sandwiches. Makes 2 servings.

Per serving: 174 cal., 11 g fat (7 g sat. fat), 32 mg chol., 204 mg sodium, 14 g carbo., 2 g fiber, 6 g pro.

Chicken and Biscuit Pockets
Prep: 20 min.   **Bake:** 10 min.

- 1 6-ounce package refrigerated buttermilk biscuits (5)
- ½ cup finely chopped cooked chicken
- ⅓ cup coarsely shredded yellow summer squash
- ¼ cup shredded Monterey Jack or cheddar cheese
- ½ cup mayonnaise
- 1 tablespoon honey mustard
- ½ cup bottled ranch salad dressing

1. Preheat oven to 400°F. Separate biscuits and flatten each with the palm of your hand to a 3½-inch circle. Divide chicken, squash, and cheese evenly on one side of each dough circle. Fold the other sides of dough circles over filling; pinch edges well to seal.* Arrange filled biscuits on an ungreased baking sheet. Bake about 10 minutes or until golden.

2. Meanwhile, in a small bowl, stir together mayonnaise and mustard. Serve mayonnaise mixture and ranch dressing as dipping sauces for warm biscuits. Makes 5 pockets.

*For a tighter seal, press edges with tines of a fork.

Per pocket: 414 cal., 34 g fat (7 g sat. fat), 30 mg chol., 663 mg sodium, 19 g carbo., 0 g fiber, 8 g pro.

Extra Saucy Chicken Sandwiches
Start to Finish: 30 min.

- 1 large onion, halved crosswise and thinly sliced
- 2 pounds skinless, boneless chicken breast halves, cut into bite-size strips
- 2 tablespoons cooking oil
- 1 14- to 16-ounce jar cheddar cheese pasta sauce
- 2 tablespoons Worcestershire sauce
- 12 slices marbled rye bread, toasted
- 1 tomato, sliced
- 12 slices bacon, crisp-cooked and drained (optional)

1. In a very large skillet, cook onion and half of the chicken in 1 tablespoon hot oil over medium-high heat for 4 to 5 minutes or until chicken is no longer pink. Transfer to a medium bowl. Add remaining chicken and remaining oil to skillet. Cook for 4 to 5 minutes or until chicken is no longer pink. Return chicken and onion mixture to skillet. Add pasta sauce and Worcestershire sauce; heat through.

2. To serve, spoon chicken mixture over half of the toasted bread slices. Top with tomato slices and, if desired, bacon. Top with remaining bread slices. Makes 6 sandwiches.

Per sandwich: 491 cal., 18 g fat (5 g sat. fat), 114 mg chol., 1,084 mg sodium, 38 g carbo., 4 g fiber, 43 g pro.

soup night

Serve some bread and maybe a salad with a bowl of soup and you have a complete meal. For some **long-simmering soups,** look in the Forget About It! chapter.

Spiced Meatball Stew
Start to Finish: 30 min.

 1   16-ounce package frozen prepared Italian-style meatballs
 3   cups green beans, cut into 1-inch pieces, or frozen cut green beans
 2   cups peeled baby carrots
 1   14.5-ounce can beef broth
 2   teaspoons Worcestershire sauce
 $\frac{1}{2}$ to $\frac{3}{4}$ teaspoon ground allspice
 $\frac{1}{2}$ teaspoon ground cinnamon
 2   14.5-ounce cans stewed tomatoes

1. In a 4-quart Dutch oven, combine the meatballs, green beans, carrots, beef broth, Worcestershire sauce, allspice, and cinnamon. Bring to boiling; reduce heat. Cover and simmer for 10 minutes.

2. Stir in the undrained tomatoes. Return to boiling; reduce heat. Cover and simmer about 5 minutes more or until vegetables are crisp-tender. Makes 8 servings.

Note: This soup freezes well. To reheat, place frozen soup in a large saucepan. Heat, covered, over medium heat about 30 minutes, stirring occasionally.

Per serving: 233 cal., 13 g fat (6 g sat. fat), 37 mg chol., 938 mg sodium, 18 g carbo., 4 g fiber, 12 g pro.

Italian Beef Soup

Start to Finish: 25 min.

- 1 pound lean ground beef
- 2 14-ounce cans reduced-sodium beef broth
- 1 16-ounce package frozen mixed vegetables
- 1 14.5-ounce can diced tomatoes
- 1½ cups tomato juice
- 1 cup dried rotini pasta
- 1 teaspoon dried Italian seasoning, crushed
- 2 cloves garlic, minced
- ¼ teaspoon salt
- ¼ cup shredded Parmesan cheese (optional)

1. In a 4-quart Dutch oven, brown beef over medium heat; drain well. Add beef broth, mixed vegetables, undrained tomatoes, tomato juice, pasta, Italian seasoning, garlic, and salt.

2. Bring to boiling; reduce heat. Simmer, uncovered, about 10 minutes or until pasta and vegetables are tender, stirring occasionally. If desired, sprinkle each serving with Parmesan cheese. Makes 6 to 8 servings.

Per serving: 227 cal., 7 g fat (3 g sat. fat), 48 mg chol., 658 mg sodium, 21 g carbo., 2 g fiber, 18 g pro.

Beef Stew with Cornmeal Dumplings

Prep: 30 min.   **Cook:** 1 hr. 40 min.

- 2 pounds beef stew meat
- 1 tablespoon cooking oil
- 1 28-ounce can diced tomatoes
- 1 cup beef broth
- ¼ cup coarse-grain Dijon-style mustard
- 1 teaspoon dried thyme, crushed
- 2 cloves garlic, minced
- ½ teaspoon dried oregano, crushed
- ½ teaspoon salt
- ½ teaspoon ground black pepper
- 1 20-ounce package refrigerated diced potatoes with onion
- 1 cup peeled baby carrots
- 1 9-ounce package frozen cut green beans
  Cornmeal Dumplings

1. In a 4-quart Dutch oven, cook beef, half at a time, in hot oil over medium heat until brown. Return all meat to pan. Add undrained tomatoes, broth, mustard, thyme, garlic, oregano, salt, and pepper. Bring to boiling; reduce heat. Cover and simmer for 1 hour. Add potatoes and carrots. Return to boiling; reduce heat. Cover and simmer for 20 minutes. Stir in beans; return to simmering.

2. Drop Cornmeal Dumplings batter from a tablespoon into small mounds on simmering stew. Cover and cook about 20 minutes more or until a wooden toothpick inserted in a dumpling comes out clean. Makes 8 servings.

Cornmeal Dumplings: In a medium bowl, stir together one 8.5-ounce package corn muffin mix, ½ cup shredded cheddar cheese, and ¼ cup sliced green onion. Stir in one lightly beaten egg and ¼ cup dairy sour cream just until moistened (batter will be thick).

Per serving: 446 cal., 13 g fat (4 g sat. fat), 104 mg chol., 1,092 mg sodium, 47 g carbo., 4 g fiber, 33 g pro.

Beef Stew with
Cornmeal Dumplings

{soup savvy}

✳ To control sodium in soup, use reduced-sodium broth. You can always add salt at the end if needed.

✳ Browning meat before adding other soup ingredients cooks out fat and gives meat color and a rich flavor.

✳ Garnish soup with crumbled bacon, crackers, sliced green onion, croutons, popcorn, shredded cheese, sour cream, snipped fresh herbs, or toasted nuts.

Quick Meatball Minestrone

Start to Finish: 25 min.

- 1   12- to 16-ounce package frozen cooked Italian-style meatballs
- 3   14-ounce cans reduced-sodium beef broth
- 1   15- to 16-ounce can Great Northern beans or cannellini beans, rinsed and drained
- 1   14.5-ounce can diced tomatoes with basil, garlic, and oregano
- 1   10-ounce package frozen mixed vegetables
- 1   cup dried small pasta (such as macaroni, small shell, mini penne, or rotini)
- 1   teaspoon sugar

    Packaged finely shredded Parmesan cheese (optional)

1. In a 4-quart Dutch oven, stir together meatballs, broth, beans, undrained tomatoes, and vegetables. Bring to boiling. Stir in pasta. Return to boiling; reduce heat. Simmer, uncovered, about 10 minutes, or until pasta is tender and meatballs are heated through. Stir in sugar. If desired, sprinkle individual servings with Parmesan cheese. Makes 6 to 8 servings.

Per serving: 413 cal., 15 g fat (7 g sat. fat), 40 mg chol., 1,242 mg sodium, 47 g carbo., 8 g fiber, 24 g pro.

Pork Stew with Gremolata

undrained tomatoes, broth, carrots, celery, thyme, bay leaf, and the 1 strip lemon peel. Bring to boiling; reduce heat. Cover and simmer about 1 hour or until meat is tender.

3. If desired, uncover stew and cook for 5 to 10 minutes more or until stew thickens slightly. Discard bay leaf and lemon peel strip. Serve stew with Gremolata and hot cooked orzo. If desired, garnish with additional lemon peel strips. Makes 4 servings.

Gremolata: In a small bowl, stir together ¼ cup snipped flat-leaf parsley, 2 teaspoons finely shredded lemon peel, and 4 cloves garlic, minced.

* Use a vegetable peeler to peel the strip of lemon peel. A peeler will give you a good-size piece of peel, but leave the bitter white pith behind.

Per serving: 491 cal., 14 g fat (3 g sat. fat), 71 mg chol., 748 mg sodium, 51 g carbo., 4 g fiber, 33 g pro.

Pork Stew with Gremolata

Prep: 30 min. **Cook:** 1 hr.

3	tablespoons all-purpose flour
½	teaspoon freshly ground black pepper
¼	teaspoon salt
1	pound boneless pork or veal sirloin, trimmed and cut into 1-inch cubes
2	tablespoons olive oil
½	cup dry white wine
1	large onion, cut into wedges
2	cloves garlic, minced
1	14.5-ounce can diced tomatoes
1	14-ounce can beef broth
1	cup bias-sliced carrot (2 medium)
1	cup chopped celery (2 stalks)
¼	teaspoon dried thyme, crushed
1	bay leaf
1	strip (4×1-inch) lemon peel*
1	recipe Gremolata
1	cup dried orzo (rosamarina), cooked according to package directions and drained
	Lemon peel strips (optional)

1. Place flour, pepper, and salt in a plastic bag. Add meat cubes, a few at a time, shaking to coat. In a large saucepan or Dutch oven, heat 1 tablespoon of the olive oil over medium-high heat; brown meat in hot oil. Using a slotted spoon, transfer meat to a medium bowl. Add wine to pan; cook for 1 minute, stirring to scrape up browned bits from bottom of pan. Add wine mixture to meat in bowl.

2. Add remaining oil to pan. Add onion; cook over medium heat for 3 to 4 minutes or until tender. Stir in garlic; cook and stir for 1 minute. Stir in meat mixture,

Good and Chunky Beef Stew

Prep: 25 min. **Cook:** 25 min.

	Nonstick cooking spray
12	ounces boneless beef sirloin steak, cut into 1-inch cubes
12	ounces tiny new potatoes, halved
1	9-ounce package frozen cut green beans (2 cups)
4	medium carrots, peeled and cut into 1-inch pieces
1	medium onion, cut into thin wedges
1	14-ounce can reduced-sodium beef broth
1	tablespoon Worcestershire sauce
1½	teaspoons dried Italian seasoning, crushed
¼	teaspoon ground black pepper
3	8-ounce cans no-salt-added tomato sauce

1. Lightly coat a 4-quart Dutch oven with cooking spray. Heat over medium-high heat. Add meat cubes. Cook for 4 to 5 minutes or to desired doneness, stirring frequently. Using a slotted spoon, remove meat from Dutch oven; set aside. Add potatoes, green beans, carrots, onion, broth, Worcestershire sauce, Italian seasoning, and pepper to Dutch oven. Bring to boiling; reduce heat. Cover and simmer about 15 minutes or until vegetables are tender.

2. Stir in tomato sauce. Return to boiling; reduce heat. Simmer, covered, for 10 minutes to blend flavors. Return meat to pan; heat through. Makes 5 servings.

Per serving: 240 cal., 3 g fat (1 g sat. fat), 41 mg chol., 280 mg sodium, 33 g carbo., 6 g fiber, 20 g pro.

Hamburger-Barley Soup

Prep: 30 min. **Cook:** 20 min.

- 1½   pounds extra-lean ground beef
- 2   cups thinly sliced carrot (4 medium)
- 1   cup chopped onion (1 large)
- 1   cup sliced celery (2 stalks)
- ½   cup chopped green sweet pepper (1 small)
- 1   clove garlic, minced
- 3   14-ounce cans beef broth
- 1   28-ounce can diced tomatoes
- 1   8-ounce can tomato sauce
- ½   cup quick-cooking barley
- 2   bay leaves
- 1   teaspoon Worcestershire sauce
- 1   teaspoon dried oregano, crushed, or
      1 tablespoon snipped fresh oregano
- ¼   teaspoon ground black pepper
- ¼   teaspoon salt
      Fresh oregano sprigs (optional)

1. In a 5- to 6-quart Dutch oven, cook beef, carrot, onion, celery, sweet pepper, and garlic over medium heat until meat is brown and vegetables are tender. Drain well; return to Dutch oven.

2. Stir in beef broth. Stir in undrained tomatoes, tomato sauce, barley, bay leaves, Worcestershire sauce, dried or snipped oregano, black pepper, and salt. Bring to boiling; reduce heat. Cover and simmer about 20 minutes or until barley is tender. Discard bay leaves. If desired, garnish with oregano sprigs. Makes 8 servings.

Per serving: 237 cal., 8 g fat (3 g sat. fat), 54 mg chol., 990 mg sodium, 20 g carbo., 3 g fiber, 19 g pro.

> For soup meat
> to get tender, it
> needs a long
> simmer. Use
> hamburger to
> **cut the
> cook time**.

Italian Pork and Pepper Soup

Prep: 20 min. **Cook:** 1 hr. 15 min.

- 1½   pounds boneless pork shoulder
- 2   tablespoons cooking oil
- ½   cup chopped onion (1 medium)
- 2   14-ounce cans beef broth
- 1   14.5-ounce can diced tomatoes with
      basil, oregano, and garlic
- 1   cup bottled roasted red sweet peppers,
      drained and cut into bite-size strips
- 2   tablespoons balsamic vinegar
- ¼   teaspoon ground black pepper
- 2   cups sliced zucchini
      Shredded Parmesan cheese (optional)

1. Trim fat from meat. Cut meat into 1-inch pieces. In a 4-quart Dutch oven, brown meat, half at a time, in hot cooking oil over medium-high heat. With second batch of meat, add onion; cook until onion is crisp-tender. Return all meat to pan.

2. Stir in broth, undrained tomatoes, roasted peppers, vinegar, and black pepper. Bring to boiling; reduce heat. Cover and simmer for 50 minutes.

3. Add zucchini. Return to boiling; reduce heat. Cover and simmer about 15 minutes more or until zucchini is tender. If desired, sprinkle each serving with Parmesan cheese. Makes 6 servings.

Per serving: 266 cal., 13 g fat (3 g sat. fat), 76 mg chol., 936 mg sodium, 11 g carbo., 2 g fiber, 25 g pro.

Fast-cooking refrigerated pasta is a **delicious addition** to quick, hearty soups.

Sausage Tortellini Soup

Sausage Tortellini Soup

Prep: 15 min.   **Cook:** 20 min.

    Nonstick cooking spray
12 ounces cooked smoked sausage links, sliced
  1 large onion, cut into thin wedges
  2 cloves garlic, minced
  3 14-ounce cans reduced-sodium chicken broth
  1 14.5-ounce can diced tomatoes with
    basil, oregano, and garlic
  1 10-ounce package frozen baby lima beans
  1 cup water
  2 9-ounce packages refrigerated cheese tortellini
  ¼ cup slivered fresh basil

1. Coat a 4-quart Dutch oven with cooking spray. Heat over medium heat. Add sausage, onion, and garlic; cook until sausage is brown and onion is tender. Drain fat.

2. Add broth, undrained tomatoes, lima beans, and the water. Bring to boiling; reduce heat. Cover and simmer for 10 minutes. Add tortellini. Return to boiling; reduce heat. Simmer, uncovered, about 5 minutes or until pasta and beans are tender. Sprinkle individual servings with basil. Makes 8 servings.

Per serving: 336 cal., 6 g fat (2 g sat. fat), 65 mg chol., 1,182 mg sodium, 46 g carbo., 3 g fiber, 24 g pro.

Chicken and Sausage Gumbo

Prep: 40 min.   **Cook:** 40 min.

  ⅓ cup all-purpose flour
  ⅓ cup cooking oil
  ½ cup chopped onion (1 medium)
  ½ cup chopped green or red sweet pepper
  ½ cup sliced celery (1 stalk)
  3 cloves garlic, minced
1½ to 2 teaspoons Cajun seasoning
  1 14-ounce can beef broth
  1 10-ounce package frozen cut okra
1½ cups chopped cooked chicken
  8 ounces cooked smoked sausage links, sliced
  3 cups hot cooked long grain or brown rice

1. In a 3-quart heavy saucepan, combine flour and oil until smooth. Cook over medium-high heat for 5 minutes, stirring constantly. Reduce heat to medium. Cook and stir for 8 to 10 minutes or until dark reddish brown.

2. Stir in onion, sweet pepper, celery, and garlic. Cook about 10 minutes or until tender, stirring frequently. Stir in Cajun seasoning, broth, and ¾ cup *water*. Add okra. Bring to boiling; reduce heat. Simmer, covered, for 15 minutes. Stir in chicken and sausage; heat through. Serve gumbo in bowls over rice. Makes 6 servings.

Per serving: 482 cal., 27 g fat (7 g sat. fat), 59 mg chol., 900 mg sodium, 34 g carbo., 2 g fiber, 24 g pro.

Easy Salmon Chowder

Prep: 15 min.   **Cook:** 10 min.

  2 cups frozen vegetables (such as broccoli,
    sweet peppers, and/or corn)
  2 tablespoons minced, seeded fresh jalapeño
    chile pepper (optional)
  1 tablespoon butter
  2 tablespoons all-purpose flour
  2 cups milk
  1 cup half-and-half or light cream
  2 cups frozen loose-pack hash brown
    potatoes with onions and peppers, thawed
  1 15-ounce can salmon, drained and flaked
  ¼ cup snipped fresh flat-leaf parsley
  2 tablespoons lemon juice
  ½ teaspoon salt
  ½ teaspoon ground black pepper

1. In a large saucepan, cook frozen vegetables and, if desired, jalapeño pepper in hot butter over medium heat for 3 to 5 minutes or until tender. Stir in flour. Stir in milk and half-and-half. Cook and stir until bubbly. Cook and stir for 2 minutes more.

2. Stir in hash brown potatoes, salmon, parsley, lemon juice, salt, and black pepper. Cook and stir until heated through. Makes 4 servings.

Per serving: 383 cal., 19 g fat (9 g sat. fat), 98 mg chol., 1,009 mg sodium, 23 g carbo., 4 g fiber, 30 g pro.

Mexican Corn Soup

Prep: 15 min. **Cook:** 10 min.

- 1 16-ounce package frozen whole kernel corn, thawed
- 1 cup chicken broth
- 1 4.5-ounce can diced green chile peppers
- 2 tablespoons butter
- 1 clove garlic, minced
- 1 teaspoon dried oregano, crushed
- ¼ teaspoon salt
- ¼ teaspoon ground black pepper
- 2 cups milk
- 1 cup chopped cooked chicken (about 5 ounces)
- 1 cup chopped tomatoes (2 medium)
- 1 cup shredded Monterey Jack cheese (4 ounces)
  Snipped fresh parsley (optional)
  Fresh oregano sprigs (optional)

1. In a blender, combine half of the corn and all of the chicken broth. Cover; blend until nearly smooth.

2. In a large saucepan, stir together corn puree, remaining corn, the chile peppers, butter, garlic, dried oregano, salt, and black pepper. Bring to boiling; reduce heat. Simmer, uncovered, for 10 minutes. Stir in milk, chicken, and tomatoes; heat through. Remove from heat. Stir in cheese until melted. If desired, sprinkle each serving with snipped parsley and garnish with oregano sprigs. Makes 6 servings.

Per serving: 279 cal., 14 g fat (8 g sat. fat), 56 mg chol., 479 mg sodium, 23 g carbo., 0 g fiber, 18 g pro.

Crab Bisque

Start to Finish: 20 min.

- 1 10.75-ounce can condensed cream of asparagus soup
- 1 10.75-ounce can condensed cream of mushroom soup
- 2¾ cups milk
- 1 cup half-and-half or light cream
- 1 6- to 6.5-ounce can crabmeat, drained, flaked, and cartilage removed
- 3 tablespoons dry sherry or milk
  Thinly sliced chives or chopped watercress (optional)

1. In a 4-quart Dutch oven, stir together cream of asparagus soup, cream of mushroom soup, milk, and half-and-half. Bring just to boiling over medium heat, stirring frequently.

2. Stir in crabmeat and dry sherry; heat through. If desired, garnish with chives. Makes 6 servings.

Shrimp Bisque: Prepare as above, except substitute cream of shrimp soup for the cream of mushroom soup and 8 ounces small cooked, peeled, and deveined shrimp for the crabmeat.

Mushroom Bisque: Prepare as above, except before adding soups and liquids to Dutch oven, cook and stir 2 cups sliced button, stemmed shiitake, and/or portobello mushrooms in 2 tablespoons hot butter until tender. Continue as directed, omitting crabmeat and chives.

Per serving: 225 cal., 12 g fat (5 g sat. fat), 51 mg chol., 882 mg sodium, 15 g carbo., 0 g fiber, 12 g pro.

Mexican Corn Soup

Crab Bisque

Thin strips of bacon curl up to make a **pretty garnish**. Or just sprinkle the soup with bacon crumbles.

Fireside Potato Chowder

Prep: 25 min. **Cook:** 15 min.

- 6 slices bacon, halved crosswise
- 1 medium onion, chopped
- 1 stalk celery, chopped
- 2 large potatoes, peeled and coarsely chopped
- 1 cup water
- 1 teaspoon Dijon-style mustard
- 1½ cups half-and-half, light cream, or milk
- 1 10.75-ounce can condensed cream of chicken soup or golden mushroom soup
- Snipped fresh parsley (optional)

1. In a large saucepan, cook bacon over medium heat until crisp. Remove bacon, reserving 1 tablespoon drippings in saucepan. Transfer bacon to paper towels. Crumble bacon; set aside, reserving some for garnish.

2. Add onion and celery to saucepan. Cook until tender. Stir in potatoes, the water, and mustard. Bring to boiling; reduce heat. Cover and simmer about 15 minutes or just until the potatoes are tender.

3. Stir in half-and-half and soup; heat through. (Do not boil.) Stir in bacon. Garnish with reserved bacon and, if desired, parsley. Makes 6 servings.

Per serving: 317 cal., 22 g fat (9 g sat. fat), 44 mg chol., 728 mg sodium, 20 g carbo., 2 g fiber, 11 g pro.

A-to-Z Vegetable Soup

Start to Finish: 45 min.

- 2 cups cut-up mixed fresh vegetables, such as zucchini, carrots, broccoli, and/or red sweet pepper
- 1 tablespoon cooking oil or olive oil
- 2 14-ounce cans reduced-sodium chicken broth
- 2 cloves garlic, minced
- 1 15-ounce can cannellini or Great Northern beans, rinsed and drained
- ½ cup dried alphabet-shape pasta or tiny shells
- 2 tablespoons fresh oregano leaves or 2 teaspoons dried oregano, crushed

1. In a large saucepan, cook vegetables in hot oil over medium heat about 5 minutes or until crisp-tender.

2. Add broth and garlic to saucepan. Bring to boiling. Stir in beans, pasta, and dried oregano (if using). Return to boiling; reduce heat. Cover and simmer about 10 minutes or until pasta is just tender. Stir in fresh oregano leaves (if using). Makes 4 servings.

Per serving: 188 cal., 4 g fat (1 g sat. fat), 0 mg chol., 717 mg sodium, 33 g carbo., 6 g fiber, 12 g pro.

Cheese-Tortellini Soup

Start to Finish: 25 min.

  3 slices packaged ready-to-serve cooked
     bacon, chopped
  ⅓ cup chopped onion (1 small)
  2 cloves garlic, minced
  4 cups reduced-sodium chicken broth
  3 cups frozen cheese-filled tortellini (12 ounces)
  1 10-ounce package frozen chopped spinach,
     thawed and drained
     Ground black pepper
     Parmesan cheese shavings (optional)

1. In a large saucepan, cook bacon over medium-high heat about 3 minutes or until crisp. Add onion; cook for 3 minutes more. Stir in garlic; cook for 1 minute more.

2. Add broth; bring to boiling. Stir in tortellini. Return to boiling; reduce heat. Simmer, uncovered, according to package directions, adding the spinach for the last 3 minutes of cooking time.

3. Season to taste with pepper and, if desired, garnish with Parmesan cheese. Makes 4 servings.

Per serving: 229 cal., 5 g fat (3 g sat. fat), 26 mg chol., 938 mg sodium, 31 g carbo., 3 g fiber, 14 g pro.

Vegetarian Gumbo

Prep: 10 min.   **Cook:** 6 hr. (low) or 3 hr. (high)

  2 15-ounce cans black beans, rinsed
     and drained
  1 28-ounce can diced tomatoes
  1 16-ounce package frozen loose-pack pepper
     stir-fry vegetables (yellow, green, and red
     sweet peppers, and onions)
  2 cups frozen cut okra
  2 to 3 teaspoons Cajun seasoning
     Hot cooked white or brown rice (optional)
     Chopped green onion (optional)

1. In a 3½- or 4½-quart slow cooker, stir together the beans, undrained tomatoes, stir-fry vegetables, okra, and Cajun seasoning.

2. Cover and cook on low-heat setting for 6 to 8 hours or on high-heat setting for 3 to 4 hours. If desired, serve over hot cooked rice and garnish with green onion. Makes 6 servings.

Per serving: 153 cal., 0 g fat (0 g sat. fat), 0 mg chol., 639 mg sodium, 31 g carbo., 10 g fiber, 12 g pro.

Cheese-Tortellini Soup

Shrimp Gumbo

Start to Finish: 40 min.

  8 ounces bulk hot Italian sausage
  ¾ cup chopped onion (1 large)
  ¾ chopped green sweet pepper (1 large)
  1 cup thinly sliced celery (2 stalks)
  3 cloves garlic, chopped
  2 14.5-ounce cans reduced-sodium
     stewed tomatoes
  1 14-ounce can reduced-sodium chicken broth
  1 teaspoon paprika
  ¼ teaspoon ground black pepper
  ⅛ to ¼ teaspoon cayenne pepper
  1 pound frozen uncooked medium shrimp,
     thawed, peeled, and deveined
  1 cup instant white rice

1. In a 4-quart Dutch oven, cook sausage, onion, sweet pepper, celery, and garlic over medium heat until sausage is brown, breaking up sausage with wooden spoon; drain well.

2. Add the undrained tomatoes, broth, paprika, black pepper, and cayenne. Bring to boiling; reduce heat. Cover and simmer for 10 minutes.

3. Add shrimp; cook, covered, about 4 minutes more, until shrimp are opaque. Remove from heat. Stir in rice. Cover and let stand for 5 minutes. Makes 6 servings.

Per serving: 338 cal., 14 g fat (5 g sat. fat), 144 mg chol., 971 mg sodium, 28 g carbo., 4 g fiber, 24 g pro.

Dried herbs are added to soup before simmering to extract the most flavor. Add fresh herbs at the end.

Tomato Basil Soup
Prep: 30 min. **Cook:** 30 min.

1	cup chopped celery (2 stalks)
¾	cup chopped carrot (1 large)
¼	cup chopped onion
2	cloves garlic, minced
1	tablespoon olive oil
2	cups tomato juice
1¼	cups reduced-sodium chicken broth
1	14.5-ounce can Italian-style stewed tomatoes
½	of a 6-ounce can tomato paste (⅓ cup)
1	teaspoon dried thyme, crushed
	Dash cayenne pepper
¾	cup milk, half-and-half,* or reduced-sodium chicken broth
1	tablespoon sugar
¼	cup snipped fresh basil

1. In a covered 4-quart Dutch oven, cook celery, carrot, onion, and garlic in hot oil over medium-low heat about 15 minutes or until tender, stirring occasionally. Add tomato juice, broth, undrained stewed tomatoes, tomato paste, thyme, and cayenne. Bring to boiling; reduce heat. Simmer, uncovered, for 30 minutes. Cool soup slightly.

2. Place half of the soup in a food processor or blender. Process until smooth. Transfer pureed soup to a bowl. Repeat with remaining soup. If using milk or half-and-half, stir about 1 cup of tomato mixture into milk, then return all of the soup to the pan. If using the ¾ cup chicken broth, return soup to pan, then stir in broth. Stir in sugar; heat through. Stir in basil. Makes 6 servings.

* If using the milk or half-and-half, soup may look slightly curdled.

Per serving: 106 cal., 3 g fat (1 g sat. fat), 2 mg chol., 632 mg sodium, 17 g carbo., 2 g fiber, 4 g pro.

Red Tomato Soup

Prep: 15 min. **Cook:** 15 min.

- ½ cup chopped carrot (1 medium)
- ¼ cup chopped onion
- ¼ cup chopped celery
- 1 tablespoon butter
- 1 28-ounce can diced tomatoes
- 1 5.5-ounce can vegetable juice (⅔ cup)
- 2 teaspoons sugar
- ½ teaspoon dried Italian seasoning, crushed
- ¼ teaspoon salt
- ⅛ teaspoon ground black pepper
- 1 to 1¼ cups water
  Crisp cheese puffs or corn chips (optional)

1. In a medium saucepan, cook carrot, onion, and celery in hot butter over medium heat for 5 to 8 minutes or until tender. Add undrained tomatoes, vegetable juice, sugar, Italian seasoning, salt, and pepper. Bring to boiling; reduce heat. Simmer, uncovered, for 10 minutes.

2. Cool slightly. Place half of the tomato mixture in a blender or food processor. Cover and blend until smooth. Transfer pureed soup to a bowl. Repeat with remaining tomato mixture. Return all of the soup to the pan. Add enough water to reach desired consistency. Heat through. If desired, serve with cheese puffs. Makes 4 servings.

Per serving: 125 cal., 3 g fat (2 g sat. fat), 8 mg chol., 661 mg sodium, 21 g carbo., 2 g fiber, 2 g pro.

Zesty Tomato-Zucchini Soup

Prep: 15 min. **Cook:** 10 min.

- 2 cups Red Tomato Soup (recipe above)
- ½ cup chopped zucchini
- ¼ to ½ teaspoon bottled hot pepper sauce
- ½ cup frozen artichoke hearts, thawed and chopped
- 2 tablespoons sliced pitted ripe olives
- ¼ cup water
  Italian-style croutons (optional)
  Finely shredded Parmesan cheese (optional)

1. In a medium saucepan, combine soup, zucchini, and hot pepper sauce. Bring to boiling, stirring occasionally; reduce heat. Simmer, uncovered, for 10 to 15 minutes or until zucchini is tender. Stir in artichoke hearts and olives. Heat through. If desired, top each serving with croutons and Parmesan cheese. Makes 2 servings.

Per serving: 159 cal., 5 g fat (2 g sat. fat), 8 mg chol., 769 mg sodium, 26 g carbo., 5 g fiber, 4 g pro.

Sweet Potato Soup
with Nutmeg and Maple Syrup

Prep: 20 min. **Cook:** 20 min.

- ½ cup chopped onion (1 medium)
- ½ cup chopped celery (1 stalk)
- 1 clove garlic, minced
- 1 tablespoon butter
- 1 sweet potato, peeled and cubed (about 2 cups)
- 2 cups reduced-sodium chicken broth
- ½ teaspoon ground nutmeg
- 1½ cups half-and-half or light cream
- 1 tablespoon maple syrup
  Dairy sour cream (optional)
  Ground nutmeg (optional)

1. In a 4-quart Dutch oven, cook onion, celery, and garlic in hot butter over medium heat until onion is tender but not brown. Add sweet potato, broth, and the ½ teaspoon nutmeg. Bring to boiling; reduce heat. Cover and simmer about 20 minutes or until potato is tender.

2. Cool slightly. Place one-third of the potato mixture in a blender or food processor. Cover and blend until smooth. Transfer pureed soup to a bowl. Repeat with remaining potato mixture. Return all of the soup to the Dutch oven. Stir in half-and-half and maple syrup; heat through. If desired, top each serving with sour cream and additional nutmeg. Makes 4 servings.

Per serving: 233 cal., 13 g fat (8 g sat. fat), 41 mg chol., 392 mg sodium, 24 g carbo., 3 g fiber, 6 g pro.

Zesty Tomato-Zucchini Soup

weeknight

Rosemary Chicken with Vegetables

solutions

Rosemary Chicken with Vegetables

Start to Finish: 30 min.

- 4 medium skinless, boneless chicken breast halves
- ½ teaspoon lemon-pepper seasoning
- 2 tablespoons olive oil
- 4 ounces refrigerated spinach or plain linguine
- 2 cloves garlic, minced
- 2 medium zucchini and/or yellow summer squash, cut into ¼-inch slices
- ½ cup apple juice
- 2 teaspoons snipped fresh rosemary or ½ teaspoon dried rosemary, crushed
- 2 tablespoons dry white wine or chicken broth
- 2 teaspoons cornstarch
- 1 cup halved cherry or grape tomatoes
- Fresh rosemary sprigs (optional)

1. Sprinkle chicken with lemon-pepper seasoning. In a large skillet, cook chicken in hot oil over medium heat for 8 to 10 minutes or until chicken is no longer pink, turning once. Transfer chicken to a platter; cover and keep warm. Meanwhile, cook pasta according to package directions; drain and keep warm.

2. Add garlic to skillet; cook for 15 seconds. Add zucchini, apple juice, and rosemary. Bring to boiling; reduce heat. Cover and simmer for 2 minutes.

3. In a small bowl, stir together wine and cornstarch; add to skillet. Cook and stir until thickened and bubbly; cook for 2 minutes more. Stir in tomatoes. Serve vegetables and pasta with chicken. If desired, garnish with rosemary sprigs. Makes 4 servings.

Per serving: 326 cal., 10 g fat (2 g sat. fat), 95 mg chol., 247 mg sodium, 25 g carbo., 2 g fiber, 33 g pro.

Making a good dinner in the midweek crunch can be your biggest challenge. Here are solutions to the puzzle of **what to serve** on weeknights.

Chicken Tacos

Start to Finish: 30 min.

- Nonstick cooking spray
- 1 cup chopped onion (2 medium)
- 1 clove garlic, minced
- 2 cups shredded cooked chicken
- 1 8-ounce can tomato sauce
- 1 4-ounce can diced green chile peppers, drained
- 12 taco shells
- 2 cups shredded lettuce
- ½ cup chopped seeded tomato (1 medium)
- ½ cup finely shredded cheddar cheese and/or Monterey Jack cheese (2 ounces)
- Salsa (optional)

1. Spray an unheated large skillet with cooking spray. Heat skillet over medium heat. Add the onion and garlic; cook until onion is tender. Stir in the chicken, tomato sauce, and chile peppers. Heat through.

2. Spoon chicken mixture into taco shells. Top with lettuce, tomato, and cheese. If desired, serve with salsa. Makes 6 servings.

Per serving: 286 cal., 13 g fat (4 g sat. fat), 51 mg chol., 473 mg sodium, 25 g carbo., 4 g fiber, 19 g pro.

Sautéed Chicken with Pasta

Start to Finish: 30 min.

8	**ounces angel hair pasta**
½	**teaspoon dried thyme, crushed**
½	**teaspoon salt**
¼	**teaspoon ground black pepper**
2	**skinless, boneless chicken breast halves, halved horizontally (about 12 ounces total)**
2	**tablespoons olive oil**
8	**ounces presliced fresh mushrooms (3 cups)**
1	**small onion, halved and sliced (about 1 cup)**
3	**cloves garlic, minced**
1½	**cups reduced-sodium chicken broth**
1	**tablespoon all-purpose flour**
1	**teaspoon Dijon-style mustard**
4	**roma tomatoes, cut into thin wedges**
¼	**cup chopped fresh Italian (flat-leaf) parsley**

1. Cook pasta according to package directions; drain and keep warm.

2. Meanwhile, combine thyme, ¼ teaspoon of the salt and the pepper in a small bowl. Sprinkle over both sides of chicken breast pieces. Heat 1 tablespoon of the oil in a very large skillet over medium-high heat. Add chicken. Reduce heat to medium and cook about 6 minutes or until chicken is no longer pink, turning once. Remove chicken from skillet; cover and keep warm.

3. Add remaining 1 tablespoon oil to the skillet. Heat over medium-high heat. Stir in mushrooms, onion, and garlic. Cook about 5 minutes or until onion is tender, stirring occasionally. Whisk together broth, flour, mustard, and remaining ¼ teaspoon salt; add to skillet. Cook and stir until slightly thickened and bubbly. Stir in tomatoes and parsley; heat through. Serve chicken and sauce with pasta. Makes 4 servings.

Per serving: 426 cal., 9 g fat (2 g sat. fat), 49 mg chol., 604 mg sodium, 53 g carbo., 4 g fiber, 31 g pro.

Ginger Chicken Stir-Fry

Start to Finish: 25 min.

1	tablespoon cooking oil or peanut oil
1	medium zucchini, thinly sliced
1	medium carrot, thinly sliced
1	small onion, thinly sliced
1	small red sweet pepper, halved and thinly sliced
½	head small green cabbage, shredded
12	ounces skinless, boneless chicken breast halves, cut into 1-inch pieces
½	cup bottled stir-fry sauce
½	teaspoon ground ginger
	Hot cooked rice
	Peanuts, cashews, or toasted sliced almonds (optional)

1. In a very large skillet, heat oil over medium-high heat. Add half of the vegetables; cook and stir about 2 minutes or until crisp-tender. Remove vegetables from skillet. Repeat with remaining vegetables; remove from skillet.

2. If necessary, add more oil to skillet. Add chicken. Cook and stir for 3 to 5 minutes or until chicken is no longer pink. Push chicken from center of skillet. Add sauce and ginger to center of skillet. Cook and stir until bubbly. Return cooked vegetables to skillet. Cook and stir about 1 minute more or until all is coated and heated through. Serve over hot cooked rice. If desired, sprinkle each serving with peanuts. Makes 6 servings.

Per serving without rice: 130 cal., 3 g fat (1 g sat. fat), 34 mg chol., 540 mg sodium, 9 g carbo., 2 g fiber, 16 g pro.

Easy Chicken and Dumplings

Prep: 25 min. **Cook:** 15 min.

1	2- to 2½-pound purchased roasted chicken
1	16-ounce package frozen mixed vegetables
1¼	cups reduced-sodium chicken broth or water
1	10.75-ounce can reduced-fat, reduced-sodium condensed cream of chicken soup
½	teaspoon dried Italian seasoning, crushed
⅛	teaspoon ground black pepper
1	11.5-ounce package refrigerated cornbread twists

1. Remove meat from chicken (discard skin and bones). Chop or shred meat (you should have 3½ to 4 cups). In a large saucepan, stir together chicken, vegetables, broth, soup, Italian seasoning, and pepper.

Ginger Chicken Stir-Fry

Easy Chicken and Dumplings

Bring to boiling; reduce heat. Cover and simmer about 15 minutes or until vegetables are tender.

2. Meanwhile, remove cornbread twists from package; cut along perforations. Lay twists on a baking sheet; roll 2 twists together to make a spiral. Repeat with remaining twists. Bake according to package directions.

3. To serve, spoon chicken mixture into bowls and serve with cornbread spirals. Makes 4 to 6 servings.

Per serving: 650 cal., 30 g fat (8 g sat. fat), 107 mg chol., 1,399 mg sodium, 57 g carbo., 5 g fiber, 42 g pro.

Mock Chicken Pot Pie

Start to Finish: 30 min.

½ of a 15-ounce package rolled refrigerated
   unbaked piecrusts (1 crust)
1 10.75-ounce can condensed
   cream of onion soup
1⅓ cups low-fat milk
3 ounces reduced-fat cream cheese
   (Neufchâtel), cut up
½ teaspoon dried sage, crushed
¼ teaspoon ground black pepper
1½ cups chopped cooked chicken
1 10-ounce package frozen mixed vegetables
½ cup uncooked instant rice

1. Preheat oven to 450°F. Let piecrust stand at room
temperature for 15 minutes as directed on package. Unroll
piecrust. Using a pizza cutter or sharp knife, cut piecrust
into strips about ½ to 1 inch wide. Place strips on a baking sheet. Bake for 6 to 8 minutes or until golden.

2. Meanwhile, for filling, in a large saucepan, combine
soup, milk, cream cheese, sage, and pepper. Cook and
stir over medium-high heat until cream cheese melts. Stir
in chicken, vegetables, and rice. Bring to boiling; reduce
heat. Cover and simmer about 10 minutes or until vegetables and rice are tender.

3. Transfer filling to a serving dish. Top with pastry
strips. Makes 4 servings.

Per serving: 587 cal., 27 g fat (12 g sat. fat), 86 mg chol., 999 mg
sodium, 58 g carbo., 2 g fiber, 25 g pro.

Chicken Quesadillas
Start to Finish: 25 min.

1   2- to 2¼-pound deli-roasted chicken
4   8- to 10-inch flour tortillas
    Fresh spinach leaves
1   cup sautéed mushrooms
2   cups shredded Monterey Jack cheese
    (8 ounces)
    Salsa (optional)
    Guacamole (optional)

1. Remove meat from chicken (discard skin and bones). Chop meat; reserve 2 cups. (Place remaining chicken in an airtight container for another use; refrigerate for up to 3 days or freeze for up to 3 months.)

2. Spoon chicken evenly on bottom halves of tortillas. Top with spinach and mushrooms. Sprinkle cheese over mushrooms. Fold tortillas in half.

3. Heat quesadillas on a griddle over medium heat until brown on both sides and cheese melts. If desired, serve with salsa and guacamole. Makes 4 servings.

Per serving: 472 cal., 28 g fat (15 g sat. fat), 120 mg chol., 513 mg sodium, 18 g carbo., 2 g fiber, 37 g pro.

Chicken Linguine with Pesto Sauce
Start to Finish: 20 min.

8   ounces dried linguine
1   10-ounce package frozen broccoli, cauliflower, and carrots
1   10-ounce container refrigerated Alfredo pasta sauce or 1 cup jarred Alfredo sauce
⅓   cup purchased basil pesto
¼   cup milk
½   of a 2- to 2¼-pound deli-roasted chicken
    Grated Parmesan cheese

1. In a 4-quart Dutch oven, cook pasta according to package directions, adding vegetables during the last 5 minutes of cooking. Drain. Return to Dutch oven.

2. While pasta is cooking, in a small bowl, combine sauce, pesto, and milk; set aside. Remove meat from chicken (discard skin and bones); chop meat.

3. Add chicken to Dutch oven. Add sauce mixture; toss to coat. Heat through over medium-low heat. If desired, stir in additional milk to reach desired consistency. Top each serving with cheese. Makes 4 servings.

Per serving: 801 cal., 48 g fat (4 g sat. fat), 109 mg chol., 546 mg sodium, 54 g carbo., 3 g fiber, 37 g pro.

Chicken Lasagna Rolls with Chive-Cream Sauce

Prep: 40 min.　**Bake:** 35 min.

- 6 dried lasagna noodles
- 1 8-ounce package reduced-fat cream cheese (Neufchâtel), softened
- ½ cup milk
- ¼ cup grated Romano or Parmesan cheese
- 1 tablespoon snipped fresh chives
- 1½ cups chopped cooked chicken
- ½ of a 10-ounce package frozen chopped broccoli, thawed and drained (1 cup)
- ½ cup bottled roasted red sweet peppers, drained and sliced
- ⅛ teaspoon ground black pepper
- 1 cup purchased marinara or pasta sauce

1. Preheat oven to 350°F. Cook noodles according to package directions. Drain noodles; rinse with cold water. Drain again. Cut each in half crosswise; set aside.

2. Meanwhile, in a bowl, beat cream cheese with an electric mixer on medium to high speed for 30 seconds. Slowly beat in milk. Stir in cheese and chives.

3. In a bowl, combine ½ cup white sauce, the chicken, broccoli, roasted peppers, and black pepper. Place about ¼ cup filling at one end of each noodle; roll up. Place rolls, seam sides down, in a 3-quart baking dish.

4. Spoon marinara sauce over rolls. Spoon remaining white sauce over top. Bake, covered, for 35 to 40 minutes or until heated through. Makes 6 servings.

Per serving: 288 cal., 13 g fat (7 g sat. fat), 65 mg chol., 412 mg sodium, 22 g carbo., 2 g fiber, 19 g pro.

Chicken and Pasta Primavera

Start to Finish: 25 min.

- 1 9-ounce package refrigerated fettuccine
- 1 cup thinly sliced carrot (2 medium)
- 1 medium zucchini, halved lengthwise and thinly sliced (1¼ cups)
- ¾ cup frozen whole kernel corn
- 12 ounces deli-roasted chicken meat, cut into ½-inch strips (about 2½ cups)
- 1½ cups chicken broth
- 4 teaspoons cornstarch
- 2 teaspoons finely shredded lemon peel
- 1 teaspoon dried basil, crushed
- ½ cup dairy sour cream
- 2 tablespoons Dijon-style mustard

1. Cook pasta according to package directions, adding carrot, zucchini, and corn to the water with pasta. If the chicken is chilled, place it in a colander. Pour the pasta, vegetables, and cooking liquid over chicken to warm it; drain. Return all to saucepan.

2. Meanwhile, in a medium saucepan, stir together broth, cornstarch, lemon peel, and basil. Cook and stir over medium heat until thickened and bubbly. Cook and stir for 2 minutes more. Remove from heat. Stir in sour cream and mustard. Pour over pasta mixture; toss gently to coat. Makes 6 servings.

Per serving: 334 cal., 10 g fat (4 g sat. fat), 98 mg chol., 547 mg sodium, 34 g carbo., 3 g fiber, 27 g pro.

{quick chicken}

If you need cooked chicken for a recipe, poach some chicken breasts. For 1½ cups chopped cooked chicken, in a skillet, combine 8 ounces skinless, boneless chicken breast halves and 1½ cups water. Cover and simmer for 12 to 14 minutes or until chicken is no longer pink.

Curry Burritos

Start to Finish: 15 min.

- 1 tablespoon cooking oil
- ½ cup purchased shredded carrots
- ½ cup snow pea pods, cut into thin strips
- Reserved mixture from Turkey and Bean Burritos (opposite) (about 1¾ cups)
- ¼ cup unsweetened coconut milk
- 2 teaspoons curry powder
- Reserved tortillas from Turkey and Bean Burritos (opposite)
- ¼ cup finely chopped peanuts
- Chutney (optional)

1. In a large skillet, heat oil over medium-high heat. Add carrots; cook and stir for 3 to 4 minutes. Add pea pods and stir for 1 minute more. Stir in reserved turkey mixture, the coconut milk, and curry powder. Bring to boiling; reduce heat. Simmer, uncovered, for 2 minutes.

2. Divide mixture among the 4 reserved tortillas. Top with peanuts. Fold bottom edges up and over filling, just until covered. Roll up, tucking in sides. If desired, serve with chutney. Makes 4 burritos.

Per burrito: 306 cal., 16 g fat (5 g sat. fat), 22 mg chol., 378 mg sodium, 30 g carbo., 5 g fiber, 14 g pro.

Turkey and Bean Burritos

Start to Finish: 35 min.

8	8-inch flour tortillas
12	ounces uncooked ground turkey
1	cup chopped onion (2 medium)
2	cloves garlic, minced
1	15-ounce can black beans or pinto beans, rinsed and drained
$\frac{1}{2}$	cup salsa
2	teaspoons chili powder
$\frac{1}{4}$	cup shredded cheddar cheese (1 ounce)
$\frac{1}{4}$	cup shredded lettuce
	Salsa (optional)
	Dairy sour cream (optional)

1. Preheat oven to 350°F. Stack tortillas; wrap in foil. Heat in the oven for 10 minutes to soften.

2. Meanwhile, for filling, in a large skillet, cook turkey, onion, and garlic over medium heat until meat is brown and onion is tender. Drain off fat. Stir in beans, the $\frac{1}{2}$ cup salsa, and the chili powder. Heat through. Reserve half of filling mixture (about 2 cups) and half of the tortillas (4) for Curry Burritos (opposite).

3. Spoon about $\frac{1}{3}$ cup of the remaining filling onto each remaining tortilla and top each with 1 tablespoon cheese and 1 tablespoon lettuce. Fold bottom edge up and over filling, just until covered. Roll up, tucking in sides. If desired, serve burritos with additional salsa and the sour cream. Makes 4 burritos.

Per burrito: 238 cal., 10 g fat (4 g sat. fat), 37 mg chol., 427 mg sodium, 26 g carbo., 4 g fiber, 15 g pro.

Simple Beef and Noodles

Return to boiling; reduce heat to low. Cover and simmer for 20 to 25 minutes or until vegetables are tender, stirring frequently.

2. Meanwhile, cook noodles according to package directions; drain. Serve meat mixture over noodles. Makes 6 servings.

Per serving: 364 cal., 8 g fat (2 g sat. fat), 87 mg chol., 903 mg sodium, 51 g carbo., 4 g fiber, 22 g pro.

Hamburger-Mash Surprise

Prep: 25 min.   **Bake:** 30 min.   **Stand:** 5 min.

- ¾   cup shredded cheddar cheese (3 ounces)
- 2   cups refrigerated mashed potatoes
- 12   ounces lean ground beef
- ½   cup chopped onion
- 2   cups sliced zucchini or yellow summer squash
- 1   14.5-ounce can diced tomatoes with basil, oregano, and garlic
- ½   of a 6-ounce can (⅓ cup) no-salt-added tomato paste
- ¼   teaspoon ground black pepper
  Paprika (optional)

1. Preheat oven to 375°F. Stir ½ cup of the cheese into the potatoes; set aside. In a large skillet, cook ground beef and onion until meat is no longer pink and onion is tender. Drain off fat. Stir in zucchini, undrained tomatoes, tomato paste, and pepper. Bring to boiling. Transfer meat mixture to a 2-quart casserole.

2. Spoon mashed potato mixture into a large pastry bag fitted with a large round tip. Starting at one end, fill in the casserole with rows of the mashed potato mixture until the meat mixture is covered. (Or spoon mashed potato mixture in mounds on top of the hot meat mixture.) Sprinkle with remaining cheese. If desired, sprinkle with paprika.

3. Bake about 30 minutes or until potatoes are golden brown. Let stand for 5 minutes before serving. Makes 6 servings.

To Make Ahead: After bringing meat mixture to a boil, divide evenly among six 10-ounce casserole dishes. Top with potatoes and cheese. Cover with plastic wrap; chill for up to 48 hours. To bake, remove plastic wrap. If desired, sprinkle with paprika. Place casseroles in a 15×10×1-inch baking pan. Cover with foil. Bake in a 375°F oven for 35 minutes. Remove foil. Bake for 5 minutes more. Let stand for 5 minutes before serving.

Per serving: 254 cal., 12 g fat (3 g sat. fat), 39 mg chol., 644 mg sodium, 21 g carbo., 3 g fiber, 16 g pro.

Simple Beef and Noodles

Prep: 15 min.   **Cook:** 20 min.

- 1   17-ounce package refrigerated cooked beef tips with gravy
- ½   teaspoon dried basil, crushed
- ¼   teaspoon ground black pepper
- 1   10.75-ounce can condensed golden mushroom soup
- ½   cup beef broth
- 1½   cups sliced fresh mushrooms
- 1   cup packaged peeled baby carrots, halved lengthwise
- 1   cup loose-pack frozen small whole onions
- 12   ounces dried wide egg noodles (6 cups)

1. In a large saucepan, combine beef tips with gravy, the basil, and pepper. Stir in soup and beef broth. Bring to boiling. Add mushrooms, carrots, and onions.

Asian Beef and Noodle Bowl

Start to Finish: 30 min.

- 4 cups water
- 2 3-ounce packages ramen noodles (any flavor)
- 2 teaspoons chili oil, or 2 teaspoons cooking oil plus ⅛ teaspoon cayenne pepper
- 12 ounces beef flank steak or top round steak, cut into thin bite-size strips
- 1 teaspoon grated fresh ginger
- 2 cloves garlic, minced
- 1 cup beef broth
- 2 tablespoons soy sauce
- 2 cups baby spinach leaves or torn fresh spinach
- 1 cup purchased shredded carrots
- ¼ cup snipped fresh cilantro

1. In a large saucepan, bring the water to boiling. If desired, break up noodles; drop noodles into the boiling water. (Discard the flavor packets or save for another use.) Return to boiling; boil for 2 to 3 minutes or just until noodles are tender but still firm, stirring occasionally. Drain noodles; set aside.

2. Meanwhile, in a very large skillet, heat oil over medium-high heat. Add beef, ginger, and garlic; cook and stir for 2 to 3 minutes or until beef is desired doneness. Carefully stir beef broth and soy sauce into skillet. Bring to boiling; reduce heat.

3. Add spinach, carrots, and cooked noodles to skillet; stir to combine. Heat through. Stir in cilantro just before serving. Makes 4 servings.

Per serving: 381 cal., 17 g fat (3 g sat. fat), 34 mg chol., 1,503 mg sodium, 30 g carbo., 2 g fiber, 26 g pro.

Combine the flavors from two family favorites. It's **a good way** to get picky eaters to try new things.

Taco Spaghetti

Taco Spaghetti

Prep: 25 min. **Bake:** 15 min.

- 5 ounces dried spaghetti, linguine, or fettuccine, broken
- 1 pound ground beef or ground raw turkey
- 1 large onion, chopped
- ¾ cup water
- ½ of a 1.25-ounce envelope taco seasoning mix (2 tablespoons)
- 1 11-ounce can whole kernel corn with sweet peppers, drained
- 1 cup sliced, pitted ripe olives
- 1 cup shredded Colby and Monterey Jack cheese or cheddar cheese (4 ounces)
- ½ cup salsa
- 1 4-ounce can diced green chile peppers, drained
- 6 cups shredded lettuce
- 1 medium tomato, cut into thin wedges
  Tortilla chips (optional)
  Dairy sour cream (optional)

1. Preheat oven to 350°F. Cook spaghetti according to package directions; drain. Set aside.

2. In a large skillet, cook ground beef and onion over medium heat until meat is brown and onion is tender. Drain off fat. Stir in water and taco seasoning. Bring to boiling; reduce heat. Simmer, uncovered, for 2 minutes, stirring occasionally. Stir in spaghetti, corn, olives, half of the shredded cheese, the salsa, and chile peppers.

3. Transfer mixture to a lightly greased 2-quart casserole. Cover and bake for 15 to 20 minutes or until heated through. Sprinkle with remaining cheese. Serve with shredded lettuce, tomato wedges, and, if desired, tortilla chips and sour cream. Makes 6 servings.

Per serving: 424 cal., 22 g fat (8 g sat. fat), 65 mg chol., 978 mg sodium, 38 g carbo., 3 g fiber, 26 g pro.

Sweet and Sour Meatballs

Start to Finish: 30 min.

- 1 20-ounce can pineapple chunks
- ¾ cup maple syrup or maple-flavored syrup
- ½ cup cider vinegar
- 1 12- to 16-ounce package frozen cooked meatballs
- 2 medium red and/or green sweet peppers
- ¼ cup cold water
- 2 tablespoons cornstarch
- ½ teaspoon salt
- 2 cups hot cooked Asian noodles or rice
  Sliced green onion (optional)

1. Drain pineapple, reserving liquid. Set pineapple aside. In a large saucepan, stir together pineapple liquid, syrup, and vinegar. Add meatballs. Bring to boiling; reduce heat. Simmer, covered, for 15 minutes.

2. Meanwhile, remove seeds from sweet peppers and cut into ¾-inch pieces. Add to meatballs. Simmer, covered, for 5 minutes more.

3. In a small bowl, stir together water, cornstarch, and salt. Stir into meatball mixture. Cook and stir for 1 to 2 minutes or until thickened and bubbly. Stir in pineapple chunks; heat through. Serve over hot cooked noodles and, if desired, sprinkle with green onion. Makes 4 servings.

Per serving: 667 cal., 23 g fat (9 g sat. fat), 30 mg chol., 972 mg sodium, 107 g carbo., 5 g fiber, 14 g pro.

Mexican Beef and Veggies

Start to Finish: 30 min.

- 12 ounces lean ground beef
- 1 medium (1¼ pounds) butternut squash, peeled, seeded, and cubed (about 3 cups)
- 2 cloves garlic, minced
- 1 teaspoon ground cumin
- ½ teaspoon salt
- ⅛ teaspoon ground cinnamon
- 1 14.5-ounce can diced tomatoes
- 1 medium zucchini, halved lengthwise and cut into ¼-inch slices
- ¼ cup water
- ¼ cup chopped fresh cilantro
- 2 to 3 cups hot cooked white or brown rice
  Bottled hot pepper sauce (optional)

1. In a large skillet, cook ground beef, squash, garlic, cumin, salt, and cinnamon over medium heat until meat is brown. Drain off fat.

2. Stir in undrained tomatoes. Bring to boiling; reduce heat. Cover and simmer about 8 minutes or until squash is just tender. Stir in zucchini and the water. Cover and simmer about 4 minutes more or until zucchini is tender. Stir in cilantro. Serve over hot cooked rice. If desired, season to taste with bottled hot pepper sauce. Makes 4 to 6 servings.

Per serving: 313 cal., 9 g fat (3 g sat. fat), 54 mg chol., 504 mg sodium, 39 g carbo., 3 g fiber, 20 g pro.

Mediterranean Mostaccioli

Start to Finish: 25 min.

- 4 ounces dried mostaccioli or gemelli pasta
- 2 cups sliced zucchini
- 8 ounces ground beef
- ½ of a medium eggplant, peeled and cubed (about 2½ cups)
- 1 14.5-ounce can diced tomatoes with basil, oregano, and garlic
- 2 tablespoons tomato paste
- ½ cup shredded carrot
- ¼ cup snipped fresh basil
- 2 tablespoons raisins (optional)
- ¼ teaspoon ground cinnamon
- 1 tablespoon balsamic vinegar (optional)
- ½ cup shredded mozzarella cheese (2 ounces)

1. Cook pasta according to package directions, adding zucchini during the last 2 minutes of cooking. Drain; keep warm.

2. Meanwhile, for sauce, in a large skillet, cook beef and eggplant over medium heat until meat is brown. Drain off fat. Stir in undrained tomatoes, tomato paste, carrot, basil, raisins (if desired), and cinnamon. Bring to boiling; reduce heat. Simmer, uncovered, about 2 minutes or until desired consistency, stirring occasionally. Remove from heat. If desired, stir in vinegar.

3. Transfer pasta mixture to a serving dish. Spoon sauce over pasta mixture. Sprinkle with cheese. Makes 4 to 6 servings.

Per serving: 334 cal., 11 g fat (5 g sat. fat), 47 mg chol., 672 mg sodium, 38 g carbo., 4 g fiber, 21 g pro.

Meatball and Red Pepper Pasta

Start to Finish: 30 min.

- 1 cup thinly sliced carrot (2 medium)
- ½ cup chopped onion (1 medium)
- 2 cloves garlic, minced
- 1 tablespoon olive oil or cooking oil
- 2 12-ounce packages frozen cooked Italian-style meatballs (24 meatballs)
- 1 26-ounce jar spicy red pepper pasta sauce
- 8 ounces dried spaghetti or bow-tie pasta
  Finely shredded Parmesan cheese

1. In a large skillet, cook carrot, onion, and garlic in hot oil over medium heat for 5 minutes or until just tender. Stir in meatballs and pasta sauce. Bring to boiling; reduce heat. Simmer, covered, about 15 minutes or until meatballs are heated through.

2. Meanwhile, cook pasta according to package directions until just tender; drain. Serve meatballs and sauce over hot cooked pasta. Sprinkle with Parmesan cheese. Makes 6 servings.

Per serving: 591 cal., 31 g fat (13 g sat. fat), 77 mg chol., 1,225 mg sodium, 46 g carbo., 8 g fiber, 28 g pro.

Curried Apple Pork Chops

Prep: 15 min.   **Cook:** 36 min.

- 4   boneless pork loin chops, cut ¾ inch thick
     Salt and ground black pepper
     Nonstick cooking spray
- 2   large sweet potatoes (about 1¼ pounds), peeled and thinly sliced
- 1   21-ounce can apple pie filling
- 2   teaspoons curry powder
- 1   8-ounce package frozen sugar snap peas

1. Trim fat from pork. Sprinkle with salt and pepper. Coat a large skillet with cooking spray. Brown pork on both sides in hot skillet over medium heat. Add sweet potatoes. Cover and cook for 15 minutes.

3. Meanwhile, stir together pie filling and curry powder; spoon over sweet potatoes. Cover and cook about 15 minutes more or until potatoes are nearly tender. Add sugar snap peas; cover and cook for 6 to 8 minutes more or until peas are crisp-tender. Makes 4 servings.

Per serving: 539 cal., 13 g fat (4 g sat. fat), 92 mg chol., 301 mg sodium, 63 g carbo., 6 g fiber, 41 g pro.

Meatballs Stroganoff

Start to Finish: 30 min.

- 1   12- to 16-ounce package frozen cooked meatballs
- 1   cup reduced-sodium beef broth
- 1   4-ounce can sliced mushrooms, drained
- 1   8-ounce carton dairy sour cream
- 2   tablespoons all-purpose flour
- ½   cup milk
- 1   tablespoon Dijon-style mustard
- 4   cups hot cooked wide egg noodles
     Snipped fresh parsley (optional)

1. In a large skillet, combine the meatballs, broth, and mushrooms. Bring to boiling; reduce heat. Cover and simmer about 15 minutes or until meatballs are heated through.

2. In a small bowl, stir together sour cream and flour. Whisk in milk and mustard. Stir sour cream mixture into skillet. Cook and stir until thickened and bubbly. Cook and stir for 1 minute more. Serve over hot cooked noodles. If desired, stir in snipped fresh parsley. Makes 6 to 8 servings.

Per serving: 424 cal., 25 g fat (12 g sat. fat), 73 mg chol., 696 mg sodium, 36 g carbo., 3 g fiber, 16 g pro.

Taco Pizza

Prep: 15 min.   **Bake:** 20 min.

- 8   ounces lean ground beef or bulk pork sausage
- ¾   cup chopped green sweet pepper (1 medium)
- 1   11.5-ounce package refrigerated corn bread twists
- ½   cup salsa
- 3   cups shredded taco cheese (12 ounces)
     Crushed tortilla chips, sour cream, chopped tomato, and/or chopped green onion (optional)

1. Preheat oven to 400°F. In a large skillet, cook beef and sweet pepper over medium heat until meat is brown. Drain off fat. Set meat mixture aside.

2. Unroll corn bread dough (do not separate into strips). Press dough into a greased 12-inch pizza pan, building up edges. Spread salsa over dough. Sprinkle with meat mixture and cheese. Bake about 20 minutes or until bottom of crust is golden brown when lifted slightly with a spatula. If desired, top with crushed tortilla chips, sour cream, tomato, and/or green onion. Cut into wedges. Makes 6 servings.

Per serving: 451 cal., 30 g fat (15 g sat. fat), 73 mg chol., 901 mg sodium, 26 g carbo., 1 g fiber, 22 g pro.

Skillet Tuna and Biscuits

Skillet Tuna and Biscuits

Start to Finish: 30 min.

- 1 10-ounce container reduced-fat refrigerated Alfredo pasta sauce
- 1 10-ounce package frozen peas and carrots
- 1 4-ounce can sliced mushrooms, drained
- 1 teaspoon lemon juice
- ¼ teaspoon dried dill weed
- 1 12-ounce can tuna, drained and flaked
- 1 cup packaged biscuit mix
- ⅓ cup fat-free milk
- ¼ cup shredded cheddar cheese (1 ounce)

1. Preheat oven to 400°F. In a large ovenproof skillet, combine pasta sauce, peas and carrots, mushrooms, lemon juice, and dill. Cook and stir over medium heat until bubbly and heated through. Remove from heat. Stir in tuna. Cover to keep warm.

2. In a medium bowl, stir together biscuit mix, milk, and half of the cheese. Drop mixture into 4 mounds on top of tuna mixture. Sprinkle with the remaining cheese. Bake for 12 to 15 minutes or until biscuits are golden. Makes 4 servings.

Per serving: 487 cal., 20 g fat (9 g sat. fat), 74 mg chol., 1,540 mg sodium, 46 g carbo., 3 g fiber, 33 g pro.

Speedy Spicy Tuna Noodle Casserole

Start to Finish: 25 min.

- 8 ounces dried wagon wheel and/or elbow macaroni (2⅔ cups)
- 1 10.75-ounce can condensed fiesta nacho cheese soup
- ½ cup milk
- 1 12-ounce can solid white tuna (water pack), drained and broken into chunks
- 1 4-ounce can or jar diced green chile peppers, drained
  Rich round crackers, tortilla chips, or corn chips (optional)

1. Cook pasta in lightly salted water according to package directions; drain. Return pasta to pan.

2. Add soup and milk to cooked pasta and stir until pasta is coated and creamy. Gently fold in tuna and chile peppers. Heat through. If desired, serve with crackers or chips. Makes 4 servings.

Per serving: 414 cal., 9 g fat (4 g sat. fat), 44 mg chol., 905 mg sodium, 51 g carbo., 2 g fiber, 31 g pro.

Shredded Pork Tacos

Shredded Pork Tacos

Prep: 30 min. **Cook:** 8 hr. (low) or 4 hr. (high)

- 1 2½- to 3-pound boneless pork shoulder roast
- 1 cup chicken broth
- ½ cup enchilada sauce or salsa
- 4 8-inch soft flour tortillas or taco shells
  Shredded lettuce, finely shredded Mexican-blend cheese, chopped tomato, sliced pitted ripe olives, and/or sliced avocado
  Dairy sour cream (optional)

1. Trim fat from pork. If necessary, cut pork to fit in a 3½- or 4-quart slow cooker. Place pork in cooker. Add broth. Cover and cook on low-heat setting for 8 to 10 hours or on high-heat setting for 4 to 5 hours. Remove meat from cooker; discard broth. Using two forks, shred meat, discarding any fat. Reserve 2 cups of the meat. (Place remaining meat in an airtight container for another use; refrigerate for up to 3 days or freeze up to 3 months.)

2. In a saucepan, combine 2 cups meat and the sauce. Cover; cook over medium-low heat about 10 minutes or until heated through, stirring occasionally. Meanwhile, warm flour tortillas according to package directions.

3. To assemble tacos, place pork mixture in center of warm tortillas or in taco shells. Top as desired with lettuce, cheese, tomato, olives, and/or avocado. If desired, serve with sour cream. Makes 4 servings.

Per serving: 616 cal., 31 g fat (10 g sat. fat), 202 mg chol., 846 mg sodium, 20 g carbo., 3 g fiber, 61 g pro.

Shrimply Divine Pasta

Start to Finish: 20 min.

- 1 6-ounce package rotini or other pasta
- 12 ounces frozen medium shrimp, thawed, peeled, and deveined
- 3 cloves garlic, minced
- 1 tablespoon olive oil
- 1 cup chicken broth
- 1 tablespoon cornstarch
- 1 teaspoon dried basil, crushed
- 1 teaspoon dried oregano, crushed
- 4 cups prewashed (packaged) baby spinach or torn spinach

Finely shredded Parmesan cheese

1. Cook pasta according to package directions. Drain well; keep pasta warm.

2. Meanwhile, rinse shrimp; pat dry with paper towels. For sauce, in a large skillet, cook garlic in hot oil over medium-high heat for 15 seconds. Add shrimp. Cook and stir for 2 to 3 minutes or until shrimp are opaque. Remove shrimp. Stir together broth, cornstarch, basil, and oregano. Add to skillet. Cook and stir until thickened and bubbly. Add the spinach. Cook for 1 to 2 minutes more or until wilted. Return shrimp to skillet; stir to combine.

3. Toss shrimp mixture and pasta together. Top with Parmesan cheese. Makes 4 servings.

Per serving: 333 cal., 7 g fat (1 g sat. fat), 136 mg chol., 422 mg sodium, 39 g carbo., 3 g fiber, 25 g pro.

Grilled Shrimp Kabobs

Prep: 20 min.　**Grill:** 6 min.

　1　pound fresh or frozen large shrimp in shells
　1　medium green and/or red sweet pepper,
　　　cut into 16 pieces
　¼　of a medium fresh pineapple, cut into chunks
　4　green onions, cut into 2- to 3-inch pieces
　¼　cup bottled low-carb barbecue sauce

1. Thaw shrimp, if frozen. Peel and devein shrimp, keeping tails intact. Rinse shrimp; pat dry with paper towels. Alternately thread shrimp, sweet pepper pieces, pineapple chunks, and green onion pieces onto 8 long metal skewers.

2. For a charcoal grill, grill kabobs on the greased grill rack of an uncovered grill directly over medium coals for 6 to 10 minutes or until shrimp are opaque, turning once and brushing with barbecue sauce halfway through grilling. (For a gas grill, preheat grill. Reduce heat to medium. Place kabobs on greased grill rack over heat. Cover and grill as above.) Makes 4 servings.

Per serving: 127 cal., 2 g fat (0 g sat. fat), 129 mg chol., 257 mg sodium, 9 g carbo., 1 g fiber, 18 g pro.

Mexican Shrimp Tostadas

Start to Finish: 20 min.

　4　tostada shells
　2　cups shredded lettuce
　1　15-ounce can black beans, rinsed and
　　　drained
　20　large shrimp, peeled, deveined,
　　　cooked, and chilled
　1　tablespoon lime juice
　1　medium tomato, cut into 16 thin wedges
　¼　cup dairy sour cream
　　　Sliced green onion
　　　Salsa

1. Place one tostada shell on each of 4 serving plates. Top with some lettuce and ¼ of the beans. Arrange 5 shrimp in a circle over the beans; sprinkle shrimp with lime juice.

2. Arrange 4 tomato wedges on each tortilla and top with a tablespoon of the sour cream and some green onion. Serve with salsa. Makes 4 servings.

Per serving: 273 cal., 6 g fat (2 g sat. fat), 227 mg chol., 670 mg sodium, 25 g carbo., 6 g fiber, 32 g pro.

Honey Mustard Tenderloin

Prep: 10 min. **Cook:** 2 min. **Roast:** 25 min.

- ½ of a 16-ounce package peeled fresh baby carrots (1½ cups)
- 12 tiny new potatoes, halved
- ⅓ cup honey mustard
- 2 tablespoons olive oil or cooking oil
- ½ teaspoon garlic pepper
- ¼ teaspoon seasoned salt
- 1 12- to 16-ounce pork tenderloin

1. Preheat oven to 425°F. Cook carrots and potatoes in a medium saucepan in lightly salted boiling water for 2 minutes; drain. Set aside.

2. In a medium bowl, stir together honey mustard, olive oil, garlic pepper, and seasoned salt; spread half of the mixture on the tenderloin. Place tenderloin on a rack in a shallow roasting pan. Insert a meat thermometer into thickest part of the tenderloin. Toss carrots and potatoes with remaining mustard mixture; spoon vegetables around the tenderloin.

3. Roast, uncovered, in the preheated oven for 25 to 35 minutes or until the meat thermometer registers 160°F, stirring the vegetables once halfway through roasting time. Makes 4 servings.

Per serving: 286 cal., 9 g fat (2 g sat. fat), 55 mg chol., 328 mg sodium, 28 g carbo., 3 g fiber, 21 g pro.

Honey Mustard Tenderloin

Orange-Sauced Fish with Broccoli

Start to Finish: 30 min.

- 1 pound fresh or frozen fish fillets, ½ to ¾ inch thick
- 1 10-ounce package frozen chopped broccoli
- 1 tablespoon water
- 1 cup water
- ½ cup orange marmalade
- ¼ teaspoon salt
- 1 cup quick-cooking couscous
  Freshly ground black pepper
- 1 tablespoon butter
- 2 teaspoons lemon juice

1. Thaw fish, if frozen. Rinse fish; pat dry with paper towels. If necessary, cut fish into 4 serving-size pieces; set aside.

2. Place broccoli in a microwave-safe 2-quart square baking dish. Sprinkle with the 1 tablespoon water. Cover with vented plastic wrap. Microwave on 100-percent power (high) for 4 to 6 minutes or until crisp-tender, giving the dish a half-turn and stirring broccoli halfway through cooking.

3. Stir the 1 cup water, 2 tablespoons of the orange marmalade, and the ¼ teaspoon salt into the broccoli. Stir in couscous. Spread couscous mixture evenly in dish. Arrange fish on top of the couscous mixture, folding under any thin edges to make fish uniform thickness; sprinkle fish with additional salt and the pepper.

4. Cover with vented plastic wrap. Microwave on 100-percent power (high) for 7 to 9 minutes or until fish just flakes when tested with a fork, giving the dish a half-turn halfway through cooking.

5. For sauce, in a small microwave-safe bowl, combine remaining marmalade, the butter, and lemon juice. Microwave on 100-percent power (high) about 1 minute or until butter melts and sauce is bubbly. Stir sauce; drizzle over fish. Makes 4 servings.

Per serving: 420 cal., 5 g fat (2 g sat. fat), 62 mg chol., 312 mg sodium, 66 g carbo., 5 g fiber, 29 g pro.

Caesar Salmon Pizzas

Prep: 15 min. **Bake:** 8 min.

2	6-inch Italian bread shells (Boboli®)
¼	cup bottled creamy Caesar salad dressing
2	cups torn fresh spinach
2	ounces smoked salmon, flaked, skin and bones removed
¼	cup walnut pieces, toasted
¼	cup finely shredded Parmesan cheese (1 ounce)
2	tablespoons thinly bias-sliced green onion (1)
1	teaspoon drained capers (optional)

1. Preheat oven to 400°F. Lightly spread bread shells with some of the Caesar dressing. Place bread shells on a baking sheet. Top bread shells with spinach, salmon, walnuts, half of the Parmesan cheese, the green onion, and, if desired, capers.

2. Bake, uncovered, for 8 to 10 minutes or just until heated through. Drizzle with remaining Caesar dressing; sprinkle with remaining Parmesan cheese. Makes 2 pizzas.

Per pizza: 652 cal., 39 g fat (6 g sat. fat), 19 mg chol., 1,480 mg sodium, 54 g carbo., 4 g fiber, 26 g pro.

{toasting nuts}

Toast nuts to give recipes an outstanding flavor boost. Spread them in a single layer in a shallow roasting pan. Bake in a 350°F oven for 5 to 10 minutes or until nuts are golden brown, stirring once or twice. Check them often to make sure they don't get too brown. They go quickly from perfect to burnt, and if they burn, you have to start over.

2. In a large skillet, heat oil over medium heat. Add garlic; cook and stir for 15 seconds. Add tomatoes; cook and stir for 2 minutes. Add asparagus stalks, broth, salt, and pepper. Cook and stir for 3 minutes. Add asparagus tips and shrimp; cook and stir for 2 to 3 minutes or until shrimp are opaque. Stir in butter until melted.

3. Add asparagus mixture and basil to pasta; toss to combine. Makes 4 servings.

Per serving: 274 cal., 6 g fat (2 g sat. fat), 137 mg chol., 362 mg sodium, 31 g carbo., 4 g fiber, 24 g pro.

Quick Stuffed Peppers Risotto
Start to Finish: 25 min.

4	small (about 5 ounces each) or 2 large (about 8 ounces each) red, green, and/or yellow sweet peppers
	Salt and ground black pepper
1	cup 1-inch pieces fresh asparagus or broccoli florets
1	8.8-ounce package cooked long grain rice
1	cup cubed cooked chicken
½	cup finely shredded Parmesan or Romano cheese (2 ounces)
¼	cup milk
½	to 1 teaspoon dried oregano, crushed
¼	teaspoon salt
⅛	teaspoon ground black pepper
¼	cup chopped walnuts, toasted if desired
	Shaved or shredded Parmesan or Romano cheese (optional)

1. Cut tops off small peppers or halve large peppers lengthwise. Remove membranes and seeds. If necessary, cut a thin slice from the bottom of the small peppers so they stand upright. In a 4-quart Dutch oven, cook peppers in enough boiling water to cover for 3 minutes. Drain well. Place on a serving platter, cut sides up. Sprinkle lightly with salt and black pepper; set aside.

2. Meanwhile, for filling, in a medium saucepan, cook asparagus, covered, in a small amount of boiling water for 1 to 2 minutes or until just tender. Drain and return to pan. Stir in rice, chicken, the ½ cup Parmesan cheese, the milk, oregano, ¼ teaspoon salt, and ⅛ teaspoon black pepper. Cook and stir over medium heat until heated through. Stir in walnuts.

3. Spoon filling into peppers. If desired, top with additional Parmesan cheese. Makes 4 servings.

Per serving: 321 cal., 13 g fat (4 g sat. fat), 43 mg chol., 581 mg sodium, 32 g carbo., 5 g fiber, 21 g pro.

Pasta with Shrimp, Asparagus, and Tomatoes

Pasta with Shrimp, Asparagus, and Tomatoes
Start to Finish: 30 min.

4	ounces dried spaghetti
12	ounces fresh or frozen peeled and deveined shrimp
16	thin spears fresh asparagus
1	teaspoon olive oil
4	cloves garlic, minced
2	cups chopped seeded roma tomatoes (6 medium)
¼	cup chicken broth
¼	teaspoon salt
¼	teaspoon ground black pepper
1	tablespoon butter
¼	cup shredded fresh basil

1. Cook pasta according to package directions. Drain; keep warm. Meanwhile, thaw shrimp if frozen. Set aside. Snap off and discard woody bases from asparagus. Remove tips; set aside. Bias-slice asparagus stalks into 1- to 1½-inch pieces; set aside.

Ravioli with Summer Vegetables

Start to Finish: 25 min.

- 1 9-ounce package refrigerated cheese-filled ravioli or tortellini
- 2 cloves garlic, minced
- 2 teaspoons olive oil or cooking oil
- 1¼ cups thinly sliced yellow summer squash (1 medium)
- 4 roma tomatoes, quartered
- 1 15-ounce can garbanzo beans, rinsed and drained
- 2 teaspoons snipped fresh thyme or ½ teaspoon dried thyme, crushed
- ¼ teaspoon ground black pepper
- 4 cups shredded fresh spinach

1. Cook ravioli according to package directions.

2. Meanwhile, in a large skillet, cook and stir garlic in 2 teaspoons hot oil for 30 seconds. Add squash, tomatoes, garbanzo beans, thyme, and pepper. Cook and stir over medium-high heat for 4 to 5 minutes or until squash is crisp-tender and mixture is heated through.

3. Drain ravioli; add to vegetable mixture. Toss lightly. Add spinach and toss lightly. Spoon into serving dishes. Makes 4 servings.

Per serving: 304 cal., 7 g fat (2 g sat. fat), 25 mg chol., 688 mg sodium, 48 g carbo., 7 g fiber, 15 g pro.

Kids' Favorite Pasta Primavera

Start to Finish: 25 min.

- 1 12-ounce package frozen cooked breaded chicken nuggets
- 8 ounces dried wagon wheel pasta (rotelle)
- 4 cups chopped or sliced assorted vegetables (broccoli, carrots, summer squash, cauliflower, and sweet peppers)
- ½ of an 8-ounce tub cream cheese spread with chives and onion
- ¼ to ½ cup milk
   Salt and ground black pepper
   Shredded Parmesan cheese

1. Heat chicken nuggets according to package directions; keep warm.

2. Meanwhile, in a Dutch oven, heat a large amount of lightly salted water to boiling. Add pasta; cook for 4 minutes. Add vegetables; cook about 5 minutes more or until pasta is tender. Drain and return to pan.

3. Add cream cheese spread to pasta mixture. Heat through. Add enough milk to thin to desired consistency. Season to taste with salt and pepper. Sprinkle with Parmesan cheese. Serve with baked chicken nuggets. Makes 4 servings.

Per serving: 643 cal., 27 g fat (12 g sat. fat), 81 mg chol., 811 mg sodium, 72 g carbo., 4 g fiber, 25 g pro.

Rice Pilaf with Oranges and Walnuts

Prep: 20 min. **Cook:** 25 min.

- 1½ cups sliced fresh mushrooms (4 ounces)
- 1 cup sliced celery (2 stalks)
- 1 cup finely chopped onion (2 medium)
- 1 tablespoon cooking oil
- 1 14-ounce can chicken broth
- ⅔ cup water
- 1 6-ounce package long grain and wild rice mix
- 2 medium oranges, peeled and sectioned, or one 11-ounce can mandarin oranges, drained
- ½ cup chopped toasted walnuts

1. In a large saucepan, cook mushrooms, celery, and onion in hot oil over medium heat about 5 minutes or until tender. Add broth and water; bring to boiling. Stir in rice mix and seasoning packet; reduce heat. Cover and simmer for 25 to 30 minutes or until rice is tender. Gently stir in oranges and walnuts. Makes 6 servings.

Per serving: 214 cal., 10 g fat (1 g sat. fat), 1 mg chol., 673 mg sodium, 29 g carbo., 3 g fiber, 6 g pro.

Veggie Nuggets

Prep: 20 min.   **Bake:** 15 min.

   Nonstick cooking spray
- 1 egg yolk
- ¼ cup milk
- ½ cup seasoned fine dry bread crumbs
- ¼ cup grated Parmesan cheese
- 2 tablespoons butter, melted (optional)
- 4 cups vegetables, such as ¼-inch-thick sliced zucchini, peeled baby carrots, broccoli florets, and/or green beans
- ¾ cup bottled ranch salad dressing
   Shredded cheddar cheese

1. Preheat oven to 400°F. Lightly coat a baking sheet with cooking spray; set aside. In a shallow dish, whisk together egg yolk and milk. In another shallow dish, stir together the bread crumbs and Parmesan cheese. Dip vegetables in egg mixture, then in bread crumb mixture to coat. Arrange vegetable pieces on the prepared baking sheet. If desired, drizzle with melted butter.

2. Bake for 15 to 20 minutes or until vegetables are tender and golden. Serve warm with ranch dressing that has been sprinkled with cheddar cheese. Makes 5 to 6 servings.

Per serving: 271 cal., 22 g fat (4 g sat. fat), 51 mg chol., 662 mg sodium, 14 g carbo., 1 g fiber, 5 g pro.

Veggie Nuggets

Ramen Noodles with Vegetables

Start to Finish: 15 min.

2   3-ounce package ramen noodles (any flavor)
1   cup purchased shredded carrot
12 ounces fresh asparagus, trimmed and cut
    into 1-inch pieces (2 cups)
1   tablespoon cooking oil
½   cup light teriyaki sauce

1. Cook noodles according to package directions (discard seasoning packet). Drain and keep warm.

2. Meanwhile, in a large skillet, cook carrot and asparagus in hot oil over medium-high heat for 3 to 5 minutes or until asparagus is crisp-tender. Stir in the cooked noodles. Add teriyaki sauce; toss to coat. Makes 4 servings.

Per serving: 291 cal., 14 g fat (4 g sat. fat), 0 mg chol., 1,396 mg sodium, 36 g carbo., 3 g fiber, 7 g pro.

Rice 'n' Bean Tostadas

Start to Finish: 30 min.

1½ cups water
1½ cups quick-cooking brown rice
½   cup chopped onion (1 medium)
1   15-ounce can chili beans with chili gravy
1   8-ounce can whole kernel corn, drained
8   tostada shells
3   cups shredded lettuce
½   cup shredded cheddar cheese (2 ounces)
1   cup quartered cherry tomatoes

1. Preheat oven to 350°F. In a large saucepan, bring water to boiling. Stir in rice and onion. Return to boiling; reduce heat. Cover and simmer for 5 minutes. Remove from heat. Stir. Cover and let stand for 5 minutes. Stir undrained chili beans and the corn into rice mixture. Heat through.

2. Meanwhile, place tostada shells on a baking sheet. Bake for 5 minutes or until heated through.

3. To assemble, place 2 tostada shells on each plate. Top tostadas with shredded lettuce and the rice-bean mixture. Sprinkle with cheddar cheese and top with tomatoes. Makes 4 servings.

Per serving: 438 cal., 12 g fat (4 g sat. fat), 15 mg chol., 621 mg sodium, 70 g carbo., 11 g fiber, 15 g pro.

Nacho-Style Scalloped Potatoes

Prep: 10 min. **Cook:** 20 min.

- 1   20-ounce package refrigerated shredded hash brown potatoes*
- 2   tablespoons cooking oil
- 12 ounces lean ground beef
- ½   cup chopped onion
- 1   11-ounce can condensed fiesta nacho cheese soup
- 1   4-ounce can diced green chile peppers
- ½   cup milk
  Dairy sour cream (optional)
  Bottled salsa (optional)
  Sliced green onion (optional)

1. In a large skillet, spread the potatoes evenly in hot oil and cook over medium heat for 6 minutes or until bottom is crisp. With a pancake turner, turn potatoes in large sections. Cook for 7 to 9 minutes more or until golden. Transfer to large bowl. In the same skillet, cook ground beef and onion until meat is brown. Drain off fat. Stir in soup, undrained chile peppers, and milk. Fold in cooked potatoes. Heat through.

2. If desired, serve with sour cream, salsa, and sliced green onion. Makes 4 servings.

*If you cannot find refrigerated potatoes, frozen shredded hash browns, thawed, can be substituted.

Per serving: 430 cal., 21 g fat (7 g sat. fat), 62 mg chol., 716 mg sodium, 40 g carbo., 3 g fiber, 22 g pro.

Grilled Steak, Mango, and Pear Salad

Prep: 15 min. **Grill:** 14 min.

- 12 ounces boneless beef top loin steak, 1 inch thick
- ½   teaspoon salt
- ¼   teaspoon ground black pepper
- 1   10-ounce package torn mixed salad greens (about 8 cups)
- 1   24-ounce jar refrigerated sliced mango, drained
- 1   medium pear, peeled, cored, and chopped
- ¾   cup refrigerated fat-free blue cheese salad dressing
  Cracked black pepper

1. Sprinkle both sides of steak with salt and the ¼ teaspoon pepper.

2. Place steak on the rack of an uncovered grill directly over medium heat. Grill until desired doneness, turning once halfway through grilling. Allow 14 to 18 minutes for medium rare (145°F) or 18 to 22 minutes for medium (160°F).

3. To serve, thinly slice steak across the grain. Arrange greens on a serving platter; top with meat, mango, and pear. Top with salad dressing. Sprinkle with cracked black pepper. Makes 4 servings.

Per serving: 307 cal., 5 g fat (2 g sat. fat), 50 mg chol., 900 mg sodium, 49 g carbo., 4 g fiber, 19 g pro.

Pulled Chicken-Peanut Salad

Start to Finish: 25 min.

- 2 tablespoons frozen orange juice concentrate, thawed
- 1 tablespoon water
- 2 teaspoons toasted sesame oil
- ¼ teaspoon salt
- ⅛ teaspoon coarsely ground black pepper
- 6 cups torn mixed salad greens
- 2 cups coarsely shredded cooked chicken
- 1 11-ounce can mandarin orange sections, drained
- ¼ cup cocktail peanuts

1. For dressing, in a small bowl, stir together juice concentrate, water, oil, salt, and pepper. Set aside.

2. Arrange greens on salad plates. Top with chicken, oranges, and peanuts. Drizzle with dressing. Makes 4 servings.

Per serving: 263 cal., 12 g fat (3 g sat. fat), 62 mg chol., 247 mg sodium, 15 g carbo., 2 g fiber, 24 g pro.

Thai-Style Beef Salad

Start to Finish: 15 min.   Chill: up to 24 hr.

- **2** tablespoons bottled Italian salad dressing
- **2** to 3 teaspoons lime juice
- **1½** teaspoons soy sauce
- **1** teaspoon snipped fresh cilantro
- **2** cups fresh spinach leaves or torn mixed salad greens
- **¼** cup purchased shredded carrot
- **½** cup shredded leftover roast beef
- **1** tablespoon chopped peanuts

1. For dressing, in a small container with a tight-fitting lid, combine dressing, lime juice, soy sauce, and cilantro; cover and shake well. Chill for up to 24 hours.

2. In an airtight container, combine spinach, carrot, beef, and peanuts. Cover and chill for up to 24 hours.

3. To serve, shake dressing; add dressing to spinach mixture and toss to coat. Makes 1 serving.

Per serving: 328 cal., 22 g fat (5 g sat. fat), 56 mg chol., 1,095 mg sodium, 10 g carbo., 3 g fiber, 25 g pro.

{sack lunch sides}

❖ Leftovers in a storage container make great lunches the next day. Throw in a couple of sides and an ice pack, and you're ready to go.

❖ Some tasty sides are crackers and cheese, apple slices, carrot sticks and ranch dip, grapes, celery and peanut butter, banana, pretzel twists, applesauce, fruit snacks, pita chips with hummus, sweet pepper strips, vanilla wafers, whole wheat crackers, low-fat yogurt, and string cheese.

Chili-Lime Chicken Salad

Prep: 15 min. **Cook:** 8 min.

- 1 pound chicken tenders*
- 2 teaspoons chili powder
-    Salt and ground black pepper
- 1 tablespoon olive oil
- ¼ cup olive oil or salad oil
- 3 tablespoons lime juice
- 2 tablespoons snipped fresh cilantro
- 1 tablespoon white wine vinegar
- ¼ teaspoon salt
-    Dash ground black pepper
- 6 cups torn romaine lettuce
- 8 cherry tomatoes, halved or quartered
- ½ of a medium avocado, pitted, peeled, and sliced

1. In a bowl, toss chicken tenders with chili powder and salt and pepper to taste. In a large skillet, heat the 1 tablespoon oil over medium-high heat. Add chicken tenders; reduce heat to medium. Cook for 8 to 12 minutes or until chicken is no longer pink, turning once.

2. Meanwhile, for dressing, in a screw-top jar, combine the ¼ cup oil, the lime juice, cilantro, vinegar, ¼ teaspoon salt, and dash pepper. Cover; shake well. Arrange lettuce on four salad plates. Top with chicken, tomatoes, and avocado. Drizzle with dressing. Makes 4 servings.

*If you can't find chicken tenders at the supermarket, make your own by cutting skinless, boneless chicken breasts lengthwise into strips.

Per serving: 284 cal., 20 g fat (3 g sat. fat), 55 mg chol., 278 mg sodium, 8 g carbo., 4 g fiber, 20 g pro.

Chicken and Grape Pasta Salad

Prep: 40 min. **Chill:** up to 24 hr.

- 1 2- to 2½-pound deli-roasted chicken or 3 cups chopped cooked chicken
- 1½ cups dried radiatore, mostaccioli, or medium shell pasta
- 3 cups fresh red and green grapes, halved and, if necessary, seeded
- 1½ cups halved small strawberries
- 1 cup chopped peeled jicama or one 8-ounce can sliced water chestnuts, drained
- ⅔ cup bottled cucumber ranch salad dressing
- ⅛ teaspoon cayenne pepper
- 1 to 2 tablespoons milk (optional)
-    Leaf lettuce

Try taco seasoning in place of chili powder for a different flavor.

Chili-Lime Chicken Salad

1. Remove meat from chicken (discard skin and bones). Tear meat into bite-size pieces. Cook pasta according to package directions. Drain pasta and rinse with cold water. Drain again.

2. In a large salad bowl, place chicken, pasta, grapes, strawberries, and jicama; toss to combine.

3. In a small bowl, stir together dressing and pepper. Pour dressing over chicken mixture. Toss lightly to coat. Cover and chill for 4 to 24 hours.

4. Before serving, if necessary, stir in enough milk (1 to 2 tablespoons) to moisten. Serve salad on lettuce-lined plates. Makes 6 servings.

Per serving: 455 cal., 20 g fat (3 g sat. fat), 67 mg chol., 269 mg sodium, 43 g carbo., 3 g fiber, 27 g pro.

Basil and Tomato Pasta Salad

Prep: 25 min. **Chill:** up to 24 hr.

- 8 ounces dried rotini, cavatelli, or penne pasta
- 6 ounces fresh green beans, trimmed and cut into 1-inch pieces, or 1 cup frozen cut green beans
- 3 medium tomatoes, cut into thin wedges (about 1 pound)
- 1 cup desired-flavor bottled vinaigrette salad dressing
- ¾ cup finely shredded Parmesan cheese (3 ounces)
- ½ cup sliced pitted kalamata olives or ripe olives
- ½ cup finely shredded fresh basil
  Shaved Parmesan cheese (optional)

1. Cook pasta according to package directions, adding green beans the last 5 minutes of cooking; drain. Rinse with cold water; drain again.

2. In a very large bowl, toss together the pasta mixture, tomatoes, salad dressing, finely shredded cheese, olives, and basil. Cover and chill for 4 to 24 hours. Toss gently before serving. If desired, top with shaved Parmesan. Makes 12 to 16 servings.

Per serving: 170 cal., 8 g fat (2 g sat. fat), 4 mg chol., 384 mg sodium, 19 g carbo., 2 g fiber, 5 g pro.

Asian Chicken and Rice Salad

Start to Finish: 25 min.

- 1　6- to 7.2-ounce box rice pilaf mix
- 2　cups shredded or chopped cooked chicken
- 1　14-ounce can whole baby corn, drained
- ½　cup chopped red sweet pepper (1 small)
- ½　cup snow pea pods, halved, or thinly sliced celery (1 stalk)
- ¼　cup sliced green onion (2)
- ½　cup bottled Asian salad dressing
- 　　Toasted sesame seeds (optional)

1. Cook rice mix according to package directions.

2. In a large bowl, stir together rice mix, chicken, corn, sweet pepper, pea pods, and green onion. Add dressing, stirring gently to combine. Serve immediately or cover and chill for up to 24 hours. If desired, sprinkle with sesame seeds before serving. Makes 4 to 6 servings.

Per serving: 429 cal., 14 g fat (3 g sat. fat), 62 mg chol., 1,057 mg sodium, 46 g carbo., 5 g fiber, 26 g pro.

Chilled Asparagus Salad

Prep: 20 min.　**Cook:** 3 min.

- ½　cup mayonnaise or salad dressing
- ¼　cup plain yogurt
- ½　teaspoon finely shredded orange peel
- ⅓　cup orange juice
- ⅛　teaspoon lemon-pepper seasoning
- 1　pound fresh asparagus spears
- 6　cups torn butterhead (Boston or Bibb) lettuce
- 1　small red onion, cut into thin wedges
- 1　11-ounce can mandarin orange sections, drained

1. For dressing, in a small bowl, stir together the mayonnaise, yogurt, orange peel, orange juice, and lemon-pepper seasoning. Set dressing aside or cover and chill for up to 6 hours.

2. Snap off and discard woody bases from asparagus. Cook, covered, in a large saucepan in a small amount of lightly salted boiling water for 3 to 5 minutes or until crisp-tender. Drain asparagus. Immediately plunge cooked asparagus into ice water. Drain well.

3. Arrange lettuce, asparagus, onion wedges, and orange sections on serving plates. Drizzle dressing over salads. Makes 4 to 6 servings.

Per serving: 277 cal., 23 g fat (4 g sat. fat), 11 mg chol., 180 mg sodium, 16 g carbo., 3 g fiber, 4 g pro.

Stack-It-Up Chicken Salad

Start to Finish: 30 min.

- 2　romaine hearts, halved crosswise
- 1　2¼- to 2½-pound deli-roasted chicken, skin and bones removed, meat coarsely chopped
- ½　of a fresh pineapple, peeled, if desired, and cut into wedges
- 1　Granny Smith apple, cored and sliced, or 1 cup red and/or green seedless grapes
- 1　medium yellow or red sweet pepper, cut into thin strips
- ½　cup bottled ginger-sesame stir-fry sauce
- ¼　cup creamy peanut butter
- ¼　teaspoon crushed red pepper
- 　　Water (optional)

1. On individual serving plates, build a stack with the romaine, chicken, pineapple, apple, and sweet pepper strips.

2. In a small bowl, whisk together the stir-fry sauce, peanut butter, and crushed red pepper. If necessary, whisk in water, 1 teaspoon at a time, until sauce reaches drizzling consistency. Serve sauce with salad. Makes 4 servings.

Per serving: 529 cal., 19 g fat (5 g sat. fat), 123 mg chol., 998 mg sodium, 44 g carbo., 5 g fiber, 45 g pro.

one-pan

Dilled Shrimp with Rice

plan

One pan is **all you need** to fix a family-friendly dinner simply and quickly. And cleanup is quicker when you use fewer pans.

Shrimp with Basil on Fettuccine

Start to Finish: 25 min.

- 1 pound fresh or frozen peeled and deveined medium shrimp (1½ pounds medium shrimp in shell)
- 6 ounces spinach or plain fettuccine
- 2 teaspoons snipped fresh basil or tarragon or 1 teaspoon dried basil or tarragon, crushed
- 2 tablespoons butter

1. Thaw shrimp, if frozen. Prepare the fettuccine according to package directions. In a large skillet, cook shrimp and basil in hot butter over medium-high heat for 2 to 3 minutes or until shrimp are opaque, stirring frequently. Serve over fettuccine. Makes 4 servings.

Per serving: 301 cal., 9 g fat (5 g sat. fat), 225 mg chol., 264 mg sodium, 24 g carbo., 1 g fiber, 29 g pro.

Dilled Shrimp with Rice

Start to Finish: 25 min.

- 1 tablespoon butter
- 1½ cups shredded carrot (3 medium)
- 1 cup sugar snap peas
- ⅓ cup sliced green onion (3)
- 1 pound cooked peeled and deveined shrimp
- 2 cups cooked rice*
- 1 teaspoon finely shredded lemon peel
- ¾ cup chicken or vegetable broth
- 1 tablespoon snipped fresh dill or 1 teaspoon dried dill weed

1. In a large skillet, melt butter over medium heat. Add carrot, sugar snap peas, and onion; cook and stir for 2 to 3 minutes or until vegetables are crisp-tender.

2. Stir shrimp, rice, lemon peel, and broth into skillet; heat through. Stir in dill. Makes 4 servings.

* For cooked rice, use leftover cooked rice or one to two 8.8-ounce pouches cooked long grain rice.

Per serving: 291 cal., 5 g fat (2 g sat. fat), 230 mg chol., 495 mg sodium, 32 g carbo., 3 g fiber, 28 g pro.

Pasta with Green Beans and Goat Cheese

Frozen vegetables cook quickly and add color and **balanced nutrition** to one-dish meals.

Pasta with Green Beans and Goat Cheese

Prep: 15 min. **Cook:** 13 min.

- 12 cups water
- ½ teaspoon salt
- 8 ounces dried linguine
- 1 9-ounce package frozen cut green beans
- 2 medium leeks, thinly sliced (about ⅔ cup)
- ½ cup chopped walnuts
- 2 tablespoons olive oil
- 1 tablespoon butter
- 1 tablespoon snipped fresh thyme or marjoram
- 4 ounces semisoft goat cheese (chèvre), crumbled
  Cracked black pepper

1. In a 4-quart Dutch oven, bring water and salt to boiling. Add linguine; boil for 5 minutes. Add green beans. Continue boiling about 5 minutes more or until linguine is tender but still firm; drain well.

2. In the same Dutch oven, cook leeks and walnuts in hot olive oil and butter over medium heat for 3 to 4 minutes or until leeks are tender and walnuts are lightly toasted. Stir in thyme. Stir in drained linguine and green beans; heat through.

3. Transfer pasta mixture to a serving platter. Sprinkle with goat cheese and pepper. Serve immediately. Makes 6 servings.

Per serving: 361 cal., 19 g fat (6 g sat. fat), 20 mg chol., 219 mg sodium, 36 g carbo., 3 g fiber, 11 g pro.

Steamed Fish and Vegetables

Start to Finish: 20 min.

- 2 6-ounce fresh or frozen cod, tilapia, or other fish fillets, ½ to ¾ inch thick
  Whole fresh basil leaves
- 2 teaspoons shredded fresh ginger
- 1 cup thinly sliced green or red sweet pepper
- 8 ounces fresh asparagus spears, trimmed

1. Thaw fish, if frozen. Rinse fish; pat dry with paper towels. Using a sharp knife, make bias cuts about ¾ inch apart into the fish fillets. (Do not cut completely through fish.) Tuck one or two basil leaves into each cut. Rub fillets with ginger.

2. Place sweet peppers and asparagus in a steamer basket. Place fish on top of vegetables. Place basket in a large, deep saucepan or wok over 1 inch of boiling water. Cover and steam for 6 to 8 minutes or until fish begins to flake when tested with a fork. Makes 2 servings.

Per serving: 143 cal., 1 g fat (0 g sat. fat), 34 mg chol., 89 mg sodium, 6 g carbo., 2 g fiber, 27 g pro.

Easy Salmon Pasta

Prep: 10 min. **Cook:** 15 min.

- 2 cups frozen loose-pack mixed vegetables or one 10-ounce package frozen mixed vegetables
- 1½ cup packaged dried corkscrew macaroni
- ¼ cup sliced green onion (2)
- 1 10.75-ounce can condensed cheddar cheese soup
- ½ cup milk
- ½ teaspoon dried dill weed
- ¼ teaspoon dry mustard
- ⅛ teaspoon ground black pepper
- 2 6-ounce cans skinless, boneless salmon or tuna, drained
  Fresh dill (optional)

1. In a large saucepan, cook frozen vegetables, pasta, and green onion in boiling water for 10 to 12 minutes or just until pasta is tender. Drain well.

2. Stir in soup, milk, dried dill weed, mustard, and pepper. Gently fold salmon into pasta mixture. Cook over low heat until heated through. If desired, garnish with fresh dill. Makes 5 servings.

Per serving: 347 cal., 9 g fat (4 g sat. fat), 56 mg chol., 327 mg sodium, 41 g carbo., 1 g fiber, 22 g pro.

Shrimp and Couscous Jambalaya
Start to Finish: 25 min.

12   ounces fresh or frozen medium shrimp
in shells
1   cup sliced celery (2 stalks)
¾   cup chopped green sweet pepper
(1 medium)
½   cup chopped onion (1 medium)
½   teaspoon Cajun seasoning
¼   teaspoon dried oregano, crushed
2   tablespoons cooking oil
1   14.5-ounce can reduced-sodium
chicken broth
1   cup quick-cooking couscous
½   cup chopped tomato (1 medium)
  Bottled hot pepper sauce (optional)
  Lemon wedges (optional)

1. Thaw shrimp, if frozen. Peel and devein shrimp.
Rinse shrimp and pat dry with paper towels; set aside.
In a large skillet, cook and stir celery, sweet pepper,
onion, Cajun seasoning, and oregano in hot oil over
medium heat until vegetables are tender. Carefully add
broth; bring to boiling.

2. Stir in the shrimp and remove from heat. Stir in
the couscous and tomato. Cover and let stand for 5 minutes. To serve, fluff mixture with a fork and transfer
mixture to a shallow serving bowl. If desired, serve
with hot pepper sauce and lemon wedges. Makes
4 servings.

Per serving: 317 cal., 8 g fat (1 g sat. fat), 98 mg chol., 462 mg
sodium, 42 g carbo., 9 g fiber, 18 g pro.

Salmon with Tropical Rice
Prep: 15 min.   **Bake:** 15 min.

1   1½-pound fresh or frozen skinless salmon
fillet, 1 inch thick
2   teaspoons olive oil
1   teaspoon lemon-pepper seasoning
1   8.8-ounce pouch cooked brown or white rice
1   medium mango, peeled, seeded,
and chopped
1   tablespoon snipped fresh cilantro
1   teaspoon finely shredded lemon peel
  Lemon wedges and cilantro sprigs (optional)

1. Preheat oven to 450°F. Thaw salmon, if frozen.
Rinse fish and pat dry with paper towels. Place fish in
a greased 3-quart rectangular baking dish. Drizzle olive
oil over fish. Sprinkle with lemon-pepper seasoning.

2. In a medium bowl, stir together rice, mango,
cilantro, and lemon peel. Spoon rice mixture around fish.
Bake for 15 minutes or until fish flakes easily when
tested with a fork.

3. To serve, cut fish into four pieces. Serve fish on top
of rice mixture. If desired, garnish each serving with
lemon wedges and cilantro sprigs. Makes 4 servings.

Per serving: 462 cal., 22 g fat (4 g sat. fat), 99 mg chol., 104 mg
sodium, 27 g carbo., 2 g fiber, 36 g pro.

{shrimp smarts}

❊ To peel shrimp, use your fingers to open the shell
lengthwise down the body's underside. Starting
at the head end, peel the shell back from the body.
Then gently pull on the tail portion of the shell
and remove it.

❊ To devein shrimp, use a sharp knife to make a
shallow slit along the shrimp's back from the
head end to the tail. Rinse under cold running
water to remove the vein, using the tip of knife
if necessary.

Microwave Meat Loaf with Tomato Sauce

Prep: 15 min.   **Cook:** 26 min.

- **1** 8-ounce can pizza sauce
- **½** cup shredded zucchini
- **¼** cup rolled oats
- **¼** cup finely chopped onion
- **3** tablespoons snipped fresh parsley
- **2** cloves garlic, minced
- **1** teaspoon dried thyme, crushed
- **¼** teaspoon salt
- **¼** teaspoon ground black pepper
- **1** pound lean ground beef
- **½** pound uncooked ground turkey breast

1. In large bowl, combine 2 tablespoons of the pizza sauce, the zucchini, oats, onion, 2 tablespoons of the parsley, half of the garlic, the thyme, salt, and pepper. Add beef and turkey; mix well. Shape meat mixture into a 7×4×2-inch loaf. Place in a greased 9-inch microwave-safe pie plate or 2-quart square baking dish.

2. Cover meat loaf with waxed paper. Microwave on 100 percent power (high) for 5 minutes, turning plate once.* Tilt plate slightly; spoon off drippings. In a bowl, stir together remaining pizza sauce, remaining parsley, and remaining garlic. Pour evenly over meat loaf. Cover with waxed paper; microwave on 50 percent power (medium) for 21 to 24 minutes or until cooked through (165°F), turning plate twice.* Makes 6 servings.

* There is no need to turn the plate if your microwave has a turntable.

Per serving: 243 cal., 12 g fat (5 g sat. fat), 66 mg chol., 380 mg sodium, 7 g carbo., 1 g fiber, 24 g pro.

Steak and Mushrooms

Start to Finish: 30 min.

4   beef tenderloin steaks, cut 1 inch thick
    (about 1 pound)
    Salt and ground black pepper
1   tablespoon olive oil
6   cloves garlic, minced
½   cup chopped red onion
1   medium green sweet pepper, cut into
    thin strips
1   8-ounce package presliced button
    mushrooms (3 cups)
¼   cup onion-flavor beef broth or beef broth
¼   cup whipping cream

Steak and Mushrooms

1. Season meat lightly with salt and pepper. In a large skillet, heat oil over medium-high heat until very hot. Add meat. Reduce heat to medium and cook for 10 to 13 minutes or to desired doneness (145°F for medium rare; 160°F for medium), turning once. Transfer steaks to a serving platter; keep warm.

2. In the same skillet cook and stir garlic, onion, sweet pepper, and mushrooms over medium-high heat about 6 minutes or until tender and most of the liquid has evaporated. Stir in broth and cream. Bring to boiling. Boil gently, uncovered, over medium heat about 4 minutes or until slightly thickened, stirring occasionally. Spoon mushroom mixture over steaks. Makes 4 servings.

Per serving: 298 cal., 18 g fat (7 g sat. fat), 90 mg chol., 191 mg sodium, 7 g carbo., 1 g fiber, 26 g pro.

Beef Enchiladas

Prep: 20 min.   **Bake:** 30 min.

1   17-ounce package refrigerated cooked
    beef roast au jus
1   10-ounce can enchilada sauce
1   cup shredded Monterey Jack cheese (4 ounces)
1   8-ounce can no-salt-added tomato sauce
8   6-inch flour tortillas
1   tomato, chopped
    Shredded lettuce
    Shredded cheddar cheese (optional)

1. Preheat oven to 350°F. Heat roast according to package directions. Remove meat from au jus. Shred the meat. Discard au jus or reserve for another use. In a medium bowl, stir together the shredded beef, ⅓ cup of the enchilada sauce, and ½ cup of the cheese.

2. To assemble, pour tomato sauce into a greased 2-quart rectangular baking dish. Spoon ¼ to ⅓ cup meat mixture near the edge of each tortilla; roll up. Place enchiladas, seam sides down, on top of tomato sauce in baking dish. Top with remaining enchilada sauce.

3. Bake, covered, about 25 minutes or until enchiladas are heated through. Sprinkle with remaining cheese. Bake, uncovered, for 5 minutes more. Serve with tomato, lettuce, and, if desired, cheese. Makes 4 servings.

Per serving: 478 cal., 22 g fat (11 g sat. fat), 89 mg chol., 1,151 mg sodium, 37 g carbo., 3 g fiber, 35 g pro.

Garlic-Mustard Steak Sandwiches

Prep: 15 min.   **Broil:** 12 min.

>   4   to 6 hoagie rolls, split
>   2   tablespoons honey mustard
>   ½   teaspoon dried marjoram or thyme,
>   crushed
>   1   clove garlic, minced
>   ¼   teaspoon coarsely ground black pepper
>   1   to 1½ pounds beef flank steak
>   1   large red onion, sliced ½ inch thick
>   4   to 6 slices Swiss cheese
>   Honey mustard (optional)

1. Preheat broiler. Place rolls, cut sides up, on the unheated rack of a broiler pan. Broil 4 to 5 inches from heat for 1 to 2 minutes or until toasted. Set aside. In a small bowl, stir together the 2 tablespoons mustard, the marjoram, garlic, and pepper. Set mustard mixture aside.

2. Trim any fat from steak. Score steak on both sides with shallow diagonal cuts at 1-inch intervals. Brush both sides of steak with mustard mixture.

3. Place steak on broiler pan. Place onion slices beside steak. Broil 4 to 5 inches from heat for 12 to 17 minutes or until steak is desired doneness (145°F for medium rare; 160°F for medium) and onion is tender, turning steak and onion once.

4. Thinly slice steak at an angle across the grain. Separate onion slices into rings. Arrange steak strips, onion rings, and cheese on roll bottoms. Broil about 1 minute or until cheese starts to melt. Add roll tops. If desired, pass additional honey mustard. Makes 4 to 6 servings.

Per serving: 685 cal., 22 g fat (9 g sat. fat), 65 mg chol., 844 mg sodium, 78 g carbo., 4 g fiber, 43 g pro.

1 teaspoon dried oregano, crushed
½ teaspoon dried basil or marjoram, crushed
¼ teaspoon ground black pepper
6 ounces dried spaghetti, broken
¼ cup grated Parmesan cheese

1. In a large saucepan, cook ground beef, fresh mushrooms (if using), onion, and garlic over medium heat until meat is brown and onion is tender. Drain off fat.

2. Stir in canned mushrooms (if using), broth, water, tomato paste, oregano, basil, and pepper. Bring to boiling. Add the broken spaghetti, a little at a time, stirring constantly. Return to boiling; reduce heat. Simmer, uncovered, for 17 to 20 minutes or until spaghetti is tender and sauce is desired consistency, stirring frequently. Serve with Parmesan cheese. Makes 4 servings.

Per serving: 362 cal., 12 g fat (5 g sat. fat), 39 mg chol., 857 mg sodium, 44 g carbo., 4 g fiber, 21 g pro.

Greek Skillet Supper
Prep: 20 min.   Cook: 15 min.

8 ounces lean ground lamb or ground beef
¾ cup chopped onion (1 large)
2 cloves garlic, minced
1 14.5-ounce can beef broth
1½ cups dried medium shell macaroni
2 cups frozen mixed vegetables
1 14.5-ounce can diced tomatoes
2 tablespoons tomato paste
2 teaspoons snipped fresh marjoram or
   1 teaspoon dried marjoram, crushed
⅛ teaspoon ground cinnamon
⅛ teaspoon ground nutmeg
½ cup crumbled feta cheese (2 ounces)
1 teaspoon snipped fresh marjoram

1. In a large skillet, cook meat, onion, and garlic over medium heat until meat is brown and onion is tender. Drain off fat. Stir in broth and macaroni. Bring to boiling; reduce heat. Cover and simmer for 10 minutes.

2. Stir in vegetables, undrained tomatoes, tomato paste, dried marjoram (if using), cinnamon, and nutmeg. Return to boiling; reduce heat. Simmer, uncovered, for 5 to 10 minutes more or until vegetables are tender. Stir in the 2 teaspoons fresh marjoram (if using). Sprinkle with feta cheese and the 1 teaspoon fresh marjoram. Makes 4 servings.

Per serving: 400 cal., 12 g fat (6 g sat. fat), 50 mg chol., 783 mg sodium, 51 g carbo., 3 g fiber, 22 g pro.

You don't have to **cook the pasta** separately for spaghetti. Add some water to the sauce and cook it all together.

One-Pot Spaghetti
Start to Finish: 40 min.

8 ounces ground beef or bulk pork sausage
1 cup sliced fresh mushrooms or one 6-ounce jar sliced mushrooms, drained
½ cup chopped onion (1 medium)
1 clove garlic, minced
1 14-ounce can chicken broth or beef broth
1¾ cups water
1 6-ounce can tomato paste

Peppered Pork Chops and Pilaf

Start to Finish: 25 min.

- **4** 3-ounce boneless pork loin chops, cut ¾ inch thick
- **2** teaspoons seasoned pepper blend
- **1** tablespoon olive oil
- **3** cups vegetables, such as broccoli, carrots, mushrooms, onions, and/or sweet peppers, cut into bite-size pieces
- **1** 14-ounce can chicken broth
- **2** cups uncooked instant brown rice
- **¼** cup roasted red sweet pepper strips

1. Sprinkle both sides of chops with the seasoned pepper blend. In a large skillet, cook chops in hot oil over medium heat for 5 minutes. Turn chops. Cook for 3 to 7 minutes more or until chops register 160°F on an instant-read thermometer. Remove chops from skillet; cover and keep warm.

2. Add vegetables, broth, and rice to skillet. Bring to boiling; reduce heat. Cover and simmer for 5 to 7 minutes or until rice is tender and vegetables are crisp-tender. Return pork chops to skillet; cover and heat through. Garnish with roasted red pepper strips. Makes 4 servings.

Per serving: 305 cal., 9 g fat (2 g sat. fat), 47 mg chol., 606 mg sodium, 32 g carbo., 4 g fiber, 24 g pro.

Oriental Pork and Vegetables

Prep: 10 min. Cook: 8 min.

- **6** ounces rice stick noodles or two 3-ounce packages ramen noodles (any flavor), broken if desired
- **2** teaspoons sesame oil or olive oil
- **1** 16-ounce package frozen stir-fry vegetables
- **1** 12-ounce pork tenderloin, cut into ¼-inch-thick slices
- **¼** cup teriyaki sauce
- **2** tablespoons plum sauce

1. Discard spice packet from ramen noodles, if using, or save for another use. Prepare noodles as directed on package. Set aside and keep warm.

2. Heat a very large nonstick skillet over medium-high heat. Add 1 teaspoon of the sesame oil. Cook and stir vegetables for 4 to 6 minutes or until crisp-tender. Remove from skillet. Set aside and keep warm.

3. Add remaining oil to skillet. Add pork and cook over medium-high heat for 4 to 6 minutes or until no longer pink, turning slices once. Stir in vegetables (drained if necessary), teriyaki sauce, and plum sauce; heat through. Toss with noodles. Makes 4 servings.

Per serving: 341 cal., 5 g fat (1 g sat. fat), 55 mg chol., 820 mg sodium, 48 g carbo., 3 g fiber, 22 g pro.

Pork and Potato Skillet

Prep: 10 min.   **Cook:** 20 min.

4	4-ounce boneless pork loin chops
¾	teaspoon seasoned salt
2	tablespoons cooking oil
⅓	cup chopped onion (1 small)
1	medium red sweet pepper, cut into ¾-inch pieces
3	cups frozen diced hash brown potatoes
2	cups frozen peas and carrots
1	teaspoon dried thyme, crushed

1. Sprinkle both sides of chops evenly with ½ teaspoon of the seasoned salt. In a very large skillet, heat 1 tablespoon of the oil over medium-high heat. Cook chops in hot oil for 3 minutes. Turn chops and cook for 3 minutes more or until brown. Remove from skillet.

2. Carefully add remaining 1 tablespoon oil to skillet. Add onion and sweet pepper; cook and stir for 1 minute. Add potatoes, peas and carrots, thyme, and remaining seasoned salt; mix well. Cook and stir for 6 minutes.

3. Place chops on top of potato mixture; cover. Reduce heat to medium. Cook for 7 to 9 minutes more or until chops are no longer pink. Makes 4 servings.

Per serving: 406 cal., 15 g fat (3 g sat. fat), 72 mg chol., 422 mg sodium, 39 g carbo., 5 g fiber, 29 g pro.

Mu Shu-Style Pork Roll-Ups

Start to Finish: 20 min.

4	10-inch flour tortillas
1	teaspoon toasted sesame oil
12	ounces lean boneless pork, cut into strips
2	cups loose-pack frozen stir-fry vegetables
¼	cup bottled plum or hoisin sauce

1. Preheat oven to 350°F. Wrap tortillas tightly in foil. Heat in oven for 10 minutes.

2. Meanwhile, in a large skillet, heat oil over medium-high heat. Add pork strips; cook and stir for 2 to 3 minutes or until no longer pink. Add vegetables. Cook and stir for 3 to 4 minutes or until vegetables are crisp-tender.

3. Spread 1 tablespoon of the plum or hoisin sauce on each tortilla; place a quarter of the meat mixture just below the center of each tortilla. Fold the bottom edge up and over the filling. Fold in the sides until they meet; roll up tortillas. Makes 4 servings.

Per serving: 296 cal., 8 g fat (2 g sat. fat), 53 mg chol., 325 mg sodium, 32 g carbo., 1 g fiber, 22 g pro.

Frozen veggies are a nutritious time-saver in the kitchen.

Pork and Potato Skillet

Mu Shu-Style Pork Roll-Ups

For carefree cleanup, **spread foil** on the broiler pan. Poke a few holes in the foil to allow juices to drain.

Glazed Teriyaki Pork Chops with Potatoes

Prep: 20 min. Broil: 9 min.

- 4 boneless pork loin chops, cut ¾ inch thick
- ¼ cup teriyaki sauce
- 12 ounces tiny new potatoes, quartered
- 1 tablespoon olive oil
- 1 tablespoon toasted sesame oil
- ¼ teaspoon salt
- ⅛ teaspoon ground black pepper
- 1 cup pea pods, halved lengthwise
  Teriyaki sauce

1. Preheat broiler. Brush both sides of chops with the ¼ cup teriyaki sauce. Arrange chops on half of the unheated rack of a broiler pan; set aside.

2. In a large bowl, toss potatoes with olive oil, sesame oil, salt, and pepper until coated. Arrange potatoes in a single layer on rack next to chops.

3. Broil 4 to 5 inches from the heat for 9 to 11 minutes or until internal temperature of chops register 160°F and potatoes are tender, turning chops and potatoes once.

4. Place pea pods in a large bowl. Add potatoes and toss to combine. Serve chops with potatoes and pea pods. Pass additional teriyaki sauce. Makes 4 servings.

Per serving: 394 cal., 15 g fat (4 g sat. fat), 86 mg chol., 626 mg sodium, 23 g carbo., 2 g fiber, 38 g pro.

Vermicelli with Sausage and Spinach

Start to Finish: 25 min.

- 1 pound cooked smoked sausage, halved lengthwise and cut in ½-inch-thick slices
- ¾ cup chopped onion (1 large)
- 2 large garlic cloves, chopped
- 2 teaspoons olive oil
- 2 14-ounce cans reduced-sodium chicken broth
- 8 ounces dried vermicelli or angel hair pasta, broken in half
- 1 9-ounce package fresh prewashed baby spinach
- ¼ teaspoon ground black pepper
- ⅓ cup whipping cream

1. In a 4-quart Dutch oven, cook sausage, onion, and garlic in hot oil over medium heat until onion is tender.

2. Add broth and ¼ cup water; bring to boiling. Add pasta; cook for 3 minutes, stirring frequently. Add spinach and pepper; cook and stir for 1 minute more. Stir in cream. Makes 4 to 6 servings.

Per serving: 782 cal., 47 g fat (18 g sat. fat), 104 mg chol., 2,556 mg sodium, 52 g carbo., 4 g fiber, 38 g pro.

Zesty Chicken with Black Beans

Start to Finish: 30 min.

- 1 pound skinless, boneless chicken breast halves, cut into 2-inch pieces
- 2 tablespoons cooking oil
- 1 6- to 7.4-ounce package Spanish rice mix
- 1 15-ounce can black beans, rinsed and drained
- 1 14.5-ounce can diced tomatoes
  Sour cream, sliced green onion, and lime wedges (optional)

1. In a large skillet, cook chicken pieces in 1 tablespoon of the oil over medium heat until no longer pink on outside. Remove chicken from skillet and keep warm.

2. Add rice mix and remaining 1 tablespoon oil to skillet; cook and stir for 2 minutes over medium heat. Stir in seasoning packet from rice mix, 1¾ cups water, the beans, and undrained tomatoes; add chicken. Bring to boiling; reduce heat. Cover and simmer for 15 to 20 minutes or until rice is tender and chicken is no longer pink inside. Remove from heat. Let stand for 5 minutes. If desired, serve with sour cream, green onion, and lime wedges. Makes 4 servings.

Per serving: 424 cal., 9 g fat (2 g sat. fat), 66 mg chol., 1,080 mg sodium, 52 g carbo., 6 g fiber, 37 g pro.

Greens, Beans, and Ham

Prep: 10 min. **Cook:** 8 min.

- **2** 15-ounce cans Great Northern beans
- **1** tablespoon olive oil
- **6** cloves garlic, minced
- **2** cups cooked smoked ham, cut into bite-size strips
- **3** cups chopped fresh spinach or one 10-ounce package frozen spinach, thawed and well drained

1. Drain beans, reserving liquid. In a large nonstick skillet, heat olive oil over medium heat. Add garlic; cook and stir for 1 minute. Add beans and ham; cook about 5 minutes or until heated through, stirring occasionally. Stir in spinach; cover and cook for 2 to 5 minutes more or until fresh greens are wilted or frozen spinach is heated through. If desired, thin mixture with some of the reserved bean liquid. Makes 4 servings.

Per serving: 353 cal., 6 g fat (1 g sat. fat), 12 mg chol., 537 mg sodium, 51 g carbo., 11 g fiber, 27 g pro.

A skillet that can do double duty on top of the stove and in the oven is **a must-have** for one-pan meals.

Popover Pizza Casserole

Popover Pizza Casserole

Prep: 30 min.   **Bake:** 25 min.

- 12 ounces uncooked ground turkey or ground beef
- ¾ cup chopped onion (1 large)
- ¾ cup chopped green sweet pepper (1 medium)
- ½ of a 3.5-ounce package sliced pepperoni
- 1 14- to 15.5-ounce jar or can pizza sauce
- 1 4-ounce can mushroom stems and pieces, drained
- 1 teaspoon dried Italian seasoning, crushed
- ½ teaspoon fennel seeds, crushed
- 2 eggs
- 1 cup milk
- 1 tablespoon cooking oil
- 1 cup all-purpose flour
- 1½ cups broccoli florets
- 1 cup shredded mozzarella cheese (4 ounces)
- 2 tablespoons grated Parmesan cheese

1. In a large ovenproof skillet, cook turkey, onion, and pepper over medium heat until meat is brown and vegetables are tender. Drain off fat. Cut pepperoni slices in half. Stir pepperoni, pizza sauce, mushrooms, Italian seasoning, and fennel seeds into meat mixture. Bring to boiling; reduce heat. Simmer, uncovered, for 10 minutes, stirring occasionally. Preheat oven to 400°F.

2. Meanwhile, for popover topping, in a small bowl, combine eggs, milk, and oil. Beat with an electric mixer on medium speed or whisk for 1 minute. Add flour; beat for 1 minute more or until smooth.

3. Top meat mixture in skillet with broccoli; sprinkle with mozzarella cheese. Pour popover topping over mixture in skillet, covering completely. Sprinkle with Parmesan cheese.

4. Bake for 25 to 30 minutes or until topping is puffed and golden brown. Makes 6 servings.

Per serving: 379 cal., 18 g fat (7 g sat. fat), 145 mg chol., 818 mg sodium, 29 g carbo., 3 g fiber, 24 g pro.

Greek Chicken and Pita Casserole

Prep: 20 min.   **Bake:** 50 min.

- 1 10.75-ounce can reduced-fat and reduced-sodium condensed cream of chicken soup
- 4 cups chopped cooked chicken (1¼ pounds)
- 2 medium zucchini, halved lengthwise and sliced into ½-inch pieces (4 cups)
- ½ cup reduced-sodium chicken broth
- ½ cup chopped red onion
- 2 cloves garlic, minced (1 teaspoon)
- ½ teaspoon Greek seasoning
- 3 6-inch pita breads, torn into bite-size pieces
- 1 cup crumbled feta cheese (4 ounces)
- ½ cup pitted kalamata olives, sliced
- 2 tablespoons olive oil
- 2 cups chopped roma tomatoes (4 large)

1. Preheat oven to 350°F. In a large bowl, combine soup, chicken, zucchini, broth, onion, garlic, and Greek seasoning; mix well. Transfer to an ungreased 3-quart rectangular baking dish. Bake, covered, about 30 minutes or until vegetables are almost tender. Stir.

2. In a medium bowl, toss together pita pieces, cheese, olives, and oil. Sprinkle pita mixture and tomatoes over chicken mixture. Bake about 20 minutes more or until top is golden. Makes 4 servings.

Per serving: 468 cal., 22 g fat (8 g sat. fat), 109 mg chol., 1,118 mg sodium, 30 g carbo., 3 g fiber, 36 g pro.

Chicken and Noodles

Prep: 15 min.   **Cook:** 25 min.

- 1 12-ounce package frozen noodles (about 3 cups)
- 3 cups reduced-sodium chicken broth
- 2 cups sliced carrot (4 medium)
- 1 cup chopped onion (2 medium)
- ½ cup sliced celery (1 stalk)
- 2 cups milk
- 1 cup frozen peas
- 3 tablespoons all-purpose flour
- ½ teaspoon salt
- ⅛ teaspoon ground black pepper
- 2 cups chopped cooked chicken
  Coarsely ground black pepper (optional)

1. In 4-quart Dutch oven, combine noodles, broth, carrot, onion, and celery. Bring to boiling; reduce heat. Cover and simmer about 20 minutes or until vegetables are tender. Stir in 1½ cups of the milk and the peas.

2. In a small bowl, stir together the remaining ½ cup milk, the flour, salt, and ⅛ teaspoon pepper. Whisk until smooth; stir into noodle mixture along with the chicken. Cook and stir until thickened and bubbly. Cook and stir for 1 minute more. If desired, season each serving with coarsely ground pepper. Makes 8 servings.

Per serving: 269 cal., 5 g fat (2 g sat. fat), 86 mg chol., 36 g carbo., 3 g fiber, 19 g pro.

Honey Chicken Sandwiches

Savory Chicken Salad

Start to Finish: 30 min.

- 1 2- to 2¼-pound deli-roasted chicken
- 1 pound sliced fresh button mushrooms
- 2 tablespoons olive oil
- ½ cup purchased dried tomato pesto
- 3 tablespoons balsamic vinegar
- ½ cup cherry tomatoes, halved
- 1 5-ounce package mixed salad greens (about 8 cups)

1. Remove and chop enough meat from chicken to make 2 cups. (Discard skin and bones.) Save remaining chicken for another use.

2. In a large skillet, cook mushrooms in hot oil over medium heat about 10 minutes or until tender, stirring occasionally. Stir in pesto and balsamic vinegar. Bring to boiling; stir in chopped chicken. Heat through. Gently stir in tomatoes. Line a platter with salad greens and top with the chicken mixture. Serve warm. Makes 4 servings.

Per serving: 419 cal., 24 g fat (6 g sat. fat), 96 mg chol., 330 mg sodium, 14 g carbo., 3 g fiber, 38 g pro.

Honey Chicken Sandwiches

Start to Finish: 20 min.

- 3 tablespoons honey
- 2 teaspoons snipped fresh thyme or ½ teaspoon dried thyme, crushed
- 1 small red onion, halved and thinly sliced
- 12 ounces cut-up cooked chicken
- 4 baked biscuits, split

1. In a medium skillet, stir together honey and thyme; stir in red onion. Cook and stir over medium-low heat just until hot (do not boil). Stir in chicken; heat through. Arrange chicken mixture on biscuit bottoms. Add tops. Makes 4 servings.

Per serving: 342 cal., 12 g fat (3 g sat. fat), 76 mg chol., 443 mg sodium, 31 g carbo., 1 g fiber, 27 g pro.

Rotini-Kielbasa Skillet

Start to Finish: 35 min.

- 2 cups dried rotini or rotelle (wagon wheel) pasta (about 6 ounces)
- 1 tablespoon olive oil
- 1 medium onion, cut into wedges
- 2 cloves garlic, minced
- 1 pound cooked turkey kielbasa, halved lengthwise and sliced diagonally
- 1 small zucchini, coarsely chopped
- 1 yellow or orange sweet pepper, cut into small strips
- 1 teaspoon dried Italian seasoning, crushed
- ⅛ teaspoon cayenne pepper
- 8 roma tomatoes, cored and chopped (about 1 pound)

1. Cook pasta according to package directions; drain. Meanwhile, in a very large skillet, heat oil over medium-high heat. Add onion and garlic; cook for 1 minute. Add kielbasa; cook until onion is tender, stirring frequently.

2. Add zucchini, sweet pepper, Italian seasoning, and cayenne; cook and stir for 5 minutes. Stir in tomatoes and cooked pasta. Heat through, stirring occasionally. Makes 6 servings.

Per serving: 267 cal., 10 g fat (2 g sat. fat), 47 mg chol., 677 mg sodium, 29 g carbo., 2 g fiber, 15 g pro.

Veggies and Chicken Tortellini
Start to Finish: 30 min.

- 1 pound skinless, boneless chicken breast halves, cut into 1-inch pieces
  Nonstick cooking spray
- 1 medium onion, thinly sliced (1 cup)
- 1 14.5-ounce can diced tomatoes with basil, garlic, and oregano
- 1 cup reduced-sodium chicken broth
- 1 large green sweet pepper, cut into ¾-inch pieces
- 1 large red sweet pepper, cut into ¾-inch pieces
- 1 cup sliced fresh mushrooms
- 1 9-ounce package refrigerated tortellini
- 1 ounce Parmesan cheese, shaved into strips

1. Coat a large skillet with nonstick cooking spray. Cook chicken in skillet over medium heat until brown, stirring often. Remove from skillet. Add onion to skillet; cook and stir until tender. Return chicken to skillet. Add undrained tomatoes, broth, sweet peppers, and mushrooms. Bring to boiling. Add tortellini. Return to boiling; reduce heat. Cover and simmer for 5 to 8 minutes or until tortellini is tender.

2. Uncover and simmer about 3 minutes more or until slightly thickened. Top with shaved Parmesan. Makes 6 servings.

Per serving: 287 cal., 6 g fat (3 g sat. fat), 66 mg chol., 720 mg sodium, 31 g carbo., 3 g fiber, 28 g pro.

Curried Chicken and Noodles
Start to Finish: 15 min.

- 2 3-ounce packages chicken-flavor ramen noodles
- 2 cups frozen broccoli, cauliflower, and carrot
- ½ cup purchased coconut milk
- 1 to 2 teaspoons curry powder
  Dash cayenne pepper
- 1 cup cubed cooked chicken breast

1. In a large saucepan, bring 5 cups water to boiling. Add noodles with seasoning packets and vegetables. Cook about 3 minutes or until vegetables are tender. Drain. Return noodle mixture to pan. Combine coconut milk, curry powder, and cayenne; stir into saucepan. Heat through. Makes 4 servings.

Per serving: 333 cal., 15 g fat (10 g sat. fat), 30 mg chol., 934 mg sodium, 32 g carbo., 3 g fiber, 18 g pro.

Skillet-Style Lasagna
Start to Finish: 35 min.

- 8 ounces uncooked lean ground chicken
- ½ cup chopped onion (1 medium)
- 2 cups purchased spaghetti sauce
- 1 cup water
- 2 cups dried extra-wide noodles
- 1½ cups coarsely chopped zucchini (1 medium)
- ½ cup fat-free ricotta cheese
- 2 tablespoons grated Parmesan cheese
- 1 tablespoon snipped fresh parsley
- ½ cup shredded part-skim mozzarella cheese (2 ounces)

1. In a large skillet, cook chicken and onion over medium heat until meat is brown. Drain off fat. Stir in spaghetti sauce and water. Bring to boiling. Stir in noodles and zucchini. Return to boiling; reduce heat. Cover and simmer for 10 minutes or until pasta is tender, stirring occasionally.

2. Meanwhile, in a small bowl, stir together ricotta cheese, Parmesan cheese, and parsley. Drop cheese mixture by spoonfuls into mounds on top of the pasta mixture in the skillet. Sprinkle each mound with mozzarella cheese. Cover and cook over low heat for 4 to 5 minutes or until cheese mixture is heated through and mozzarella is melted. Remove from heat. Let stand for 10 minutes before serving. Makes 6 servings.

Per serving: 186 cal., 3 g fat (2 g sat. fat), 45 mg chol., 519 mg sodium, 21 g carbo., 2 g fiber, 17 g pro.

Maryland Fried Chicken with Creamy Gravy

Prep: 20 min. **Cook:** 55 min.

1	egg, lightly beaten
3	tablespoons milk
1	cup finely crushed saltine crackers (28 crackers)
1	teaspoon dried thyme, crushed
½	teaspoon paprika
⅛	teaspoon ground black pepper
2½	to 3 pounds meaty chicken pieces (breasts, thighs, and drumsticks)
2	to 3 tablespoons cooking oil
1	cup milk
	Creamy Gravy

1. In a small bowl, combine the egg and the 3 tablespoons milk. In a shallow bowl, stir together crushed crackers, thyme, paprika, and pepper. Dip chicken pieces, 1 at a time, in egg mixture then roll in cracker mixture.

2. In a large skillet, brown chicken in hot oil over medium heat for 10 to 15 minutes, turning occasionally. Drain well.

3. Add the 1 cup milk to skillet. Heat just to boiling. Reduce heat to medium-low; cover tightly. Cook for 35 minutes. Uncover; cook about 10 minutes more or until chicken is no longer pink (170°F for breasts; 180°F for thighs and drumsticks). Transfer chicken to a serving platter, reserving drippings for gravy. Cover chicken and keep warm. Prepare Creamy Gravy. Makes 6 servings.

Creamy Gravy: Skim fat from drippings. Reserve 3 tablespoons of the drippings in skillet. In a screw-top jar, combine ¾ cup milk, 3 tablespoons all-purpose flour, ¼ teaspoon salt, and ⅛ teaspoon ground black pepper; cover and shake until well combined. Add to skillet. Stir in an additional 1 cup milk. Cook over medium heat, stirring constantly, until thickened and bubbly. Cook and stir for 1 minute more. (If desired, thin with additional milk.) Makes about 1¾ cups.

Per serving: 404 cal., 20 g fat (5 g sat. fat), 131 mg chol., 423 mg sodium, 19 g carbo., 1 g fiber, 35 g pro.

Thai Rice Noodles

Prep: 20 min. **Cook:** 8 min.

12	ounces fresh rice noodles (rice ribbon noodles)
3	tablespoons cooking oil
12	ounces skinless, boneless chicken breast halves, cut into bite-size pieces
2	cloves garlic, minced
1	tablespoon minced fresh ginger
2	cups broccoli florets
2	medium carrots, cut into thin, bite-size strips (1 cup)
1	small onion, cut into thin wedges (⅓ cup)
¼	cup oyster sauce
1	tablespoon brown sugar

1. Cut rice noodles into 1×3-inch strips; set aside. In a large skillet, heat 2 tablespoons of the oil over medium-high heat until very hot. Carefully add noodles; cook and stir for 3 to 4 minutes or until edges of noodles just begin to turn golden. Remove noodles from skillet; set aside.

2. Add remaining oil to skillet. Add chicken, garlic, and ginger; cook and stir for 2 to 3 minutes or until chicken is no longer pink. Add broccoli, carrots, and onion; cook and stir for 2 to 3 minutes more or until vegetables are crisp-tender. Stir in the oyster sauce, brown sugar, and noodles; heat through. Makes 4 servings.

Per serving: 341 cal., 12 g fat (2 g sat. fat), 49 mg chol., 507 mg sodium, 37 g carbo., 2 g fiber, 22 g pro.

Maryland Fried Chicken with Creamy Gravy

Thyme Chicken Marsala
Start to Finish: 30 min.

- 2 **medium skinless, boneless chicken breast halves (about 10 ounces total)**
- **Salt and ground black pepper**
- 1 **tablespoon all-purpose flour**
- 2 **tablespoons olive oil**
- 1 **medium carrot, cut into thin bite-size strips (½ cup)**
- 1 **small red or yellow sweet pepper, cut into thin bite-size strips**
- 2 **cloves garlic, minced**
- ¼ **teaspoon salt**
- ¼ **teaspoon ground black pepper**
- ⅓ **cup dry Marsala**
- 1 **tablespoon snipped fresh thyme**
- **Hot cooked linguine (optional)**

1. Place each chicken piece between 2 pieces of plastic wrap. Working from the center to the edges, pound lightly with the flat side of a meat mallet until ¼ inch thick. Remove plastic wrap. Sprinkle chicken lightly with salt and pepper. Coat the chicken with flour, shaking off excess. Set aside.

2. In a large skillet, heat 1 tablespoon of the oil over medium heat. Add carrot strips; cook and stir for 3 minutes. Add sweet pepper strips, garlic, salt, and black pepper; cook and stir 4 to 5 minutes or until vegetables are crisp-tender. Divide the vegetable mixture between 2 dinner plates. Cover and keep warm.

3. In the same skillet, heat the remaining 1 tablespoon oil. Add chicken. Cook for 4 to 5 minutes or until chicken is tender and no longer pink, turning once. Place the chicken on top of cooked vegetables.

4. Add Marsala and thyme to skillet. Scrape up any browned bits from the bottom of the skillet. Spoon Marsala mixture over chicken. If desired, serve with linguine. Makes 2 servings.

Per serving: 354 cal., 16 g fat (3 g sat. fat), 82 mg chol., 555 mg sodium, 11 g carbo., 2 g fiber, 34 g pro.

condensed
cream
of
chicken
soup

CONDENSED CREAM OF MUSHROOM SOUP

forget

Greek-Style Beef and Vegetables

Prep: 15 min.   **Cook:** 6 hr. (low) or 3 hr. (high) + 30 min.

1	pound ground beef
1	cup chopped onion (1 large)
3	cloves garlic, minced
1	14-ounce can beef broth
3	cups frozen mixed vegetables
1	14.5-ounce can diced tomatoes
3	tablespoons tomato paste
1	teaspoon dried oregano, crushed
$\frac{1}{8}$	teaspoon ground cinnamon
$\frac{1}{8}$	teaspoon ground nutmeg
2	cups dried medium shell macaroni
1	cup shredded Monterey Jack or crumbled feta cheese (4 ounces)

1. In a large skillet, cook ground beef, onion, and garlic over medium heat until meat is brown and onion is tender. Drain off fat. Place in a 3½- or 4-quart slow cooker. Stir in broth, mixed vegetables, undrained tomatoes, tomato paste, oregano, cinnamon, and nutmeg.

2. Cover and cook on low-heat setting for 6 to 8 hours or on high-heat setting for 3 to 4 hours. If using low-heat setting, turn to high-heat setting. Add pasta. Cover and cook about 30 minutes more or until pasta is tender. Top each serving with cheese. Makes 6 servings.

Per serving: 446 cal., 16 g fat (7 g sat. fat), 64 mg chol., 539 mg sodium, 46 g carbo., 5 g fiber, 28 g pro.

Let your slow cooker fix dinner. Just load it up in the morning, turn it on, and **forget about it.** You'll come home to a hot, comforting meal.

about it!

BBQ Brisket Sandwiches

Prep: 15 min. **Cook:** 10 hr. (low)

4	pounds fresh beef brisket (2 pieces)
2	cups chopped onion (2 large)
1	cup ketchup
½	cup cider vinegar
2	tablespoons packed brown sugar
2	tablespoons Worcestershire sauce
1	tablespoon liquid smoke (optional)
1	teaspoon salt
½	teaspoon ground black pepper
	Hamburger buns
	Purchased deli coleslaw

1. Trim fat from meat; set meat aside. In a bowl, combine onion, ketchup, vinegar, brown sugar, Worcestershire sauce, liquid smoke (if using), salt, and pepper. Pour ⅓ of onion mixture into a 4- or 5-quart slow cooker; add meat. Pour remaining onion mixture over meat. Cover and cook on low-heat setting for 10 to 11 hours.

2. Transfer meat to cutting board. Chop or shred meat; place in a large bowl. Skim and discard fat from sauce. Add enough sauce to meat to moisten. Serve on buns with coleslaw. Makes 16 servings.

Per serving meat mixture only: 320 cal., 7 g fat (2 g sat. fat), 51 mg chol., 633 mg sodium, 33 g carbo., 2 g fiber, 30 g pro.

Salsa Swiss Steak

Prep: 20 min. **Cook:** 9 hr. (low) or 4½ hr. (high)

2	pounds beef round steak, 1 inch thick
1	to 2 large red sweet peppers, cut into strips
1	medium onion, sliced
1	10.75-ounce can condensed cream of mushroom soup
1	cup salsa
2	tablespoons all-purpose flour
1	teaspoon dry mustard

1. Trim fat from meat. Cut meat into 6 serving-size pieces. In a 3½- or 4-quart slow cooker, place meat, peppers, and onion. In a bowl, stir together soup, salsa, flour, and mustard. Pour over meat and vegetables in cooker.

2. Cover and cook on low-heat setting for 9 to 10 hours or on high-heat setting for 4½ to 5 hours. If desired, serve with hot cooked rice, corn bread, or mashed potatoes. Makes 6 servings.

Per serving: 251 cal., 6 g fat (2 g sat. fat), 65 mg chol., 574 mg sodium, 10 g carbo., 1 g fiber, 37 g pro.

Southwestern Steak Roll-Ups

Prep: 15 min. **Cook:** 7 hr. (low) or 3½ hr. (high)

1	16-ounce package frozen loose-pack pepper stir-fry vegetables (yellow, green, and red peppers, and onion)
1	pound beef flank steak
1	14.5-ounce can Mexican-style stewed tomatoes
1	small jalapeño pepper, seeded and finely chopped* (optional)
2	teaspoons chili powder
4	to 8 flour tortillas, warmed**

1. Place frozen vegetables in a 3½- or 4-quart slow cooker. Trim fat from meat. If necessary, cut meat to fit in cooker. Place meat on top of vegetables in cooker. In a medium bowl, stir together undrained tomatoes, jalapeño pepper (if using), and chili powder. Pour over meat in cooker.

2. Cover and cook on low-heat setting for 7 to 8 hours or on high-heat setting for 3½ to 4 hours. Remove meat from cooker; slice against the grain. Using a slotted spoon, remove vegetables from cooker. Divide meat and vegetables among warm tortillas; roll up tortillas. Makes 4 servings.

*Note: Because fresh jalapeños and other chile peppers contain volatile oils that can burn your skin and eyes, avoid direct contact with chiles as much as possible. When working with chile peppers, wear plastic or rubber gloves. If your bare hands do touch chile peppers, wash hands well with soap and water.

**To warm tortillas: Stack tortillas and wrap tightly in foil. Heat in a 350°F oven about 10 minutes or until heated through.

Per serving: 389 cal., 12 g fat (5 g sat. fat), 46 mg chol., 647 mg sodium, 36 g carbo., 4 g fiber, 32 g pro.

{a step ahead}

If your morning schedule doesn't allow time to prep ingredients for the slow cooker, do most of the work the night before. Chop vegetables, brown ground meats completely, put the items in separate containers, and refrigerate overnight. Place everything in the slow cooker in the morning, and away you go!

Easy Goulash

Prep: 20 min. **Cook:** 6 hr. (low) or 3 hr. (high)
Stand: 5 min.

1   pound lean ground beef
½   of a 24-ounce package frozen loose-pack
     diced hash brown potatoes with onion and
     peppers (about 3½ cups)
1   15-ounce can tomato sauce
1   14.5-ounce can diced tomatoes with basil,
     garlic, and oregano
½   cup shredded cheddar cheese (2 ounces)
     Hot cooked noodles

1. In a large skillet, cook ground beef over medium heat until brown. Drain off fat.

2. In a 3½- or 4-quart slow cooker, stir together the cooked beef, frozen potatoes, tomato sauce, and undrained tomatoes.

3. Cover and cook on low-heat setting for 6 to 8 hours or on high-heat setting for 3 to 4 hours. Turn off cooker. Sprinkle cheese over meat mixture. Let stand about 5 minutes or until cheese melts. Serve over noodles. Makes 4 servings.

Per serving: 535 cal., 33 g fat (14 g sat. fat), 109 mg chol., 1,371 mg sodium, 34 g carbo., 4 g fiber, 27 g pro.

Saucy Cheeseburger Sandwiches

Prep: 20 min.   **Cook:** 6 hr. (low) or 3 hr. (high)

2½ pounds lean ground beef
1 10.75-ounce can condensed tomato soup
1 cup finely chopped onion (2 medium)
¼ cup water
2 tablespoons tomato paste
1 tablespoon Worcestershire sauce
1 tablespoon yellow mustard
2 teaspoons dried Italian seasoning, crushed
¼ teaspoon ground black pepper
2 cloves garlic, minced
12 to 15 hamburger buns, split and toasted
12 to 15 slices American cheese (9 to 12 ounces)

1. In a large skillet, brown ground beef over medium heat. Drain off fat. Transfer meat to a 3½- or 4-quart slow cooker. Stir in soup, onion, the water, tomato paste, Worcestershire sauce, mustard, Italian seasoning, pepper, and garlic.

2. Cover and cook on low-heat setting for 6 to 8 hours or on high-heat setting for 3 to 4 hours. Serve on hamburger buns with cheese. Makes 12 to 15 servings.

Per serving: 382 cal., 17 g fat (8 g sat. fat), 80 mg chol., 734 mg sodium, 28 g carbo., 1 g fiber, 26 g pro.

Easy Cheesy Sloppy Joes

Prep: 25 minutes   **Cook:** 4½ hr. (low) or 2 hr. (high)

3 pounds lean ground beef
1 cup chopped onion (2 medium)
2 10.75-ounce cans condensed fiesta nacho cheese soup
¾ cup ketchup
18 hamburger or cocktail buns, split and toasted
Pickles (optional)

1. In a large skillet, cook ground beef and onion over medium heat until meat is brown and onion is tender. Drain off fat.

2. In a 3½- or 4-quart slow cooker, stir together meat mixture, soup, and ketchup.

3. Cover and cook on low-heat setting for 4½ hours or on high-heat setting for 2 hours. Serve meat mixture in toasted buns. If desired, garnish with pickles. Makes 18 servings.

Per serving: 288 cal., 11 g fat (4 g sat. fat), 50 mg chol., 563 mg sodium, 27 g carbo., 1 g fiber, 19 g pro.

Slow-Cooker Chili

Prep: 25 min.   **Cook:** 10 hr. (low) or 5 hr. (high)

1½ pounds ground beef
2 15-ounce cans red kidney beans or small red beans, rinsed and drained
2 14.5-ounce cans Mexican-style stewed tomatoes
1 16-ounce jar salsa
¾ cup chopped onion (1 large)
¾ cup chopped green sweet pepper (1 medium)
1 clove garlic, minced
Toppers (sliced green onion, corn chips, chopped tomato, and/or shredded cheddar)

1. In a large skillet, cook beef over medium heat until brown. Drain off fat. Transfer meat to a 4- or 5-quart slow cooker. Add beans, undrained tomatoes, the salsa, onion, sweet pepper, and garlic to cooker; stir to combine.

2. Cover and cook on low-heat setting for 10 to 12 hours or on high-heat setting for 5 to 6 hours. Serve chili with desired toppers. Makes 6 servings.

Per serving: 496 cal., 26 g fat (10 g sat. fat), 74 mg chol., 1,270 mg sodium, 40 g carbo., 10 g fiber, 32 g pro.

Beefy Minestrone

Prep: 20 min. **Cook:** 8 hr. (low) or 4 hr. (high)

- 1 pound ground beef
- 1 14-ounce can reduced-sodium beef broth
- 1¼ cups water
- 1 10-ounce package frozen mixed vegetables
- 1 14.5-ounce can diced tomatoes, undrained
- 1 10.75-ounce can condensed reduced-sodium and reduced-fat tomato soup
- 1 tablespoon dried minced onion
- 1 teaspoon dried Italian seasoning, crushed
- ¼ teaspoon garlic powder
- Fish-shape crackers, oyster crackers, or other crackers (optional)

1. In a large skillet, cook ground beef over medium heat until brown. Drain off fat. Transfer meat to a 3½- or 4-quart slow cooker. Stir in remaining ingredients, except crackers.

2. Cover and cook on low-heat setting for 8 to 10 hours or on high-heat setting for 4 to 5 hours. If desired, top each serving with crackers. Makes 4 to 6 servings.

Per serving: 346 cal., 15 g fat (6 g sat. fat), 71 mg chol., 684 mg sodium, 26 g carbo., 5 g fiber, 27 g pro.

{follow the rules}

For best results, follow the one-half to two-thirds rule, which says that a slow cooker must be at least half full and no more than two-thirds full. Most recipes give a range for the size of slow cooker that will work for that recipe. Be sure to use a slow cooker that is within the specified range so the food cooks properly.

Cajun Pork

Keep a lid on it! Try **not to peek** under the lid. Slow-cooker recipes work best in long, slow, moist heat.

Cajun Pork
Prep: 20 min. **Cook:** 6 hr. (low) or 3 hr. (high) + 30 min.

    Nonstick cooking spray
2½ to 3 pounds boneless pork shoulder, trimmed and cut into 1-inch cubes
 2 medium yellow sweet peppers, cut into 1-inch pieces
 1 tablespoon Cajun seasoning
 1 14.5-ounce can diced tomatoes with green pepper and onion
 1 16-ounce package frozen cut okra
 1 6-ounce package quick-cooking brown rice, cooked according to package directions
    Bottled hot pepper sauce (optional)

1. Lightly coat a large skillet with cooking spray. Heat over medium heat. Cook meat, half at a time, in hot skillet over medium heat until brown. Drain off fat.

2. In a 3½- or 4-quart slow cooker, place meat and sweet peppers. Sprinkle with Cajun seasoning. Top with undrained tomatoes.

3. Cover and cook on low-heat setting for 7 to 8 hours or on high-heat setting for 3½ to 4 hours. If using low-heat setting, turn to high-heat setting. Stir in frozen okra. Cover and cook for 30 minutes more. Serve over rice. If desired, pass hot pepper sauce. Makes 6 to 8 servings.

Per serving: 233 cal., 8 g fat (3 g sat. fat), 77 mg chol., 444 mg sodium, 15 g carbo., 4 g fiber, 25 g pro.

Spaghetti Sauce with Italian Sausage
Prep: 15 min. **Cook:** 8 hr. (low) or 4 hr. (high)

 ½ pound bulk Italian sausage
 ¼ pound lean ground beef
 ½ cup chopped onion
 1 clove garlic, minced
 1 14.5-ounce can diced tomatoes
 1 8-ounce can reduced-sodium tomato sauce
 1 4-ounce can sliced mushrooms, drained
 ½ cup chopped green sweet pepper (1 small)
 2 tablespoons quick-cooking tapioca
 1 bay leaf
 1 teaspoon dried Italian seasoning, crushed
 ⅛ teaspoon ground black pepper
    Dash salt
    Hot cooked spaghetti
    Snipped fresh oregano (optional)

1. In a large skillet, cook sausage, ground beef, onion, and garlic until meat is brown and onion is tender. Drain off fat.

2. In a 3½- or 4-quart slow cooker, stir together the undrained tomatoes, tomato sauce, mushrooms, sweet pepper, tapioca, bay leaf, Italian seasoning, black pepper, and salt. Stir in meat mixture.

3. Cover and cook on low-heat setting for 8 to 10 hours or high-heat setting for 4 to 5 hours. Discard bay leaf. Serve sauce over hot cooked spaghetti. If desired, sprinkle with fresh oregano. Makes 4 to 5 servings.

For 5- or 6-quart slow cooker: Double all ingredients. Prepare as above. Makes 8 to 10 servings.

Per serving: 481 cal., 24 g fat (9 g sat. fat), 79 mg chol., 788 mg sodium, 40 g carbo., 5 g fiber, 25 g pro.

Pork Chops O'Brien

Prep: 20 min.   **Cook:** 7 hr. (low) or $3\frac{1}{2}$ hr. (high)

        Nonstick cooking spray
    5   cups loose-pack frozen diced hash brown
        potatoes with onion and peppers, thawed
    1   10.75-ounce can reduced-fat and reduced-
        sodium condensed cream of mushroom soup
 $\frac{1}{2}$ cup bottled roasted red sweet peppers,
        drained and chopped
 $\frac{1}{2}$ cup dairy sour cream
 $\frac{1}{2}$ cup shredded Colby and Monterey Jack
        cheese (2 ounces)
 $\frac{1}{4}$ teaspoon ground black pepper
    4   pork loin chops, cut $\frac{3}{4}$ inch thick
    1   tablespoon cooking oil
    1   2.8-ounce can french-fried onions

1. Lightly coat a $3\frac{1}{2}$- or 4-quart slow cooker with cooking spray; set aside. In a large bowl, stir together hash brown potatoes, soup, sweet peppers, sour cream, cheese, and black pepper. Transfer potato mixture to the slow cooker.

2. Trim fat from chops. In a large skillet, brown chops on both sides in hot oil over medium heat. Drain off fat. Place chops on top of hash brown mixture in slow cooker.

3. Cover and cook on low-heat setting for 7 to 9 hours or on high-heat setting for $3\frac{1}{2}$ to $4\frac{1}{2}$ hours. Sprinkle with french-fried onions. Makes 4 servings.

Per serving: 670 cal., 29 g fat (9 g sat. fat), 92 mg chol., 639 mg sodium, 64 g carbo., 4 g fiber, 37 g pro.

Ribs and Kraut

Prep: 20 min.   **Cook:** 7 hr. (low) or $3\frac{1}{2}$ hr. (high)

    1   14-ounce can sauerkraut, drained
    1   large sweet onion, sliced (2 cups)
    2   medium tart cooking apples, peeled, cored,
        and sliced (about 2 cups)
    2   pounds boneless pork country-style ribs
    1   cup apple juice
        Snipped fresh chives

1. In a $3\frac{1}{2}$- or 4-quart slow cooker place sauerkraut, onion, and apples. Top with ribs. Pour juice over all.

2. Cover and cook on low-heat setting for 7 to 8 hours or on high-heat setting for $3\frac{1}{2}$ to 4 hours. Use a slotted spoon to serve. Sprinkle each serving with chives. Makes 6 to 8 servings.

Per serving: 312 cal., 12 g fat (4 g sat. fat), 96 mg chol., 541 mg sodium, 19 g carbo., 4 g fiber, 30 g pro.

Cuban Pork Sandwiches

Prep: 30 min.   **Cook:** 10 hr. (low) or 5 hr. (high)

    1   3- to $3\frac{1}{2}$-pound boneless pork shoulder roast
 $\frac{3}{4}$ cup reduced-sodium chicken broth
    1   medium onion, cut into wedges
    1   cup packed fresh cilantro leaves
 $\frac{1}{4}$ cup water
    2   tablespoons vinegar
    4   cloves garlic, minced
    1   teaspoon salt
    1   teaspoon ground cumin
    1   teaspoon dried oregano, crushed
 $\frac{1}{4}$ teaspoon ground black pepper
    2   red onions, thinly sliced
    1   tablespoon cooking oil
 $\frac{1}{4}$ cup lime juice
    8   ciabatta or French rolls, split

1. Trim fat from pork roast; set aside. In a $3\frac{1}{2}$- to 5-quart slow cooker, stir together broth, onion wedges, cilantro, water, vinegar, garlic, salt, cumin, oregano, and pepper. Add meat to slow cooker; spoon onion mixture over meat.

2. Cover and cook on low-heat setting for 10 to 12 hours or on high-heat setting for 5 to 6 hours.

3. Just before serving, in a large skillet, cook red onions in hot oil over medium-high heat until tender but not brown. Carefully add lime juice to skillet. Cook and stir until lime juice is evaporated.

4. Transfer meat to a cutting board, reserving liquid in cooker; cool meat slightly. Using two forks, shred meat; discard fat. Serve meat and red onions on rolls. If desired, strain juices in cooker and serve with sandwiches for dipping. Makes 8 servings.

Per serving: 381 cal., 13 g fat (4 g sat. fat), 110 mg chol., 721 mg sodium, 25 g carbo., 2 g fiber, 38 g pro.

Pulled Pork with Root Beer Sauce

Prep: 15 min. **Cook:** 8 hr. (low) or 4 hr. (high)

1   2½- to 3-pound pork sirloin roast
½   teaspoon salt
½   teaspoon ground black pepper
1   tablespoon cooking oil
2   medium onions, cut into thin wedges
1   cup root beer*
6   cloves garlic, minced
3   cups root beer* (two 12-ounce cans or bottles)
1   cup bottled chili sauce
¼   teaspoon root beer concentrate (optional)
8   to 10 hamburger buns, split (toasted, if desired)
   Lettuce leaves and tomato slices (optional)

1. Trim fat from meat. If necessary, cut meat to fit into a 3½- to 5-quart slow cooker. Sprinkle meat with the salt and pepper. In a large skillet, brown meat on all sides in hot oil over medium heat. Drain off fat. Transfer meat to cooker. Add onion, the 1 cup root beer, and the garlic.

2. Cover and cook on low-heat setting for 8 to 10 hours or on high-heat setting for 4 to 5 hours.

3. Meanwhile, for sauce, in a medium saucepan, stir together the 3 cups root beer and the chili sauce. Bring to boiling; reduce heat. Simmer, uncovered, stirring occasionally, about 30 minutes or until mixture is reduced to 2 cups. If desired, add root beer concentrate.

4. Transfer meat to a cutting board or serving platter. Using a slotted spoon, transfer onion to serving platter; discard cooking juices. Using 2 forks, pull meat apart into shreds. If desired, line buns with lettuce leaves and tomato slices. Place meat and onion on rolls. Drizzle meat with some of the root beer sauce. Makes 8 to 10 servings.

  *Note: Do not use diet root beer.

Per serving: 433 cal., 12 g fat (3 g sat. fat), 89 mg chol., 877 mg sodium, 45 g carbo., 3 g fiber, 35 g pro.

Ranch Pork Roast

Prep: 15 min. **Cook:** 9 hr. (low) or 4½ hr. (high)

1   2½- to 3-pound boneless pork shoulder roast
   Nonstick cooking spray
1   pound new red-skinned potatoes, halved
1   10.75-ounce can condensed cream of chicken soup
1   8-ounce package cream cheese, cubed and softened
1   0.4-ounce envelope ranch salad dressing mix
   Freshly ground black pepper (optional)

1. Trim fat from meat. Lightly coat a large skillet with cooking spray; heat skillet over medium heat. In hot skillet, brown roast on all sides. Remove from heat.

2. Place potatoes in a 3½- or 4-quart slow cooker. Place meat over potatoes. In a medium bowl, whisk together soup, cream cheese, and salad dressing mix. Spoon over meat and potatoes in cooker.

3. Cover and cook on low-heat setting for 9 to 10 hours or on high-heat setting for 4½ to 5 hours. If desired, serve with freshly ground black pepper. Makes 6 servings.

Per serving: 521 cal., 31 g fat (15 g sat. fat), 173 mg chol., 757 mg sodium, 16 g carbo., 1 g fiber, 42 g pro.

Pulled Pork with Root Beer Sauce

Ranch Pork Roast

Cranberry Pork Roast

Prep: 25 min. **Cook:** 6 hr. (low) or 3 hr. (high)

- 1   3-pound boneless pork top loin roast (double loin, tied)
- 1   tablespoon cooking oil
     Salt and ground black pepper
- 1   16-ounce can whole cranberry sauce
- ½   cup cranberry juice
- ¼   cup sugar
- 1   teaspoon dry mustard
- ¼   teaspoon ground cloves
- 2   tablespoons cornstarch
- 2   tablespoons cold water
     Hot cooked rice pilaf, rice, or noodles (optional)

1. In a large skillet, brown meat on all sides in hot oil over medium heat. Place meat in a 3½- to 5-quart slow cooker; sprinkle lightly with salt and pepper. In a medium bowl, stir together cranberry sauce, cranberry juice, sugar, mustard, and cloves. Pour over meat in cooker. Cover and cook on low-heat setting for 6 to 7 hours or on high-heat setting for 3 to 3½ hours.

2. Transfer meat to a platter; cover and keep warm. Skim fat from juices. Measure 2 cups of juices; transfer to a medium saucepan. In a small bowl, stir together cornstarch and water; add to saucepan. Cook and stir over medium heat until thickened and bubbly; cook and stir for 2 minutes more. Serve with roast and, if desired, rice pilaf, rice, or noodles. Makes 8 to 10 servings.

Per serving: 404 cal., 11 g fat (3 g sat. fat), 100 mg chol., 24 mg sodium, 38 g carbo., 1 g fiber, 37 g pro.

White and Green Chili

Prep: 20 min.   **Cook:** 7 hr. (low) or $3\frac{1}{2}$ hr. (high)

$1\frac{1}{2}$	**pounds lean ground pork**
1	**cup chopped onion (2 medium)**
2	**15-ounce cans Great Northern beans, rinsed and drained**
1	**16-ounce jar green salsa**
1	**14-ounce can chicken broth**
$1\frac{1}{2}$	**teaspoons ground cumin**
2	**tablespoons snipped fresh cilantro**
$\frac{1}{3}$	**cup dairy sour cream (optional)**
	Fresh cilantro sprigs (optional)

1. In a large skillet, cook ground pork and onion over medium heat until meat is brown and onion is tender. Drain off fat. Transfer meat mixture to a $3\frac{1}{2}$- or 4-quart slow cooker. Stir in beans, salsa, broth, and cumin.

2. Cover and cook on low-heat setting for 7 to 8 hours or on high-heat setting for $3\frac{1}{2}$ to 4 hours.

3. Stir in the 2 tablespoons cilantro. If desired, top each serving with sour cream and garnish with cilantro sprig. Makes 6 servings.

Per serving: 348 cal., 9 g fat (4 g sat. fat), 53 mg chol., 613 mg sodium, 39 g carbo., 9 g fiber, 26 g pro.

Chicken Curry Soup

Prep: 15 min. **Cook:** 4 hr. (low) or 2 hr. (high) + 15 min.

- 1 10.75-ounce can condensed cream of chicken or celery soup
- 1 cup water
- 2 teaspoons curry powder
- 1¼ pounds skinless, boneless chicken thighs or breast halves, cut into ¾-inch pieces
- 2 cups sliced carrot (4 medium)
- 1 13.5-ounce can unsweetened coconut milk
- 1 red sweet pepper, cut into bite-size strips
- ½ cup sliced green onion (4)
  Chopped peanuts (optional)
  Toasted coconut (optional)

1. In a 3½- or 4-quart slow cooker, stir together soup, water, and curry powder. Add chicken and carrot to cooker. Stir to combine.

2. Cover and cook on low-heat setting for 4 to 5 hours or on high-heat setting for 2 to 2½ hours. If using high-heat setting, turn to low-heat setting. Stir in coconut milk, sweet pepper, and green onion. Cover and cook for 15 minutes more. If desired, top individual servings with chopped peanuts and/or toasted coconut. Makes 6 servings.

Per serving: 309 cal., 19 g fat (12 g sat. fat), 80 mg chol., 479 mg sodium, 13 g carbo., 2 g fiber, 22 g pro.

Finger Lickin' BBQ Chicken

Prep: 10 min. **Cook:** 7 hr. (low) or 3½ hr. (high)

- 2½ to 3 pounds chicken drumsticks, skinned if desired
- 1 cup bottled barbecue sauce
- ⅓ cup apricot or peach preserves
- 2 teaspoons yellow mustard

1. Place chicken in a 3½- or 4-quart slow cooker. In a small bowl, stir together barbecue sauce, preserves, and mustard. Pour over chicken.

2. Cover and cook on low-heat setting for 7 to 8 hours or on high-heat setting for 3½ to 4 hours. Transfer chicken to a serving dish; cover and keep warm. If desired, transfer liquid in cooker to a medium saucepan. Bring to boiling; reduce heat. Simmer, uncovered, for 10 minutes or until desired consistency. Serve sauce with chicken. Makes 4 to 6 servings.

Per serving: 456 cal., 17 g fat (4 g sat. fat), 154 mg chol., 963 mg sodium, 37 g carbo., 2 g fiber, 38 g pro.

Chicken legs and thighs are flavorful, economical cuts for the slow cooker.

Creamy Pasta and Vegetables

Creamy Pasta and Vegetables

Prep: 20 min. **Cook:** 5 hr. (low) or 2½ hr. (high)

- 2 26- to 32-ounce jars tomato-basil pasta sauce or your favorite purchased pasta sauce
- 1 medium zucchini, halved lengthwise and cut into ½-inch-thick slices
- 1 medium yellow summer squash, halved lengthwise and cut into ½-inch-thick slices
- ½ cup chopped onion (1 medium)
- ¼ cup dry white wine or cranberry juice
- ½ of an 8-ounce package cream cheese, cubed
  Hot cooked fusilli pasta or spaghetti
  Finely shredded Parmesan cheese

1. In a 3½- or 4-quart slow cooker, stir together pasta sauce, zucchini, yellow squash, onion, and wine.

2. Cover and cook on low-heat setting for 5 to 7 hours or on high-heat setting for 2½ to 3½ hours. Stir in cream cheese until melted. Serve over hot cooked pasta. Top individual servings with Parmesan cheese. Makes 10 servings.

Per serving: 460 cal., 15 g fat (8 g sat. fat), 36 mg chol., 1,067 mg sodium, 56 g carbo., 4 g fiber, 24 g pro.

> Turkey tenderloins are large strips of white meat that come from the rib side of a turkey breast. They are a **low-cost option** to chicken breast.

Texas Turkey Bonanza

Texas Turkey Bonanza

Prep: 20 min.   **Cook:** 8 hr. (low) or 4 hr. (high) + 30 min.

- 2 **cups dry black-eyed peas**
- 1 **to 3 fresh jalapeño chile peppers, seeded and quartered lengthwise***
- 1½ **teaspoons dried sage, crushed**
- 1 **teaspoon salt**
- 3 **cups water**
- 1 **pound turkey breast tenderloins or pork tenderloin, cut into 1½-inch pieces**
- 2 **medium yellow summer squash, cut into wedges**
- ½ **cup finely chopped red onion (1 medium)**
  Snipped fresh cilantro
  Lime Sour Cream (optional)

1. Rinse black-eyed peas. In a large saucepan, combine peas and enough water to cover peas by 2 inches. Bring to boiling; reduce heat. Simmer, uncovered, for 10 minutes. Drain and rinse peas.

2. In a 4- or 5-quart slow cooker, stir together drained peas, the jalapeño peppers, sage, and salt. Stir in the 3 cups water. Add turkey.

3. Cover and cook on low-heat setting for 8 to 10 hours or on high-heat setting for 4 to 5 hours.

4. If using low-heat setting, turn to high-heat setting. Stir in squash. Cover and cook about 30 minutes more or until squash is crisp-tender. Sprinkle each serving with red onion and cilantro. If desired, top with Lime Sour Cream. Makes 6 servings.

Lime Sour Cream: In a small bowl, stir together ½ cup dairy sour cream, ½ teaspoon finely shredded lime peel, and 1 tablespoon lime juice. Cover and chill until ready to serve.

*Note: Because hot chile peppers, such as jalapeños, contain volatile oils that can burn your skin and eyes, avoid direct contact with chiles as much as possible. When working with chile peppers, wear plastic or rubber gloves. If your bare hands do touch the chile peppers, wash your hands well with soap and water.

Per serving: 144 cal., 1 g fat (0 g sat. fat), 47 mg chol., 423 mg sodium, 13 g carbo., 4 g fiber, 21 g pro.

Chicken with Mushroom Stuffing

Prep: 40 min. **Cook:** 4 hr. (high)

　　Nonstick cooking spray
- 2　tablespoons finely shredded lemon peel
- 1　tablespoon ground sage
- 1　tablespoon seasoned salt
- 1½　teaspoons ground black pepper
- 8　small chicken legs (drumstick-thigh portion) (about 5 pounds), skinned
- ¼　cup butter
- 4　cups quartered or sliced fresh mushrooms, such as cremini, shiitake, and/or button
- 2　cloves garlic, thinly sliced
- 8　cups sourdough baguette cut into 1-inch pieces (about 10 ounces)
- 1　cup coarsely shredded carrot (2 medium)
- 1　cup chicken broth
- ¼　cup chopped walnuts, toasted
- 3　tablespoons snipped fresh Italian parsley

1. Lightly coat the inside of a 6-quart slow cooker with cooking spray. Reserve 1 teaspoon lemon peel. In a bowl, stir together the remaining lemon peel, the sage, salt, and pepper. Rub three-quarters of sage mixture on chicken legs. Place legs in slow cooker.

2. Meanwhile, in a large skillet, cook mushrooms and garlic in hot butter over medium heat for 3 to 5 minutes or until just tender. Stir in remaining sage mixture. Transfer mushroom mixture to a large bowl. Add baguette pieces and carrot. Drizzle with broth, tossing gently to combine. Lightly pack stuffing on top of chicken in cooker.

3. Cover and cook on high-heat setting for 4 to 5 hours. Using a slotted spoon, transfer stuffing and chicken to a serving platter; discard juices in cooker. In a small bowl, combine reserved 1 teaspoon lemon peel, the walnuts, and parsley. Sprinkle nut mixture over chicken before serving. Makes 8 servings.

Per serving: 412 cal., 17 g fat (5 g sat. fat), 146 mg chol., 1,450 mg sodium, 27 g carbo., 3 g fiber, 39 g pro.

Chicken and Shrimp with Orzo

Prep: 15 min. **Cook:** 6 hr. (low) or 3 hr. (high) + 5 min.

- 12　ounces skinless, boneless chicken thighs
- 1　cup chopped onion (1 large)
- 3　cloves garlic, minced
- 1　14.5-ounce can diced tomatoes with basil, garlic, and oregano; or diced tomatoes with onion and garlic
- 2　tablespoons tomato paste
- ½　cup port wine or chicken broth
- 2　tablespoons lemon juice
- 2　bay leaves
- ½　teaspoon salt
- ¼　teaspoon crushed red pepper
- 1　8-ounce package frozen, peeled, cooked shrimp, thawed and drained
- 1　9-ounce package frozen artichoke hearts, thawed and coarsely chopped
- 2　cups hot cooked orzo (rosamarina)
- ½　cup crumbled feta cheese (2 ounces)

1. Cut chicken thighs into quarters. Place the onion and garlic in a 3½- to 5-quart slow cooker. Top with the chicken pieces. In a medium bowl, stir together the undrained tomatoes, tomato paste, wine, lemon juice, bay leaves, salt, and crushed red pepper. Pour over chicken in cooker.

2. Cover and cook on low-heat setting for 6 to 7 hours or on high-heat setting for 3 to 3½ hours.

3. If using low-heat setting, turn to high-heat setting. Remove bay leaves. Stir in shrimp and artichoke hearts. Cover; cook for 5 minutes more. Serve chicken and shrimp mixture over hot cooked orzo. Sprinkle with feta cheese. Makes 4 to 5 servings.

Per serving: 615 cal., 21 g fat (9 g sat. fat), 187 mg chol., 1,203 mg sodium, 56 g carbo., 4 g fiber, 46 g pro.

Chicken and Noodles with Vegetables

Prep: 25 min. Cook: 8 hr. (low) or 4 hr. (high)

2	cups sliced carrot (4 medium)
1½	cups chopped onion (3 medium)
1	cup sliced celery (2 stalks)
2	tablespoons snipped fresh parsley
1	bay leaf
3	medium chicken legs (drumstick-thigh portion) (about 2 pounds total), skinned
2	10.75-ounce cans reduced-fat and reduced-sodium condensed cream of chicken soup
½	cup water
1	teaspoon dried thyme, crushed
¼	teaspoon ground black pepper
10	ounces dried wide noodles (about 5 cups)
1	cup frozen peas
	Salt (optional)
	Ground black pepper (optional)

1. In a 3½- or 4-quart slow cooker, stir together carrot, onion, celery, parsley, and bay leaf. Place chicken on top of vegetables. In a large bowl, stir together soup, water, thyme, and the ¼ teaspoon pepper. Pour over chicken in cooker.

2. Cover and cook on low-heat setting for 8 to 9 hours or on high-heat setting for 4 to 4½ hours. Remove chicken from slow cooker; cool slightly. Discard bay leaf.

3. Cook noodles according to package directions; drain. Meanwhile, stir peas into mixture in slow cooker. Remove chicken from bones; discard bones. Shred or chop meat; stir into mixture in slow cooker.

4. To serve, spoon chicken mixture over noodles. If desired, season to taste with salt and additional pepper. Makes 6 servings.

Per serving: 406 cal., 7 g fat (2 g sat. fat), 122 mg chol., 532 mg sodium, 56 g carbo., 5 g fiber, 28 g pro.

Cajun Shrimp and Rice

Prep: 20 min.   **Cook:** 5 hr. (low) or 3 hr. (high) + 15 min.

- 2   14.5-ounce cans diced tomatoes
- 1   14-ounce can reduced-sodium chicken broth
- 1   cup chopped onion (1 large)
- 1   cup chopped green sweet pepper (1 large)
- 1   6-ounce package long grain and wild rice mix
- ¼   cup water
- ½   teaspoon salt-free Cajun seasoning
- 2   cloves garlic, minced
- 1   pound cooked peeled and deveined shrimp

1. In a 3½- or 4-quart slow cooker, stir together undrained tomatoes, broth, onion, pepper, rice mix (with seasoning packet), water, Cajun seasoning, and garlic.

2. Cover and cook on low-heat setting for 5 to 6 hours or on high-heat setting for 3 to 3½ hours. If using low-heat setting, turn to high-heat setting. Stir in shrimp. Cover and cook for 15 minutes. Makes 6 servings.

Per serving: 219 cal., 1 g fat (0 g sat. fat), 148 mg chol., 1,001 mg sodium, 32 g carbo., 4 g fiber, 21 g pro.

Lemon-Lime Chili Chicken

Prep: 15 min.   **Cook:** 5 hr. (low) or 2½ hr. (high)

- 2   tablespoons chili powder
- 1   teaspoon salt
- ½   teaspoon black pepper
- 3   to 3½ pounds meaty chicken pieces (breast halves, thighs, and drumsticks), skinned
- 1   medium zucchini or yellow summer squash, halved lengthwise and cut into 1-inch pieces
- 1   medium onion, cut into wedges
- ¼   cup reduced-sodium chicken broth
- ¼   cup lime juice
- ¼   cup lemon juice
- 2   cloves garlic, minced

1. In a small bowl, combine chili powder, salt, and pepper. Rub spice mixture over chicken. Place chicken in a 4- or 5-quart slow cooker. Add zucchini and onion. In a small bowl, stir together broth, lime juice, lemon juice, and garlic. Pour over chicken mixture in cooker.

2. Cover and cook on low-heat setting for 5 to 6 hours or on high-heat setting for 2½ to 3 hours. Transfer chicken and vegetables to a serving platter. Discard cooking liquid. Makes 6 to 8 servings.

Per serving: 156 cal., 4 g fat (1 g sat. fat), 76 mg chol., 525 mg sodium, 6 g carbo., 1 g fiber, 24 g pro.

Barley Vegetable Soup

Prep: 25 min.   **Cook:** 8 hr. (low) or 4 hr. (high)

- 1   15-ounce can red beans, rinsed and drained
- 1   10-ounce package frozen whole kernel corn
- ½   cup medium pearl barley
- 1   14.5-ounce can no-salt-added stewed tomatoes
- 2   cups sliced fresh mushrooms
- 1   cup chopped onion (2 medium)
- ½   cup coarsely chopped carrot (1 medium)
- ½   cup coarsely chopped celery (1 stalk)
- 3   cloves garlic, minced
- 2   teaspoons dried Italian seasoning, crushed
- ¼   teaspoon ground black pepper
- 5   cups reduced-sodium vegetable broth or chicken broth

1. In a 3½- to 5-quart slow cooker, stir together beans, corn, barley, undrained tomatoes, mushrooms, onion, carrot, celery, garlic, Italian seasoning, and pepper. Pour broth over all.

2. Cover and cook on low-heat setting for 8 to 10 hours or on high-heat setting for 4 to 5 hours. Makes 6 servings.

Per serving: 216 cal., 1 g fat (0 g sat. fat), 0 mg chol., 797 mg sodium, 15 g carbo., 9 g fiber, 11 g pro.

Cheesy Mexican-Style Vegetable Soup

Prep: 15 min. **Cook:** 6 hr. (low) or 3 hr. (high)

- 2 **cups chopped zucchini**
- ¾ **cup chopped red or green sweet pepper (1 medium)**
- ½ **cup chopped onion (1 medium)**
- 1 **15-ounce can black beans, rinsed and drained**
- 1 **10-ounce package frozen whole kernel corn**
- 1 **14.5-ounce can diced tomatoes with green chiles**
- 1 **16-ounce jar cheddar cheese pasta sauce**
- 1 **cup reduced-sodium chicken broth or vegetable broth**
   Coarsely crushed tortilla chips (optional)
   Sliced fresh jalapeño peppers (optional)

1. In a 3½- or 4-quart slow cooker, place zucchini, sweet pepper, onion, beans, and corn. Pour undrained tomatoes over vegetables and beans. In a small bowl, stir together cheese sauce and broth; pour over all.

2. Cover and cook on low-heat setting for 6 to 8 hours or on high-heat setting for 3 to 4 hours. If desired, top individual servings with crushed tortilla chips and jalapeño slices. Makes 5 to 6 servings.

Per serving: 289 cal., 14 g fat (5 g sat. fat), 35 mg chol., 1,381 mg sodium, 36 g carbo., 7 g fiber, 12 g pro.

Southwestern White Chili

Prep: 20 min. **Cook:** 8 hr. (low) or 4 hr. (high)

- 3 **15.5-ounce cans Great Northern beans, drained and rinsed**
- 4 **cups reduced-sodium chicken broth**
- 3 **cups chopped cooked chicken**
- 2 **4-ounce cans diced green chile peppers**
- 1 **cup chopped onion (2 medium)**
- 4 **cloves garlic, minced**
- 2 **teaspoons ground cumin**
- 1 **teaspoon dried oregano, crushed**
- ¼ **teaspoon cayenne pepper**
- 2 **cups shredded Monterey Jack cheese (8 ounces)**

1. In a 3½- to 5-quart slow cooker, stir together beans, broth, chicken, chile peppers, onion, garlic, cumin, oregano, and cayenne.

2. Cover and cook on low-heat setting for 8 to 10 hours or on high-heat setting for 4 to 5 hours. Stir in the cheese until melted. Makes 8 servings.

Per serving: 429 cal., 14 g fat (7 g sat. fat), 72 mg chol., 570 mg sodium, 41 g carbo., 9 g fiber, 37 g pro.

Southwestern Pinto Bean Soup

Prep: 15 min. **Stand:** 1 hr.
Cook: 8 hr. (low) or 4 hr. (high) + 30 min.

- 2 **cups dry pinto beans**
- 5 **cups cold water**
- 2 **14-ounce cans reduced-sodium chicken broth**
- ½ **cup water**
- ¾ **cup chopped onion (1 large)**
- 3 **cloves garlic, minced**
- 1 **teaspoon ground cumin**
- ¼ **teaspoon cayenne pepper**
- 1 **14.5-ounce can fire-roasted diced tomatoes**
   Shredded Monterey Jack cheese (optional)
   Snipped fresh cilantro or sliced green onions (optional)
   Crackers (optional)

1. Rinse beans. In a Dutch oven, combine rinsed beans and the 5 cups cold water. Bring to boiling; reduce heat. Simmer, uncovered, for 10 minutes. Remove from heat. Cover and let stand for 1 hour. Drain and rinse beans again.

2. In a 3½- or 4-quart slow cooker, stir together the beans, broth, the ½ cup water, onion, garlic, cumin, and cayenne.

3. Cover and cook on low-heat setting for 8 to 10 hours or on high-heat setting for 4 to 5 hours.

4. Stir in undrained tomatoes; cover and cook for 30 minutes more. If desired, partially mash mixture with a potato masher, leaving soup chunky. If desired, top individual servings with cheese and cilantro and serve with crackers. Makes 6 servings.

Per serving: 309 cal., 5 g fat (3 g sat. fat), 14 mg chol., 772 mg sodium, 46 g carbo., 10 g fiber, 18 g pro.

{good timing}

For recipes that may be ready before you get home, start the slow cooker with an automatic timer (like those used for lamps). Just make sure the timer is set to start within 2 hours of adding ingredients to the cooker and that the food is well chilled when it goes in. Dinner will be ready at just the right time!

Sausage-Corn Chowder

Prep: 15 min.   **Cook:** 8 hr. (low) or 4 hr. (high)

12 ounces cooked smoked turkey sausage, halved lengthwise and cut into ½-inch slices
3 cups frozen loose-pack diced hash brown potatoes with onion and peppers
2 medium carrots, coarsely chopped
2½ cups water
1 15- to 16.5-ounce can no-salt-added cream-style corn
1 10.75-ounce can condensed golden mushroom soup
½ cup roasted red sweet pepper strips
1 teaspoon dried thyme, crushed

1. Place sausage, frozen potatoes, and carrots in a 3½- to 5-quart slow cooker. In a large bowl, stir together water, corn, soup, red pepper strips, and thyme. Add to cooker; stir to combine.

2. Cover and cook on low-heat setting for 8 to 10 hours or on high-heat setting for 4 to 5 hours. Makes 6 servings.

Per serving: 258 cal., 7 g fat (2 g sat. fat), 40 mg chol., 893 mg sodium, 37 g carbo., 4 g fiber, 13 g pro.

Here's a trick when time is tight. Throw a cozy casserole together on the weekend, **stash it in the fridge** or freezer, then pop it into the oven on the night you need it most.

make now,

Baked Penne with Meat Sauce

Prep: 30 min.   **Bake:** 75 min.   **Freeze:** up to 1 month

  8   ounces dried penne pasta
  1   14.5-ounce can diced tomatoes
  ½   of a 6-ounce can (⅓ cup) Italian-style
        tomato paste
  ⅓   cup dry red wine or tomato juice
  ⅓   cup water
  ½   teaspoon sugar
  ½   teaspoon dried oregano, crushed, or
        2 teaspoons snipped fresh oregano
  ¼   teaspoon salt
  ¼   teaspoon ground black pepper
  1   pound lean ground beef
  ½   cup chopped onion (1 medium)
  ¼   cup sliced pitted ripe olives
  1   cup shredded reduced-fat mozzarella cheese
        (4 ounces)

1. Cook pasta according to package directions; drain well.

2. In a medium bowl, stir together undrained tomatoes, tomato paste, wine, water, sugar, dried oregano (if using), salt, and pepper. Set aside.

3. In a large skillet, brown ground beef and onion over medium heat. Drain off fat. Stir in tomato mixture. Bring to boiling; reduce heat. Cover and simmer for 10 minutes. Stir in pasta, fresh oregano (if using), and olives.

4. Divide the pasta mixture among six 10- to 12-ounce individual casseroles (or one 3-quart rectangular baking dish.)* Cover with freezer wrap, label, and freeze for up to 1 month.

5. To serve, preheat oven to 350°F. Remove freezer wrap; cover each casserole with foil. Bake about 70 minutes or until heated through. Sprinkle with mozzarella cheese. Bake, uncovered, about 5 minutes more or until cheese melts. (Or thaw casseroles overnight in the refrigerator. Bake as directed about 45 minutes or until heated through.) Makes 6 servings.

*To serve in a 3-quart baking dish: Cover dish with foil. Bake about 1½ hours or until heated through, stirring carefully once. Sprinkle with mozzarella cheese. Bake, uncovered, about 5 minutes more or until cheese melts. (Or thaw baking dish overnight in the refrigerator. Bake as directed about 55 minutes or until heated through, stirring carefully once.)

Per serving: 342 cal., 10 g fat (4 g sat. fat), 51 mg chol., 465 mg sodium, 37 g carbo., 2 g fiber, 22 g pro.

serve later

Shortcut Lasagna

Prep: 30 min. **Bake:** 40 min. **Stand:** 5 min.
Freeze: up to 3 months

- **8   ounces ground beef**
- **8   ounces bulk Italian sausage**
- **1   26-ounce jar tomato-basil pasta sauce**
- **1   egg**
- **1   15-ounce carton low-fat ricotta cheese**
  or cream-style cottage cheese
- **1   2.25-ounce can sliced pitted ripe olives**
- **9   no-boil lasagna noodles**
- **1   8-ounce package sliced mozzarella**
  cheese
- **¼   cup grated Parmesan cheese**
  Snipped fresh basil (optional)

1. Preheat oven to 350°F. In a large saucepan, brown beef and sausage over medium heat. Drain off fat. Stir pasta sauce into saucepan; bring to boiling.

2. Meanwhile, in a medium bowl, beat egg lightly with a fork. Stir in ricotta cheese and olives.

3. To assemble lasagna, spread about 1 cup of the hot meat mixture in the bottom of two 9×5-inch loaf pans or dishes. Cover with three noodles, breaking noodles as necessary to fit in pans and making sure that noodles do not touch edges of pans. Cover with one-third of the ricotta mixture, one-third of the remaining meat mixture, and one-third of the mozzarella cheese. Repeat with two more layers of noodles, meat mixture, ricotta cheese mixture, and mozzarella. (Make sure noodles are covered with sauce.) Sprinkle with Parmesan cheese.

4. Cover pans with foil. Bake for 30 minutes. Uncover and bake for 10 to 15 minutes more or until cheese is golden and noodles are tender. Let stand for 5 minutes before serving. If desired, garnish with fresh basil. Makes 8 servings.

Per serving: 492 cal., 26 g fat (12 g sat. fat), 109 mg chol., 987 mg sodium, 34 g carbo., 2 g fiber, 31 g pro.

{make it ahead}

Prepare as directed. Cool baked lasagna slightly. Chill lasagna in pans for at least 1 hour. Using two spatulas, carefully remove lasagnas from pans. Transfer to large resealable plastic bags. Seal and freeze for up to 3 months. Thaw in refrigerator for 1 to 2 days. Carefully return the lasagnas to the loaf pans. Bake in a 350°F oven for 40 to 45 minutes or until heated through.

Beef and Sweet Pepper Pasta

Start to Finish: 35 min.   **Chill:** up to 2 days
Freeze: up to 1 month

1   12-ounce package frozen cooked
    Italian meatballs
8   ounces dried pappardelle pasta or fettuccine
1   medium fennel bulb, trimmed and cut into
    bite-size strips
1   medium onion, quartered and thinly sliced
1   cup thinly sliced carrot (2 medium)
4   cloves garlic, minced
1   tablespoon olive oil
1   26-ounce jar spicy red pepper pasta sauce or
    mushroom and ripe olive pasta sauce
    Salt and ground black pepper
1   cup shredded part-skim mozzarella cheese
    (4 ounces)
½   cup finely shredded Parmesan or Romano
    cheese (2 ounces)

1. Heat meatballs according to package directions;
set aside. Cook pasta according to package directions;
drain and return to pan.

2. In a large skillet, cook fennel, onion, carrot, and
garlic in hot oil over medium heat for 6 to 8 minutes or
until vegetables are tender. Add vegetable mixture,
meatballs, and pasta sauce to pasta; toss to coat. Heat
through. Season to taste with salt and pepper. Top each
serving with the shredded cheeses. Makes 6 servings.

To Make Ahead: Prepare as above, except do not heat
vegetables, meatballs, and pasta through. Transfer to a
storage container or resealable plastic freezer bag. Refrigerate pasta mixture for up to 2 days or freeze for up
to 1 month. If frozen, thaw pasta mixture in the refrigerator for 1 to 2 days. To serve, transfer pasta mixture to
a large saucepan; add ¼ cup water. Heat over medium
heat for 15 to 20 minutes or until heated through, gently
stirring occasionally. Season to taste with salt and pepper. Top each serving with the shredded cheeses.

Per serving: 506 cal., 23 g fat (10 g sat. fat), 57 mg chol., 1,107 mg
sodium, 47 g carbo., 7 g fiber, 26 g pro.

Baked Rotini with Ham

Prep: 25 min.   **Bake:** 25 min.   **Stand:** 10 min.
Chill: up to 24 hr.

8   ounces dried tricolor rotini (3 cups)
1   16- to 17-ounce jar Alfredo pasta sauce
½   cup milk
½   cup shredded mozzarella cheese (2 ounces)
½   cup chopped cooked ham (2 ounces)
1   teaspoon dried Italian seasoning, crushed
⅛   teaspoon ground black pepper
¼   cup grated Parmesan cheese

1. Cook rotini according to package directions; drain
and return to pan. Stir in Alfredo sauce, milk, mozzarella,
ham, Italian seasoning, and pepper.

2. Transfer rotini mixture to four 7- to 8-ounce individual au gratin dishes or ramekins or a 1½-quart au
gratin dish. Sprinkle with Parmesan cheese. Cover and
chill for up to 24 hours.

3. To serve, preheat oven to 350°F. Cover with foil and
bake for 25 to 30 minutes for the individual dishes or
about 45 minutes for the casserole dish or until mixture
is heated through. Let stand for 10 minutes. Stir before
serving. Makes 4 servings.

Per serving: 503 cal., 28 g fat (13 g sat. fat), 121 mg chol., 1,084 mg
sodium, 51 g carbo., 2 g fiber, 20 g pro.

Spicy Tomato Sauce

Prep: 15 min.　**Cook:** 15 min.　**Chill:** up to 3 days
Freeze: up to 3 months

- ½ **pound uncooked bulk sweet or hot Italian sausage**
- ½ **pound ground beef**
- ½ **cup chopped onion (1 medium)**
- 2 **cloves garlic, minced**
- 2 **14.5-ounce cans diced tomatoes with garlic and onion**
- 2 **teaspoons dried basil, crushed**
- ¼ **teaspoon crushed red pepper (optional)**
  Hot cooked pasta

1. In a large skillet, cook sausage, ground beef, onion, and garlic until meat is brown. Drain off fat. Stir in undrained tomatoes, basil, and, if desired, crushed red pepper. Bring to boiling; reduce heat. Simmer, uncovered, for 15 to 18 minutes or until desired consistency.

2. Serve immediately over hot cooked pasta or divide sauce between two storage containers. Cover and refrigerate for up to 3 days or freeze for up to 3 months. If frozen, thaw overnight in the refrigerator. To serve, place desired amount of sauce in a saucepan; heat through. Serve over hot cooked pasta. Makes 4 cups.

Per ¼ cup sauce: 106 cal., 7 g fat (3 g sat. fat), 21 mg chol., 338 mg sodium, 5 g carbo., 1 g fiber, 5 g pro.

Homemade Pesto

Start to Finish: 15 min.　**Chill:** up to 2 days
Freeze: up to 3 months

- 3 **cups firmly packed fresh basil leaves (3 ounces)**
- ⅔ **cup walnuts**
- ⅔ **cup grated Parmesan or Romano cheese**
- ½ **cup olive oil**
- 4 **cloves garlic, peeled and quartered**
- ½ **teaspoon salt**
- ¼ **teaspoon ground black pepper**
  Hot cooked pasta

1. In a food processor or blender, combine basil, nuts, cheese, oil, garlic, salt, and pepper. Cover; process until nearly smooth, stopping and scraping sides as needed.

2. Place pesto in a storage container. Cover the surface with plastic wrap, then cover the container. Chill for up to 2 days. Or freeze in a standard ice cube tray by spooning 2 tablespoons pesto into each slot; cover tightly with plastic wrap. Freeze for up to 3 months. Thaw at room temperature before using.

3. To serve, toss 2 tablespoons pesto with 1 cup hot cooked pasta. Makes 1¼ cups.

Per 2 tablespoons pesto: 365 cal., 19 g fat (3 g sat. fat), 5 mg chol., 200 mg sodium, 40 g carbo., 3 g fiber, 10 g pro.

Roasted Red Pepper Sauce

Prep: 15 min.　**Cook:** 5 min.　**Chill:** up to 1 week
Freeze: up to 3 months

- 2 **12-ounce jars roasted red sweet peppers, drained**
- 1 **cup chopped onion (1 large)**
- 4 **cloves garlic, minced**
- 1 **tablespoon olive oil**
- 1 **tablespoon sugar**
- 1 **tablespoon balsamic vinegar**
- 1 **teaspoon dried thyme, crushed**
- ½ **teaspoon dried oregano, crushed**
- ¼ **teaspoon salt**
- ⅛ **teaspoon ground black pepper**
  Hot cooked pasta
  Finely shredded Parmesan cheese (optional)

1. Place sweet peppers in a food processor. Process until smooth; set aside.

2. In a medium saucepan, cook onion and garlic in hot oil over medium-high heat until tender. Add pureed peppers, the sugar, vinegar, thyme, oregano, salt, and pepper. Cook and stir until heated through.

3. Serve immediately over hot cooked pasta or divide sauce among ½-cup storage containers. Cover and refrigerate for up to 1 week or freeze for up to 3 months. If frozen, thaw overnight in the refrigerator. To serve, place desired amount of sauce in a saucepan; heat through. Serve over hot cooked pasta. If desired, sprinkle with Parmesan cheese. Makes 2½ cups.

Per ½ cup sauce: 75 cal., 3 g fat (0 g sat. fat), 0 mg chol., 120 mg sodium, 12 g carbo., 2 g fiber, 1 g pro.

{matching pasta}

Choose the pasta that best complements your sauce. Light, thin sauces are best paired with thin, delicate pastas, such as angel hair (capellini) or thin spaghetti (vermicelli). Heavy sauces go with sturdy pasta shapes, such as fettuccine, linguine, or lasagna. Chunky sauces are best with pastas with holes or ridges, such as mostaccioli, ziti, or rotini.

Homemade Alfredo Sauce

Start to Finish: 20 min.   **Chill:** up to 3 days
Freeze: up to 3 months

- 1¼ **cups whipping cream**
- 1 **cup chicken broth**
- 1 **tablespoon cornstarch**
- ¼ **teaspoon ground black pepper**
- ⅛ **teaspoon ground nutmeg**
- 1 **tablespoon olive oil**
- 4 **cloves garlic, minced**
- ½ **cup grated Parmesan cheese**
  Hot cooked pasta

1. In a bowl, stir together cream, broth, cornstarch, pepper, and nutmeg; set aside. In a medium saucepan, heat oil over medium heat. Add garlic; cook and stir for 30 seconds. Add broth mixture; cook and stir until thickened and bubbly. Cook and stir for 2 minutes more. Stir in cheese.

2. Serve immediately over hot cooked pasta or divide mixture among ½-cup storage containers. Cover and refrigerate for up to 3 days or freeze for up to 3 months. If frozen, thaw overnight in the refrigerator. To serve, place desired amount of sauce in a saucepan; heat through. Serve over hot cooked pasta. Makes 2½ cups.

Per ¼ cup sauce: 139 cal., 14 g fat (8 g sat. fat), 45 mg chol., 169 mg sodium, 2 g carbo., 0 g fiber, 2 g pro.

Pizza Supreme

Prep: 30 min. **Bake:** 25 min. **Freeze:** up to 1 month

- 1 15-ounce can pizza sauce
- 2 12-inch (10-ounces each) thin Italian bread shells (Boboli®)
- 1 pound bulk Italian sausage, ground beef, or ground pork, cooked and drained; or 1½ cups diced cooked ham (6 ounces)
- 1 cup sliced fresh mushrooms or sliced green sweet pepper
- ½ cup sliced green onion (4) or sliced pitted ripe olives
- 3 cups shredded mozzarella cheese (12 ounces)

1. Spread pizza sauce evenly on crusts. Top pizzas with meat, vegetables, and cheese.

2. Cover pizzas with plastic wrap and freeze until firm. Wrap frozen pizza in moisture- and vapor-proof wrap. Wrap in heavy foil or place in a large resealable freezer bag; seal. Freeze for up to 1 month.

3. To serve, preheat oven to 375°F. Unwrap frozen pizza and place on baking sheet. Bake about 25 minutes or until cheese is bubbly. (For crisper crust, bake pizza directly on oven rack.) Makes 3 to 4 servings per pizza.

Per serving: 685 cal., 37 g fat (14 g sat. fat), 100 mg chol., 1,586 mg sodium, 18 g carbo., 2 g fiber, 36 g pro.

Pizza Supreme

Chicken and Bean Burritos

Prep: 25 min. **Bake:** 15 min. **Freeze:** up to 3 months

- Nonstick cooking spray
- 1 medium red sweet pepper, cut into thin strips
- ½ cup chopped onion (1 medium)
- 2 cloves garlic, minced
- 1 16-ounce can fat-free refried beans
- 2 skinless, boneless chicken breast halves, cooked and shredded (about 1½ cups)
- 8 8-inch flour tortillas
- 1 cup shredded Monterey Jack cheese or cheddar cheese (4 ounces)
- Avocado, tomato, and/or salsa (optional)

1. Preheat oven to 350°F. Coat a large skillet with cooking spray. Cook sweet pepper, onion, and garlic in hot skillet over medium heat until tender. Remove from heat. Stir in beans and chicken. Meanwhile, wrap tortillas tightly in foil. Heat in oven for 10 minutes.

2. To assemble each burrito, spoon about ⅓ cup of filling onto each tortilla just below center. Top with cheese. Fold edge nearest filling up and over just until filling is covered. Fold in 2 sides and roll up.

3. Arrange burritos, seam sides down, on a baking sheet. Cover with foil and bake for 10 minutes. Uncover and bake for 5 minutes more. If desired, serve burritos with avocado, tomato, and/or salsa. Makes 8 burritos.

To Make Ahead: Prepare burritos as directed, but do not bake. Wrap each burrito in foil and place in a freezer container. Freeze for up to 3 months. To serve, place frozen burritos, loosely wrapped in foil, on a baking sheet and bake in a 350°F oven for 30 minutes. Open foil and bake for 10 to 15 minutes more or until heated through.

Per burrito: 242 cal., 8 g fat (3 g sat. fat), 35 mg chol., 482 mg sodium, 25 g carbo., 4 g fiber, 17 g pro.

Wrap and freeze individual burritos. Then bake up just as many as you need.

Parmesan Chicken and Broccoli

Prep: 30 min.　**Bake:** 40 min.　**Freeze:** up to 3 months

- 1　cup converted rice
- ½　cup sliced green onion (4)
- 12　ounces skinless, boneless chicken breast halves, cut into strips
- ¾　teaspoon dried Italian seasoning, crushed
- 1　clove garlic, minced
- 1　tablespoon cooking oil
- 1　16-ounce jar reduced-fat Alfredo pasta sauce
- 3　cups frozen cut broccoli
- ⅓　cup grated Parmesan cheese
- ¼　cup diced cooked ham
- 1　2-ounce jar diced pimientos, drained
　　Ground black pepper

1. Preheat oven to 350°F. Cook rice according to package directions; remove from heat and stir in half the green onion. Divide rice mixture among four 12-ounce individual au gratin dishes or casseroles; set aside.

2. In a large skillet, cook the chicken strips, Italian seasoning, and garlic in hot oil over medium heat for 4 to 6 minutes or until chicken is no longer pink. Remove from heat. Stir in Alfredo sauce, broccoli, cheese, ham, and pimientos. Season to taste with ground black pepper. Spoon chicken mixture over rice. Bake, covered, for 15 minutes. Uncover and bake about 15 minutes more or until heated through. Makes 4 servings.

To Make Ahead: Cover and freeze unbaked dishes for up to 3 months. To serve, thaw overnight in the refrigerator. Remove freezer wrap; cover each dish with foil. Bake in a 350°F oven for 20 minutes. Uncover and bake about 20 minutes more or until heated through.

Per serving: 660 cal., 25 g fat (12 g sat. fat), 109 mg chol., 1,277 mg sodium, 71 g carbo., 5 g fiber, 39 g pro.

Turkey and Vegetable Bake

Prep: 40 min.　**Bake:** 30 min.　**Stand:** 15 min.
Chill: up to 3 days

- 2　cups sliced fresh mushrooms
- ¾　cup chopped red or yellow sweet pepper
- ½　cup chopped onion (1 medium)
- 2　cloves garlic, minced
- 2　tablespoons butter
- ¼　cup all-purpose flour
- ¾　teaspoon salt
- ½　teaspoon dried thyme, crushed
- ¼　teaspoon ground black pepper
- 2　cups fat-free milk
- 1　10-ounce package frozen chopped spinach, thawed and well drained
- 2　cups cooked brown or white rice*
- 2　cups chopped cooked turkey or chicken
- ½　cup finely shredded Parmesan cheese
- 2　cups soft bread crumbs
- 3　tablespoons butter, melted

1. Preheat oven to 350°F. In a very large skillet, cook mushrooms, sweet pepper, onion, and garlic in the 2 tablespoons hot butter over medium heat until tender. Stir in flour, salt, thyme, and black pepper. Add milk all at once; cook and stir until thickened and bubbly. Stir in spinach, cooked rice, turkey, and ¼ cup of the Parmesan cheese.

2. Spoon turkey mixture into a 1½- to 2-quart oval or rectangular baking dish. In a bowl, stir together bread crumbs, melted butter, and remaining cheese. Sprinkle over turkey mixture. Bake for 30 to 35 minutes or until heated through. Let stand 15 minutes before serving. Makes 6 servings.

*For the 2 cups of cooked rice, purchase a family size (14.8-ounce) pouch cooked original long grain or whole grain brown rice. Measure out 2 cups rice.

To Make Ahead: Prepare as above, except increase milk to 2½ cups and do not put crumb mixture on top of turkey mixture. Do not bake. Cover and chill for up to 3 days. Place crumb mixture in a separate airtight container and chill for up to 3 days. To serve, bake, covered, in a 350°F oven for 30 minutes. Uncover and sprinkle with crumb mixture. Bake, uncovered, for 20 to 25 minutes more or until heated through. Let stand for 15 minutes before serving.

Per serving: 466 cal., 16 g fat (8 g sat. fat), 64 mg chol., 918 mg sodium, 53 g carbo., 16 g fiber, 37 g pro.

Chicken Chowder

Prep: 40 min. **Cook:** 15 min. **Chill:** up to 3 days
Freeze: up to 1 month

- 1 tablespoon olive oil or cooking oil
- 1 pound skinless, boneless chicken breast halves, cut into bite-size pieces
- ½ cup chopped onion (1 medium)
- ¾ cup coarsely chopped red, green, or yellow sweet pepper (1 medium)
- 3 cloves garlic, minced
- 2 or 3 jalapeño chile peppers, seeded and finely chopped
- 8 ounces zucchini and/or yellow summer squash, coarsely chopped
- 2 14-ounce cans reduced-sodium chicken broth
- 1 10-ounce package frozen baby lima beans
- 2 teaspoons ground cumin
- 2 teaspoons ground coriander
- ¼ teaspoon salt
- ¼ teaspoon ground black pepper
- 1 8-ounce carton dairy sour cream
- 2 tablespoons all-purpose flour
  Snipped fresh cilantro (optional)
  Shredded Monterey Jack (optional)

1. In a 4-quart Dutch oven, heat oil over medium heat. Add chicken, onion, sweet pepper, garlic, and jalapeño peppers; cook and stir until chicken is no longer pink and vegetables are tender. Add zucchini; cook for 2 minutes more. Add broth, lima beans, cumin, coriander, salt, and black pepper. Bring to boiling; reduce heat. Simmer, uncovered, for 5 minutes.

2. In a small bowl, stir together the sour cream and flour. Whisk into soup mixture. Cook and stir until thickened and bubbly; cook and stir for 1 minute more. Season to taste with additional salt and black pepper. If desired, sprinkle each serving with cilantro and cheese. Makes 6 servings (8 cups).

Make Ahead: Prepare as above through Step 1. Transfer soup to an airtight container. Cover and refrigerate for up to 3 days or freeze for up to 1 month. (If frozen, thaw overnight in the refrigerator.) To serve, transfer chowder to a 4-quart Dutch oven. Bring to boiling, stirring frequently. Add sour cream mixture. Cook and stir until thickened and bubbly; cook and stir for 1 minute more. Serve as above.

Per serving: 291 cal., 12 g fat (6 g sat. fat), 62 mg chol., 730 mg sodium, 21 g carbo., 5 g fiber, 25 g pro.

Chicken Mac and Cheese

Prep: 40 min. **Bake:** 20 min. **Stand:** 10 min.
Chill: up to 24 hr. **Freeze:** up to 1 month

- 1 pound skinless, boneless, chicken breast halves, cut into bite-size pieces
- 1 to 2 teaspoons dried Italian herb blend, crushed
- 1 tablespoon olive oil
- 8 ounces dried mostaccioli, ziti, or penne pasta
- ½ cup chopped onion (1 medium)
- 2 cloves garlic, minced
- 3 tablespoons butter
- 3 tablespoons all-purpose flour
- 2 tablespoons tomato paste
- 3 cups milk
- 2 cups shredded smoked cheddar cheese or Swiss cheese (8 ounces)
- 2 cups soft sourdough or French bread crumbs
- ½ cup finely shredded Parmesan or Romano cheese (2 ounces)
- 3 tablespoons butter, melted

1. Preheat oven to 350°F. In a large skillet, cook chicken, Italian seasoning, *salt*, and *ground black pepper* in hot oil over medium heat until chicken is no longer pink. Remove from skillet; set aside.

2. Cook pasta according to package directions until just tender. Drain; return pasta to pan.

3. Meanwhile, in same skillet, cook onion and garlic in 3 tablespoons hot butter over medium heat until tender. Stir in flour until well combined. Stir in tomato paste. Add milk. Cook and stir until mixture is thickened and bubbly; reduce heat. Add cheddar cheese; stir until almost melted. Remove from heat; season to taste with additional salt and pepper. Add sauce and chicken to cooked pasta; stir to coat. Spoon mixture into a 2-quart square baking dish. In a small bowl, stir together bread crumbs, Parmesan cheese, and 3 tablespoons melted butter. Sprinkle crumb mixture over pasta mixture.

4. Bake, uncovered, for 20 to 25 minutes or until crumb mixture is golden and edges are bubbly. Let stand for 10 minutes before serving. Makes 6 servings.

To Make Ahead: Prepare as above, except place crumb mixture in a resealable plastic bag. Cover unbaked casserole with foil. Refrigerate casserole and bread crumb mixture for up to 24 hours or freeze for up to 1 month. (If frozen, thaw overnight in refrigerator.) Bake, covered, in a 350°F oven for 20 minutes. Uncover and top with bread crumb mixture. Bake, uncovered, for 35 to 40 minutes more or until crumb mixture is golden and edges are bubbly. Let stand for 10 minutes before serving.

Per serving: 675 cal., 34 g fat (18 g sat. fat), 132 mg chol., 771 mg sodium, 49 g carbo., 1 g fiber, 42 g pro.

Meat Loaf

Prep: 20 min. **Bake:** 1 hr. 10 min. **Stand:** 10 min.
Chill: up to 24 hr. **Freeze:** up to 1 month

- 2 eggs, lightly beaten
- ¾ cup milk
- ⅔ cup fine dry bread crumbs
- ¼ cup finely chopped onion
- 2 tablespoons snipped fresh parsley
- 1 teaspoon salt
- ½ teaspoon dried sage, basil, or oregano, crushed
- ⅛ teaspoon ground black pepper
- 1½ pounds lean ground beef, lamb, or pork
- ¼ cup ketchup
- 2 tablespoons packed brown sugar
- 1 teaspoon dry mustard

1. Preheat oven to 350°F. In a medium bowl, combine eggs and milk; stir in bread crumbs, onion, parsley, salt, sage, and pepper. Add beef; mix well. Lightly pat mixture into an 8×4×2-inch loaf pan.

2. Bake for 1 to 1¼ hours or until internal temperature registers 160°F. Spoon off fat. In a small bowl, stir together ketchup, sugar, and mustard; spread over meat loaf. Bake for 10 minutes more. Let stand for 10 minutes before slicing. Makes 8 servings.

To Make Ahead: Cover and refrigerate unbaked meat loaf for up to 24 hours or freeze for up to 1 month. (If frozen, thaw overnight in refrigerator.) Bake, uncovered, for 1¼ to 1½ hours or until internal temperature registers 160°F. Spoon off fat. In a small bowl, stir together ketchup, sugar, and mustard; spread over meat loaf. Bake for 10 minutes more. Let stand for 10 minutes before slicing.

Per slice: 225 cal., 10 g fat (4 g sat. fat), 108 mg chol., 676 mg sodium, 13 g carbo., 1 g fiber, 19 g pro.

Ham Balls in Barbecue Sauce

Prep: 20 min. **Bake:** 45 min. **Chill:** up to 24 hr.
Freeze: up to 1 month

2	eggs, lightly beaten
1½	cups soft bread crumbs (2 slices)
½	cup finely chopped onion (1 medium)
2	tablespoons milk
1	teaspoon dry mustard
¼	teaspoon ground black pepper
12	ounces ground cooked ham
12	ounces ground pork or ground beef
¾	cup packed brown sugar
½	cup ketchup
2	tablespoons vinegar
1	teaspoon dry mustard

1. Preheat oven to 350°F. In a bowl, combine eggs, crumbs, onion, milk, 1 teaspoon mustard, and pepper. Add ham and pork; mix well. Shape into 12 balls, using ⅓ cup mixture for each. Place ham balls in a greased 2-quart rectangular baking dish.

Ham Balls in Barbecue Sauce

2. In a bowl, stir together brown sugar, ketchup, vinegar, and remaining 1 teaspoon mustard. Stir until sugar is dissolved. Pour over ham balls.

3. Bake, uncovered, about 45 minutes or until temperature in center of ham balls registers 160°F. Transfer ham balls to a serving platter. Makes 6 servings.

Tip: If desired, use 1 cup of purchased barbecue sauce in place of the sauce mixture in step 2.

To Make Ahead: Cover and refrigerate unbaked ham balls for up to 24 hours, or place unbaked ham balls in an airtight container and freeze for up to 1 month. If frozen, thaw in the refrigerator. Bake as directed.

Per 2 ham balls: 427 cal., 19 g fat (7 g sat. fat), 143 mg chol., 1,107 mg sodium, 42 g carbo., 1 g fiber, 23 g pro.

Bean and Beef Enchilada Casserole

Prep: 25 min. **Bake:** 40 min. **Chill:** up to 24 hr.

½	pound lean ground beef
½	cup chopped onion (1 medium)
1	teaspoon chili powder
½	teaspoon ground cumin
1	15-ounce can pinto beans, rinsed and drained
1	4-ounce can diced green chile peppers
1	8-ounce carton regular or light dairy sour cream
2	tablespoons all-purpose flour
¼	teaspoon garlic powder
8	6-inch corn tortillas
1	10-ounce can enchilada sauce or one 10.5-ounce can tomato puree
1	cup shredded cheddar cheese (4 ounces)

1. In a large skillet, cook ground beef, onion, chili powder, and cumin over medium heat until meat is brown. Drain off fat. Stir in beans and undrained chile peppers; set aside. In a small bowl, stir together sour cream, flour, and garlic powder; set aside .

2. Place half of the tortillas in the bottom of a lightly greased 2-quart rectangular baking dish, cutting to fit. Top with half the meat mixture, half the sour cream mixture, half the enchilada sauce, and ½ cup cheese. Repeat layers, except reserve remaining ½ cup cheese. Cover and chill for up to 24 hours.

3. To serve, preheat oven to 350°F. Remove plastic wrap; cover dish with foil. Bake for 35 to 40 minutes or until bubbly. Sprinkle with remaining ½ cup cheese. Bake, uncovered, about 5 minutes more or until cheese melts. Makes 6 servings.

Per serving: 429 cal., 24 g fat (12 g sat. fat), 64 mg chol., 632 mg sodium, 36 g carbo., 6 g fiber, 19 g pro.

Eight-Layer Casserole

Prep: 30 min. Bake: 55 min. Stand: 10 min.
Chill: up to 24 hr.

- **3**   **cups dried medium noodles (6 ounces)**
- **1**   **pound ground beef**
- **2**   **8-ounce cans tomato sauce**
- **1**   **teaspoon dried basil, crushed**
- **½**   **teaspoon sugar**
- **½**   **teaspoon garlic powder**
- **1**   **8-ounce carton dairy sour cream**
- **1**   **8-ounce package cream cheese, softened**
- **½**   **cup milk**
- **⅓**   **cup chopped onion (1 small)**
- **1**   **10-ounce package frozen chopped spinach, cooked and well drained**
- **1**   **cup shredded cheddar cheese (4 ounces)**

1. Preheat oven to 350°F. Cook noodles according to package directions; drain. Set aside. Meanwhile, in a large skillet, cook beef over medium heat until brown. Drain off fat. Stir in tomato sauce, basil, sugar, garlic powder, and ¼ teaspoon each *salt* and *ground black pepper*. Bring to boiling; reduce heat. Simmer, uncovered, for 5 minutes.

2. In a medium mixing bowl, beat together the sour cream and cream cheese with an electric mixer on medium speed until smooth. Stir in milk and onion. In a greased 2-quart casserole or 2-quart square baking dish, layer half of the noodles (about 2 cups), half of the meat mixture (about 1½ cups), half of the cream cheese mixture (about 1 cup), and all of the spinach. Top with the remaining meat mixture and noodles. Cover and chill remaining cream cheese mixture until needed.

3. Cover casserole with lightly greased foil. Bake about 45 minutes or until heated through. Uncover; spread remaining cream cheese mixture over top. Sprinkle with the cheddar cheese. Bake, uncovered, about 10 minutes more or until cheese melts. Let stand for 10 minutes before serving. Makes 8 servings.

To Make Ahead: Cover unbaked casserole with lightly greased foil and refrigerate for up to 24 hours. Bake in a 350°F oven for 1 hour to 1 hour 10 minutes or until heated through. Uncover; spread remaining cream-cheese mixture over top. Sprinkle with the cheddar cheese. Bake, uncovered, about 10 minutes more or until cheese melts. Let stand for 10 minutes before serving.

Per serving: 472 cal., 30 g fat (17 g sat. fat), 127 mg chol., 683 mg sodium, 25 g carbo., 3 g fiber, 27 g pro.

Three-Cheese Lasagna

Three-Cheese Lasagna

Prep: 50 min. **Bake:** 35 min. **Stand:** 15 min.
Chill: up to 24 hr.

- 2 medium eggplants, chopped (11 cups)
- 2 large red onions, halved crosswise and thickly sliced (about 2 cups)
- 2 cloves garlic, minced
- 1 cup snipped fresh basil
- ¼ cup olive oil
- 12 dried lasagna noodles
- 2 cups shredded Gruyère cheese (8 ounces)
- 1 15-ounce carton ricotta cheese
- 12 ounces goat cheese (chèvre)
- 1 cup whipping cream
- 2 eggs
- ½ teaspoon salt
- ½ teaspoon ground black pepper
- ¼ teaspoon crushed red pepper
- 2 teaspoons finely shredded lemon peel

1. Preheat oven to 450°F. In a roasting pan, combine eggplant, onion, and garlic. Add ½ cup of the basil and the oil; toss to coat. Roast, uncovered, for 30 to 35 minutes or until vegetables are very tender, stirring once.

2. Meanwhile, cook lasagna noodles according to package directions; drain. Set aside. For filling, in a food processor, combine 1½ cups of the Gruyère cheese, the ricotta, goat cheese, cream, eggs, salt, black pepper, and crushed red pepper. Process until just combined.

3. Reduce oven temperature to 375°F. Spoon one-third of the eggplant mixture evenly in the bottom of a 3-quart rectangular baking dish. Layer with 4 noodles and one-third of the filling. Repeat layers twice, starting with eggplant and ending with filling. Sprinkle with remaining ½ cup Gruyère cheese. Cover with lightly greased foil. Bake for 20 minutes. Uncover and bake for 15 to 20 minutes more or until heated through. Let stand for 15 minutes before serving. Sprinkle top with ½ cup basil and the lemon peel. Makes 12 servings.

To Make Ahead: Cover unbaked lasagna with lightly greased foil and refrigerate for up to 24 hours. Bake, covered, in a 375°F oven for 40 minutes. Uncover and bake for 20 to 25 minutes more or until heated through. Let stand 15 minutes before serving. Top as directed.

Per serving: 439 cal., 30 g fat (16 g sat. fat), 114 mg chol., 315 mg sodium, 23 g carbo., 3 g fiber, 20 g pro.

Cheese adds gooey goodness to casseroles. Use your favorite in recipes.

Dried Tomato Casserole

Dried Tomato Casserole

Prep: 25 min. **Chill:** overnight **Bake:** 40 min. **Stand:** 10 min.

- 2 9-ounce packages refrigerated four-cheese ravioli or beef ravioli
- ½ to one 8-ounce jar oil-pack dried tomatoes, drained and chopped
- 1½ cups shredded cheddar cheese (6 ounces)
- 1½ cups shredded Monterey Jack cheese (6 ounces)
- ½ cup grated Parmesan cheese (2 ounces)
- 8 eggs, lightly beaten
- 2½ cups milk
- 1 to 2 tablespoons snipped fresh basil

1. Grease a 3-quart rectangular or oval baking dish. Place uncooked ravioli evenly in dish. Sprinkle with tomatoes. Top with cheeses; set aside. In a large bowl, whisk together eggs and milk. Pour over layers in dish. Cover and chill overnight.

2. Preheat oven to 350°F. Bake, uncovered, about 40 minutes or until top is golden and center is set. Let stand for 10 minutes before serving. Sprinkle with basil or parsley just before serving. Makes 12 servings.

Per serving: 353 cal., 21 g fat (11 g sat. fat), 213 mg chol., 490 mg sodium, 20 g carbo., 1 g fiber, 21 g pro.

Vegetable Shepherd's Pie

until tender; drain. Mash potatoes. Add butter, thyme, and salt. Gradually beat in enough milk to make potatoes light and fluffy. Stir in 1 cup of the cheese until melted.

3. Spread lentil mixture in a 2- to $2\frac{1}{2}$-quart au gratin dish. Spoon potato mixture over lentil mixture. Cover dish with plastic wrap; chill overnight.

4. To serve, preheat oven to 350°F. Remove plastic wrap; cover dish with foil. Bake for 50 minutes. Uncover and bake for 10 to 15 minutes more or until heated through. Sprinkle with remaining $\frac{1}{2}$ cup cheese. Makes 6 servings.

Per serving: 449 cal., 16 g fat (10 g sat. fat), 42 mg chol., 1,122 mg sodium, 58 g carbo., 17 g fiber, 20 g pro.

Make-Ahead Chili-Cheese Hoagies
Prep: 35 min.　**Cool:** 30 min.　**Chill:** up to 24 hr.
Bake: 35 min.

- 1　**pound lean ground beef**
- 1　**cup chopped onion (1 large)**
- 1　**cup chopped green and/or red sweet pepper (1 large)**
- 2　**cloves garlic, minced**
- 1　**14.5-ounce can diced tomatoes**
- $\frac{1}{2}$　**teaspoon ground cumin**
- $\frac{1}{4}$　**teaspoon ground black pepper**
- 8　**thin slices Monterey Jack cheese (8 ounces)**
- 8　**thin slices cheddar cheese (8 ounces)**
- 　**Pickled jalapeños (optional)**
- 8　**French-style rolls or hoagie buns**

1. In a large skillet, cook ground beef, onion, sweet pepper, and garlic over medium heat until meat is brown. Drain off fat. Add undrained tomatoes, cumin, and black pepper. Bring to boiling; reduce heat. Simmer, uncovered, about 15 minutes or until thick, stirring occasionally. Cool the mixture for 30 minutes or chill the mixture until ready to assemble the sandwiches.

2. Split rolls lengthwise. Hollow out roll bottoms, leaving a $\frac{1}{4}$-inch-thick shell. Place a slice of Monterey Jack cheese, cut to fit, on bottom half of roll. Spoon meat mixture on top of cheese. Place a slice of cheddar cheese on top of meat. If desired, sprinkle with pickled jalapeños. Top with roll top. Repeat with remaining rolls. Wrap each roll in parchment paper, then in foil. Refrigerate for 2 to 24 hours.

3. Preheat oven to 375°F. Place wrapped sandwiches on a baking sheet. Bake for 35 to 40 minutes or until cheese melts and filling is hot. Makes 8 sandwiches.

Per sandwich: 738 cal., 31 g fat (15 g sat. fat), 91 mg chol., 1,274 mg sodium, 79 g carbo., 5 g fiber, 36 g pro.

Vegetable Shepherd's Pie
Prep: 25 min.　**Cook:** 30 min.　**Bake:** 1 hr.
Chill: overnight

- 1　**14-ounce can vegetable broth or chicken broth**
- $\frac{3}{4}$　**cup water**
- 1　**cup dry lentils, rinsed and drained**
- 3　**cloves garlic, minced**
- $1\frac{1}{2}$　**pounds parsnips or carrots, peeled and cut into $\frac{1}{2}$-inch-thick slices (about $3\frac{1}{2}$ cups)**
- 6　**purple boiling onions (8 ounces), quartered, or 1 medium red onion, cut into wedges**
- 1　**14.5-ounce can diced tomatoes with Italian herbs**
- 2　**tablespoons tomato paste**
- 4　**medium potatoes, peeled and cut up**
- 3　**tablespoons butter**
- 1　**tablespoon snipped fresh thyme or 1 teaspoon dried thyme, crushed**
- $\frac{1}{2}$　**teaspoon salt**
- $\frac{1}{4}$　**to $\frac{1}{3}$ cup milk**
- $1\frac{1}{2}$　**cups shredded Colby and Monterey Jack or cheddar cheese (6 ounces)**

1. In a large saucepan, stir together broth, water, lentils, and garlic. Bring to boiling; reduce heat. Cover and simmer for 20 minutes. Add parsnips and onions. Return to boiling; reduce heat. Cover and simmer for 10 to 15 minutes more or until vegetables and lentils are just tender. Remove from heat. Stir in undrained tomatoes and tomato paste.

2. Meanwhile, in a 2-quart saucepan, cook potatoes in lightly salted boiling water for 20 to 25 minutes or

Pork and Noodles

Prep: 30 min.   **Chill:** up to 24 hr.

8   ounces dried Chinese egg noodles or
    fine noodles
1½ pounds fresh asparagus spears, trimmed and
    cut into 2-inch-long pieces, or one 16-ounce
    package frozen cut asparagus
4   medium carrots, cut into thin ribbons
    or bite-size strips (2 cups)
1   pound cooked lean pork, cut into
    thin strips
1   recipe Soy-Sesame Vinaigrette
    Sesame seeds (optional)
    Sliced green onion (optional)

1. Cook noodles according to package directions;
drain. Rinse with cold water until cool; drain.

2. If using fresh asparagus, cook in a covered saucepan in a small amount of lightly salted boiling water for
4 to 6 minutes or until crisp-tender. (Or, if using frozen
asparagus, cook according to package directions.)
Drain well.

3. In a large bowl, combine noodles, asparagus, carrots, and pork. Cover and chill for 2 to 24 hours.

4. To serve, pour Soy-Sesame Vinaigrette over salad;
toss gently to coat. If desired, sprinkle with sesame
seeds and green onion. Makes 8 servings.

Soy-Sesame Vinaigrette: In a screw-top jar, combine
½ cup reduced-sodium soy sauce, ¼ cup rice vinegar or
vinegar, ¼ cup honey, 2 tablespoons salad oil, and
2 teaspoons toasted sesame oil. Cover and shake well
to mix. Chill for 2 to 24 hours.

Per serving: 338 cal., 12 g fat (3 g sat. fat), 71 mg chol., 654 mg
sodium, 35 g carbo., 3 g fiber, 23 g pro.

{ menu 1 }

Creamy Cheddar Dip, p. 146
Fruit and Broccoli Salad, p. 146
Parmesan Dinner Rolls, p. 145
Maple Chicken Fettuccine, p. 147
Brownie-Walnut Pie, p. 146

{ menu 2 }

Spiral-Sliced Ham with Plum-Easy
Mustard Sauce, p. 148
Volcano Potatoes, p. 149
Vegetable Medley au Gratin, p. 149
Ice Cream with
Orange-Praline Sauce, p. 149

{ menu 3 }

Sirloin with Mustard
and Chives, p. 150
Greens and Berry Salad, p. 150
New Potato Bake, p. 151
Root Beer Float Cake, p. 151

{ menu 4 }

Apple-Pecan Pork Chops, p. 153
Autumn Vegetable Pilaf, p. 152
Home Run Garlic Rolls, p. 152
Pumpkin Pear Cake, p. 152

{ menu 5 }

Meatball Lasagna, p. 154
Sicilian Escarole Salad, p. 155
Pesto Biscuits, p. 155
Peanutty Ice Cream Pie, p. 155

sunday dinner together

> If there's no time for a sit-down meal during the week, **bring the family together** for a relaxing meal on the weekend. Get everyone involved in the meal prep.

Parmesan Dinner Rolls

Prep: 25 min. **Rise:** 30 min. **Bake:** 12 min.

- 1 16-ounce package hot roll mix
- ¼ cup finely shredded Parmesan cheese
- 1 teaspoon dried basil, crushed
- 2 tablespoons sugar
- 1 tablespoon milk
- 2 tablespoons finely shredded Parmesan cheese

1. In a large bowl, prepare hot roll mix according to package directions through the resting step, stirring the ¼ cup Parmesan cheese, the basil, and sugar into the flour mixture. Divide dough in half.

2. Grease twenty-four 1¾-inch muffin cups. Divide each dough half into 12 portions (24 portions total). Gently pull each dough portion into a ball, tucking edges beneath. Arrange balls, smooth sides up, in the prepared muffin cups. Cover; let rise in a warm place until nearly double in size (about 30 minutes).

3. Preheat oven to 400°F. Brush roll tops with milk; sprinkle with the 2 tablespoons Parmesan cheese. Bake for 12 to 15 minutes or until golden brown. Remove rolls from muffin cups and serve warm. Makes 24.

Per roll: 89 cal., 2 g fat (0 g sat. fat), 9 mg chol., 145 mg sodium, 15 g carbo., 0 g fiber, 3 g pro.

Brownie-Walnut Pie

Creamy Cheddar Dip

Prep: 10 min. **Chill:** 4 to 48 hr.

1   16-ounce carton dairy sour cream
1   1.4-ounce envelope dry vegetable soup mix
½   cup shredded cheddar cheese (2 ounces)
    Snipped fresh parsley (optional)
    Assorted vegetable dippers (such as blanched
    asparagus spears, cherry tomatoes, pea pods,
    red sweet pepper strips, radishes, zucchini
    slices, and/or cauliflower florets)

1. In a medium bowl, stir together sour cream and soup mix. Stir in cheddar cheese. Cover and chill for at least 4 hours or up to 48 hours. If desired, sprinkle with snipped parsley. Serve with vegetable dippers. Makes 1¾ cups dip.

Per 2 tablespoons dip: 94 cal., 8 g fat (5 g sat. fat), 19 mg chol., 248 mg sodium, 3 g carbo., 0 g fiber, 2 g pro.

Fruit and Broccoli Salad

Prep: 15 min. **Chill:** 1 hr.

½   of a 16-ounce package broccoli slaw mix
    (about 2½ cups)
1   cup seedless red and/or green grapes, halved
1   medium apple, cored and chopped
⅓   to ½ cup bottled poppy seed salad dressing
2   medium oranges, peeled, seeded, and
    sectioned*
½   cup coarsely chopped pecans or walnuts,
    toasted if desired**
    Red Bibb lettuce

1. In a large bowl, combine broccoli slaw, grapes, and apple. Pour salad dressing over broccoli mixture; add oranges and toss gently to coat. Cover and chill for 1 to 4 hours. Sprinkle with nuts; toss again. Spoon salad into lettuce-lined dishes. Makes 6 to 8 servings.

***To section oranges:** Hold peeled oranges over a bowl to catch the juices. Cut down against inside membrane of one segment on both sides and release segment. Repeat with remaining segments, removing any seeds.

****To toast nuts:** Preheat oven to 350°F. Spread nuts in a single layer in a baking pan. Bake for 5 to 10 minutes or until light brown, stirring once or twice.

Per serving: 234 cal., 16 g fat (2 g sat. fat), 6 mg chol., 17 mg sodium, 22 g carbo., 3 g fiber, 3 g pro.

Brownie-Walnut Pie

Prep: 30 min. **Bake:** 50 min. **Cool:** 1 hr.

½   cup butter
3   ounces unsweetened chocolate, cut up
3   eggs, lightly beaten
1½   cups sugar
½   cup all-purpose flour
1   teaspoon vanilla
1   cup chopped walnuts
1   9-inch unbaked pastry shell*
    Coffee or vanilla ice cream
    Caramel ice cream topping

1. Preheat oven to 350°F. For filling, in a heavy small saucepan, stir the butter and chocolate over low heat until melted and smooth. Cool for 20 minutes.

2. In a large bowl, stir together the eggs, sugar, flour, and vanilla. Stir in the cooled chocolate mixture and the walnuts. Pour filling into pastry shell.

3. Bake for 50 to 55 minutes or until a knife inserted near the center comes out clean. Cool on a wire rack for 1 hour. Serve each slice warm with ice cream and drizzled with caramel topping. Makes 10 to 12 servings.

*If you don't have time to make your own piecrust dough, use purchased refrigerated piecrust dough.

Per serving with ½ cup ice cream: 655 cal., 42 g fat (19 g sat. fat), 156 mg chol., 193 mg sodium, 65 g carbo., 3 g fiber, 10 g pro.

Maple Chicken Fettuccine

Start to Finish: 25 min.

10 ounces dried fettuccine
5 skinless, boneless chicken breast halves
(about 1½ pounds total)
Salt
Ground black pepper
1 tablespoon olive oil
1 16-ounce package frozen (yellow, green, and
red) peppers and onion stir-fry vegetables
¾ cup chicken broth
1 tablespoon cornstarch
1 teaspoon snipped fresh rosemary
⅛ teaspoon ground black pepper
¼ cup maple syrup

1. Cook pasta according to package directions; drain. Set aside and keep warm.

2. Meanwhile, season chicken with salt and pepper. In a very large skillet, cook chicken in hot oil over medium heat for 10 to 12 minutes or until an instant-read thermometer inserted in chicken registers 170°F, turning chicken once. Remove chicken from skillet; keep warm.

3. Increase heat to medium-high. Add the vegetables to skillet; stir for 6 to 8 minutes or until vegetables are crisp-tender.

4. In a small bowl, stir together broth, cornstarch, rosemary, and the ⅛ teaspoon pepper. Add to skillet. Cook and stir until thickened and bubbly. Cook and stir for 1 minute more. Stir in maple syrup.

5. To serve, arrange hot pasta on individual plates or in shallow bowls. Top with chicken. Spoon peppers and sauce over chicken. Makes 5 servings.

Per serving: 466 cal., 6 g fat (1 g sat. fat), 79 mg chol., 285 mg sodium, 60 g carbo., 2 g fiber, 40 g pro.

Spiral-Sliced Ham with Plum-Easy Mustard Sauce

Prep: 10 min.   **Roast:** 2 hr.   **Stand:** 20 min.

1	7- to 8-pound fully cooked spiral-sliced ham
1	18-ounce jar red plum jam
2	tablespoons honey mustard
½	teaspoon ground black pepper

1. Preheat oven to 300°F. Place ham in a roasting pan according to package directions (discard flavor or seasoning packet). Roast about 2 hours or until an instant-read thermometer inserted in ham reads 140°F.

2. Remove ham from oven; cover with foil and let stand for 20 minutes before serving.

3. Meanwhile, in a small saucepan, heat jam over medium-low heat until melted and bubbly, stirring occasionally. Stir in honey mustard and pepper. Pass sauce with ham. Makes 16 servings.

Per serving: 261 cal., 7 g fat (3 g sat. fat), 49 mg chol., 1,125 mg sodium, 34 g carbo., 2 g fiber, 14 g pro.

Volcano Potatoes

Prep: 15 min.   **Bake:** 65 min.

- 3   **20-ounce packages refrigerated mashed potatoes**
- ¾ **cup whipping cream**
- ¾ **cup shredded Gruyère, Havarti, or American cheese (3 ounces)**
- **Freshly cracked black pepper**

1. Preheat oven to 300°F. Spoon potatoes into a 2-quart casserole. Bake, covered, for 50 minutes. Meanwhile, in a medium mixing bowl, beat cream on medium speed of an electric mixer to soft peaks; fold in cheese.

2. Remove potatoes from oven. (Time this so the ham comes out at the same time and is resting while the potatoes finish baking.) Increase oven temperature to 375°F. Uncover potatoes. With a large spoon, make a hole in the center of the potatoes by pushing from the center to the sides. Spoon the whipping cream mixture into the hole. Sprinkle top with cracked pepper.

3. Bake, uncovered, for 15 to 20 minutes more or until top is golden. Makes 10 servings.

Per serving: 243 cal., 13 g fat (6 g sat. fat), 37 mg chol., 300 mg sodium, 24 g carbo., 1 g fiber, 7 g pro.

Ice Cream with Orange-Praline Sauce

Start to Finish: 15 min.

- 1   **12-ounce jar caramel ice cream topping**
- ½ **cup orange marmalade**
- ⅔ **cup coarsely chopped pecans, toasted**
- ½ **gallon vanilla, cinnamon, pumpkin, or eggnog ice cream**

1. In a small saucepan, stir together ice cream topping and marmalade; cook over medium-low heat until marmalade is melted, stirring occasionally. Stir in pecans; heat through. Spoon warm sauce over scoops of ice cream. Makes 10 servings.

Per serving: 484 cal., 24 g fat (13 g sat. fat), 109 mg chol., 156 mg sodium, 61 g carbo., 1 g fiber, 7 g pro.

Vegetable Medley au Gratin

Prep: 20 min.   **Bake:** 65 min.

- 1   **10.75-ounce can condensed cream of chicken and mushroom soup**
- ½ **cup dairy sour cream**
- ½ **teaspoon dried dill weed**
- 2   **16-ounce packages loose-pack frozen broccoli, cauliflower, and carrots, thawed**
- ⅔ **cup crushed stone-ground wheat crackers (about 15 crackers)**
- ⅓ **cup finely chopped walnuts**
- ¼ **cup finely shredded Parmesan cheese**
- 2   **tablespoons butter, melted**

1. Preheat oven to 300°F. In a large bowl, stir together soup, sour cream, and dill; stir in vegetables. Transfer to a 2-quart rectangular baking dish. Cover with foil.

2. Bake, covered, for 50 minutes. In a small bowl, stir together crushed crackers, walnuts, cheese, and melted butter. Uncover baking dish and sprinkle crumb mixture over top. Increase oven temperature to 375°F. Bake, uncovered, about 15 minutes more or until topping is browned. Makes 10 servings.

To Make Ahead: Prepare and cover unbaked vegetable and crumb mixtures separately. Chill overnight. Bake as directed.

Per serving: 160 cal., 11 g fat (4 g sat. fat), 15 mg chol., 440 mg sodium, 11 g carbo., 3 g fiber, 5 g pro.

Sirloin with Mustard and Chives

Start to Finish: 20 min.

- 4 boneless beef sirloin or ribeye steaks, cut about ¾ inch thick (about 1½ pounds)
- 2 teaspoons garlic-pepper seasoning
- ½ cup light dairy sour cream
- 2 tablespoons Dijon-style mustard
- 1 tablespoon snipped fresh chives

1. Sprinkle both sides of steaks with 1½ teaspoons of the seasoning. Grill steaks on the rack of an uncovered grill directly over medium heat to desired doneness, turning once halfway through cooking time. (Allow 9 to 11 minutes for medium rare [145°F] and 11 to 13 minutes for medium [160°F].) Transfer steaks to a serving platter and keep warm.

2. Meanwhile, in a small bowl, stir together sour cream, mustard, chives, and remaining seasoning. Spoon sour cream mixture over steaks. Makes 4 servings.

Per serving: 256 cal., 9 g fat (4 g sat. fat), 112 mg chol., 421 mg sodium, 2 g carbo., 0 g fiber, 37 g pro.

Greens and Berry Salad

Start to Finish: 15 min.

- 1 8-ounce package torn mixed greens (about 8 cups)
- ½ cup crumbled blue cheese (optional)
- 2 ¼-inch-thick slices red onion, separated into rings
- 1 cup fresh raspberries or sliced fresh strawberries
- 1 2-ounce package slivered almonds, toasted (⅓ cup)
- ¼ cup bottled balsamic vinaigrette salad dressing
- 1 teaspoon Dijon-style mustard

1. In a large salad bowl, combine the greens, blue cheese (if desired), onion, raspberries, and almonds.

2. In a small bowl, whisk together the salad dressing and mustard. Pour dressing over the salad. Toss well to coat. Makes 4 to 6 servings.

Per serving: 157 cal., 12 g fat (1 g sat. fat), 0 mg chol., 215 mg sodium, 11 g carbo., 5 g fiber, 5 g pro.

New Potato Bake

Prep: 15 min. Bake: 25 min. Stand: 10 min.

- 1½ pounds tiny new potatoes, quartered
- 5 cups fresh baby spinach
- ⅓ cup chopped green onion (4)
- 1 tablespoon butter
- 1 tablespoon all-purpose flour
- ¼ teaspoon salt
- ⅛ teaspoon cayenne pepper
   Dash ground nutmeg
- 1 cup milk
- 1 cup shredded Swiss cheese (4 ounces)
   Nonstick cooking spray
- 1 tablespoon fine dry bread crumbs

1. Preheat oven to 375°F. In a large saucepan, cook the potatoes, covered, in lightly salted boiling water for 8 minutes. Stir in spinach. Drain well.

2. In small saucepan, cook green onion in hot butter over medium heat about 3 minutes or until softened. Stir in flour, salt, cayenne, and nutmeg. Stir in milk. Cook and stir over medium heat until thickened and bubbly. Add ½ cup of the cheese; stir until melted.

3. Lightly coat a 2-quart square baking dish with cooking spray. Layer half of the potato mixture in the prepared dish; spoon half the sauce over the potato mixture. Sprinkle with half the remaining cheese. Top with remaining potato mixture and remaining sauce. Sprinkle with remaining cheese. Top evenly with bread crumbs.

4. Bake for 25 to 30 minutes or until potatoes are tender and crumbs are brown. Let stand for 10 minutes before serving. Makes 6 to 8 servings.

Tip: Make 12 to 16 servings by doubling all ingredients and assembling in a 3-quart rectangular baking dish.

Per serving: 223 cal., 9 g fat (6 g sat. fat), 29 mg chol., 229 mg sodium, 25 g carbo., 3 g fiber, 11 g pro.

Root Beer Float Cake

Prep: 25 min. Cool: about 2 hr.

- 1 2-layer-size caramel or yellow cake mix
   Root beer
- 1½ teaspoons vanilla
- 1 teaspoon finely shredded lemon peel
   Celebration Icing
   Crushed root beer-flavor hard candies (optional)
   Maraschino cherries (optional)

1. Preheat oven to 350°F. Prepare cake mix according to package directions, except substitute root beer for the liquid and add vanilla and lemon peel. Pour batter into a greased 13×9×2-inch baking pan. Bake according to package directions. Cool completely in pan on a wire rack.

2. Spread Celebration Icing over cooled cake. If desired, sprinkle with crushed root beer-flavor hard candies and/or garnish with cherries. Makes 12 servings.

Celebration Icing: In a medium mixing bowl, beat ⅓ cup softened butter with an electric mixer until smooth. Gradually add 1 cup powdered sugar, beating well. Slowly beat in 3 tablespoons root beer and 1 teaspoon vanilla. Gradually beat in 2 cups more powdered sugar. If necessary, beat in a little more root beer or powdered sugar to make icing spreading consistency.

For a double-layer cake: Allow cake to cool in pan for 10 minutes. Remove from pan and cool completely. Cut cooled cake in half crosswise. Frost the top of one cake piece with some of the frosting. Top with remaining cake half and frost top of layers.

Per serving: 347 cal., 8 g fat (4 g sat. fat), 14 mg chol., 321 mg sodium, 69 g carbo., 0 g fiber, 2 g pro.

Pumpkin Pear Cake

Prep: 25 min. **Bake:** 35 min. **Cool:** 35 min.

1	cup packed brown sugar
⅓	cup butter, melted
1½	teaspoons cornstarch
2	15-ounce cans pear halves in light syrup
½	cup coarsely chopped pecans
1	2-layer-size spice cake mix
1	cup canned pumpkin

1. Preheat oven to 350°F. In a small bowl, stir together brown sugar, butter, and cornstarch. Drain pears, reserving 3 tablespoons of the syrup. Stir reserved syrup into brown sugar mixture. Pour mixture into a 13×9×2-inch baking pan. If desired, cut pear halves into fans by making 3 or 4 lengthwise cuts ¼ inch from the stem end of each pear half to the bottom of the pear half. Arrange pear halves on top of syrup in pan, cored sides down. Sprinkle pecans evenly into pan.

2. Prepare cake mix according to package directions, except decrease oil to 2 tablespoons and add pumpkin. Slowly pour cake batter into pan, spreading evenly.

3. Bake for 35 to 40 minutes or until a wooden toothpick inserted near the center comes out clean. Cool in pan on a wire rack for 5 minutes. Run a thin metal spatula around edges of cake. Carefully invert cake into a 15×10×1-inch baking pan or onto a very large serving platter with slightly raised sides. Cool about 30 minutes before serving. Serve warm. Makes 16 servings.

Per serving: 337 cal., 15 g fat (4 g sat. fat), 51 mg chol., 254 mg sodium, 51 g carbo., 2 g fiber, 3 g pro.

Home Run Garlic Rolls

Prep: 20 min **Rise:** 1½ hr. **Bake:** 15 min.

1	16-ounce loaf frozen white or whole wheat bread dough, thawed
1	tablespoon butter, melted
2	cloves garlic, minced
2	tablespoons grated Parmesan cheese

1. Lightly grease a 13×9×2-inch baking pan; set aside. Shape dough into 24 balls. Place balls in prepared pan. Cover; let rise in a warm place until nearly double (1½ to 2 hours).

2. Preheat oven to 350°F. In a small bowl, stir together melted butter and garlic. Brush butter mixture over tops of rolls. Sprinkle with Parmesan cheese. Bake for 15 to 20 minutes or until golden. Remove rolls from pans and cool slightly on a wire rack. Serve warm. Makes 24 rolls.

Per 2 rolls: 55 cal., 1 g fat (0 g sat. fat), 2 mg chol., 99 mg sodium, 9 g carbo., 0 g fiber, 1 g pro.

Autumn Vegetable Pilaf

Start to Finish: 35 min.

1	6- to 7.2-ounce package rice pilaf mix
2	tablespoons olive oil
2	tablespoons cider vinegar
2	cloves garlic, minced
1	teaspoon dried thyme, crushed
1	large sweet potato or carrot, peeled and cut into ½-inch cubes
1	medium zucchini, halved lengthwise and cut into 1-inch pieces
1	small red onion, cut into wedges
⅓	cup chopped pecans or walnuts, toasted

1. Heat oven to 400°F. Cook rice mix according to package directions, except omit butter or oil.

2. Meanwhile, in a large bowl, stir together the oil, vinegar, garlic, and thyme. Add sweet potato, zucchini, and onion, stirring to coat. Spread vegetables in a single layer in a 15×10×1-inch baking pan. Roast for 20 to 25 minutes or until vegetables are light brown and tender, stirring occasionally.

3. Stir roasted vegetables and the nuts into hot rice pilaf. Makes 6 servings.

Per serving: 233 cal., 9 g fat (1 g sat. fat), 0 mg chol., 328 mg sodium, 34 g carbo., 3 g fiber, 4 g pro.

Apple-Pecan Pork Chops

Start to Finish: 20 min.

4 boneless pork loin chops (¾ to 1 inch thick)
   Salt
   Ground black pepper
2 tablespoons butter
1 medium red apple, cored and thinly sliced
¼ cup chopped pecans
2 tablespoons packed brown sugar

1. Sprinkle chops with salt and pepper. Set aside. In a large skillet, melt butter over medium heat until it sizzles. Add apples; cook and stir for 2 minutes. Push apples to side of skillet. Add pork chops; cook for 4 minutes. Turn chops over, moving apples aside as needed. Spoon apples over chops. Sprinkle with pecans and brown sugar.

2. Cover and cook for 4 to 8 minutes more or until an instant-read thermometer inserted in centers of chops registers 160°F. Spoon apples and cooking juices over chops. Makes 4 servings.

Per serving: 250 cal., 13 g fat (5 g sat. fat), 66 mg chol., 360 mg sodium, 12 g carbo., 1 g fiber, 22 g pro.

Meatball Lasagna

Prep: 25 min.   **Bake:** 45 min.   **Stand:** 15 min.

- 9   dried lasagna noodles
- ½   of a 15-ounce container ricotta cheese
- 1½ cups shredded mozzarella cheese (6 ounces)
- ¼   cup grated Parmesan cheese
- 1   16-ounce package frozen cooked Italian-style meatballs (½-ounce size), thawed
- 1   16-ounce jar tomato pasta sauce

1. Preheat oven to 375°F. Cook lasagna noodles according to package directions. Drain noodles; rinse with cold water. Drain well; set aside.

2. In a small bowl, stir together ricotta, 1 cup mozzarella cheese, and the Parmesan cheese; set aside. In a medium bowl, stir together meatballs and one-third (about 1 cup) of the pasta sauce; set aside.

3. To assemble, spread a small amount of the reserved sauce over bottom of a 2-quart square baking dish. Layer three cooked noodles in the dish. Spoon meatball mixture over noodles. Layer three more noodles over meatballs. Spread half of the remaining sauce over noodles. Spoon ricotta mixture over sauce and spread evenly. Top with remaining noodles and remaining sauce.

4. Cover dish with foil. Bake for 35 minutes. Remove foil and sprinkle remaining mozzarella over lasagna. Bake, uncovered, about 10 minutes more or until cheese melts. Let stand for 15 minutes before serving. Makes 8 to 9 servings.

Per serving: 410 cal., 21 g fat (11 g sat. fat), 66 mg chol., 897 mg sodium, 31 g carbo., 4 g fiber, 23 g pro.

Pesto Biscuits

Prep: 15 min. **Bake:** 10 min.

2¼ cups packaged biscuit mix
½ cup milk
¼ cup purchased basil pesto
2 teaspoons olive oil
2 tablespoons finely shredded Parmesan cheese

1. Preheat oven to 450°F. In a bowl, stir together biscuit mix, milk, and pesto until soft dough forms.

2. Turn dough out onto a lightly floured surface. Knead 10 times or until nearly smooth. Pat dough ½ inch thick. Using a 2½-inch round cutter, cut out dough. Place rounds on an ungreased baking sheet. Brush lightly with olive oil and sprinkle with cheese.

3. Bake about 10 minutes or until golden. Serve warm. Makes 10 to 12 biscuits.

Per serving: 165 cal., 8 g fat (2 g sat. fat), 4 mg chol., 426 mg sodium, 19 g carbo., 1 g fiber, 4 g pro.

Peanutty Ice Cream Pie

Prep: 30 min. **Freeze:** 6 hr.

1½ cups coarsely ground peanuts
3 tablespoons butter, melted
2 tablespoons sugar
¼ cup flaked coconut
¼ cup light-color corn syrup
¼ cup peanut butter
3 tablespoons chopped peanuts
1 quart vanilla ice cream
  Chopped candy-coated milk chocolate pieces or peanuts (optional)

1. Lightly grease a 9-inch pie plate. In a medium bowl, combine ground peanuts, butter, and sugar. Press mixture firmly onto bottom and up sides of the prepared pie plate. Chill for 15 minutes.

2. Meanwhile, in a small bowl, stir together coconut, corn syrup, peanut butter, and the 3 tablespoons chopped peanuts. Place ice cream in a large chilled bowl; stir ice cream just to soften. Stir in the coconut mixture just until combined. Spoon into chilled crust. If desired, sprinkle chopped chocolate pieces or peanuts over pie. Cover; freeze about 6 hours or until firm. Remove from freezer and place the pie on a warm, damp towel for a few minutes before cutting into wedges. Makes 8 servings.

Per serving: 493 cal., 36 g fat (14 g sat. fat), 57 mg chol., 269 mg sodium, 36 g carbo., 3 g fiber, 13 g pro.

Sicilian Escarole Salad

Sicilian Escarole Salad

Start to Finish: 20 min.

  Dressing
6 cups torn escarole or romaine
6 cups torn leaf lettuce
1 English cucumber or cucumber, quartered lengthwise and sliced into ½ inch chunks
1 cup pitted ripe olives or kalamata olives, chopped
1 cup thinly sliced red or Vidalia onion
3 cups assorted stir-ins*

1. Prepare Dressing; set aside. In a very large bowl, combine escarole, lettuce, cucumber, olives, and onion. Add desired stir-ins. Just before serving, pour Dressing over salad and toss to coat. Makes 12 to 16 servings.

Dressing: In a screw-top jar, combine ⅓ cup olive oil; 2 tablespoons white wine vinegar; one 2-ounce can anchovy fillets, drained and chopped; 3 cloves garlic, minced; ½ teaspoon each dried basil and oregano, crushed; ¼ teaspoon each salt and crushed red pepper; and ⅛ teaspoon ground black pepper. Cover; shake well.

***Stir-ins:** Chopped roasted red sweet peppers, drained and rinsed cannellini beans, drained and flaked canned tuna, croutons, tomato slices, snipped fresh basil or oregano, cubed salami, cubed Asiago cheese, or shredded provolone cheese.

Per serving (without stir-ins): 93 cal., 8 g fat (1 g sat. fat), 4 mg chol., 319 mg sodium, 4 g carbo., 2 g fiber, 2 g pro.

Peanut Butter Pretzel Pops

snack attack

Snacks should do more than just fill the void in your tummy. It's best to **get some** nutritional **benefit** from them, too. These recipes help you strike that balance.

Peanut Butter Pretzel Pops

Prep: 25 min.   **Bake:** 8 min. per batch

- 1   18-ounce roll chocolate chip cookie dough or refrigerated peanut butter cookie dough
- 1   cup finely chopped dry roasted peanuts or honey-roasted peanuts
- 10   to 12 pretzel rods, halved crosswise

1.   Preheat oven to 375°F. Lightly grease cookie sheets; set aside. Roll dough into twenty to twenty-four 1¼-inch balls. Place peanuts in a shallow dish. Roll dough balls in peanuts, pressing to coat dough balls evenly. Reshape dough into balls if necessary. Insert the cut end of a halved pretzel rod into each dough ball, pressing the pretzel to but not through the end of the dough ball. Place 3 inches apart on prepared cookie sheets.

2.   Bake for 8 to 10 minutes or until tops are light brown. Let cool for 1 minute on cookie sheets. Transfer to a wire rack; cool completely. Makes 20 to 24 cookies.

Per cookie: 178 cal., 10 g fat (2 g sat. fat), 7 mg chol., 222 mg sodium, 19 g carbo., 0 g fiber, 4 g pro.

No-Bake Butterscotch-Pretzel Treats

Prep: 25 min.   **Chill:** 2 hr.

    Nonstick cooking spray
- 1½   cups powdered sugar
- 1   cup creamy peanut butter
- 6   tablespoons butter, melted
- 2   cups crushed pretzels (about 6½ ounces)
- 1   11-ounce package butterscotch-flavored pieces (about 2 cups)
- ¼   cup whipping cream
- ½   cup coarsely crushed pretzels
- ½   cup chopped peanuts

1.   Line a 13×9×2-inch pan with foil. Lightly coat the foil with cooking spray; set aside. In a large bowl, stir together powdered sugar, peanut butter, and melted butter. Stir in the 2 cups crushed pretzels. Press mixture firmly over the bottom of the prepared pan.

2.   In a heavy medium saucepan, combine butterscotch pieces and whipping cream. Stir over low heat until pieces are just melted. Carefully spoon and spread butterscotch mixture over crumb mixture in pan. Sprinkle the ½ cup coarsely crushed pretzels and the peanuts evenly over butterscotch mixture; press gently.

3.   Cover and chill for at least 2 hours. Cut into bars to serve. Store in the refrigerator for up to 1 week. Makes about 36 bars.

Per bar: 166 cal., 10 g fat (5 g sat. fat), 7 mg chol., 154 mg sodium, 17 g carbo., 1 g fiber, 3 g pro.

Pepper Pecans
Start to Finish: 25 min.

- ½ cup sugar
- 3 tablespoons water
- 1 teaspoon garlic salt
- ½ teaspoon paprika
- ¼ teaspoon ground black pepper
- ¼ teaspoon cayenne pepper
- 3 cups pecan halves
- Nonstick cooking spray

1. Preheat oven to 325°F. In a large skillet, stir together sugar, water, garlic salt, paprika, black pepper, and cayenne. Bring to boiling over medium heat; boil gently, uncovered, for 2 minutes. Stir in pecan halves until well coated.

2. Line a 15×10×1-inch baking pan with foil; coat foil with cooking spray. Spread nuts in a single layer on foil. Bake for 15 to 20 minutes or until browned, stirring occasionally. Cool in pan; break apart large clusters. Store in an airtight container at room temperature for up to 1 week. Makes 3 cups.

Per ¼ cup: 218 cal., 19 g fat (2 g sat. fat), 0 mg chol., 80 mg sodium, 12 g carbo., 3 g fiber, 3 g pro.

Dried Fruit Snack Mix
Start to Finish: 10 min.

- ½ cup dried tart red cherries or raisins
- ½ cup dried pineapple, chopped
- ½ cup small pretzel twists
- ½ cup puffed corn cereal or round toasted oat cereal

1. In a large bowl, stir together all ingredients. Store in an airtight container in the freezer for up to 1 week. Makes 2 cups.

Per ½ cup: 162 cal., 1 g fat (0 g sat. fat), 0 mg chol., 120 mg sodium, 38 g carbo., 2 g fiber, 2 g pro.

No-Nuts Cereal Snack

Prep: 10 min. **Bake:** 10 min.

- 2 cups puffed corn cereal
- 2 cups round toasted oat cereal
- 1 cup small fish-shape cheese crackers
- 1 cup chow mein noodles
- 3 tablespoons cooking oil
- 1 0.4-ounce envelope dry buttermilk salad dressing mix (1 tablespoon)

1. Preheat oven to 350°F. In a 13×9×2-inch baking pan, stir together cereals, crackers, and chow mein noodles. Drizzle oil over top; toss to coat. Sprinkle with dressing mix; toss to coat. Bake for 10 minutes, stirring once. Cool in pan. Store in an airtight container at room temperature for up to 1 week. Makes 6 servings.

Per serving: 236 cal., 12 g fat (2 g sat. fat), 1 mg chol., 449 mg sodium, 28 g carbo., 2 g fiber, 4 g pro.

Cinnamon Bagel Fries

Start to Finish: 10 min.

- 1 4-inch plain or cinnamon-raisin bagel, split
- 1 tablespoon butter, melted
- 1 tablespoon sugar
- ½ teaspoon ground cinnamon

1. Toast bagel halves. Place warm bagel halves on a cutting board. Using a serrated knife, slice into ¼- to ½-inch-wide strips. Place bagel strips in a large resealable plastic bag; drizzle with butter. Seal bag; shake to coat. Add sugar and cinnamon; seal bag and shake again. Serve warm. Makes 2 servings.

Per serving: 198 cal., 6 g fat (4 g sat. fat), 15 mg chol., 279 mg sodium, 30 g carbo., 1 g fiber, 5 g pro.

Goldfish Trail Mix

Start to Finish: 10 min.

- 1 cup bite-size fish-shape crackers
- 1 cup round toasted oat cereal with honey
- 1 cup pretzel sticks or twists
- 1 cup raisins, dried cherries, dried cranberries, and/or chopped dried pineapple

1. In a large bowl, stir together all ingredients. Transfer to an airtight container and store at room temperature for up to 2 weeks. Makes 4 cups.

Per ½ cup: 121 cal., 2 g fat (0 g sat. fat), 2 mg chol., 173 mg sodium, 26 g carbo., 1 g fiber, 2 g pro.

Chili Mixed Nuts

Prep: 10 min. **Bake:** 15 min.

- 3 cups mixed nuts or peanuts
- 2 tablespoons butter, melted
- 1 tablespoon chili powder
- 1 tablespoon lime juice
- 1 teaspoon garlic salt

1. Preheat oven to 325°F. Spread nuts in a single layer in a 15×10×1-inch baking pan. In a small bowl, stir together butter, chili powder, lime juice, and garlic salt. Drizzle over nuts. Toss to coat.

2. Bake for 15 minutes, stirring twice. Spread nuts on a large piece of foil to cool. Store in an airtight container at room temperature for up to 2 weeks or freeze for up to 3 months. Makes 3 cups.

Per ¼ cup: 223 cal., 20 g fat (4 g sat. fat), 5 mg chol., 104 mg sodium, 9 g carbo., 3 g fiber, 6 g pro.

Nutty Corn and Fruit Mix

Nutty Corn and Fruit Mix
Start to Finish: 15 min.

 1 package (6- to 7-cup yield) plain microwave
     popcorn
     Nonstick cooking spray
 2 to 3 tablespoons grated Parmesan cheese
 2 cups shoestring potato sticks
1½ cups peanuts or almonds
 1 cup mixed dried fruit

1. Pop popcorn according to package directions. Pour popcorn into a very large bowl; coat popcorn lightly with cooking spray.

2. Sprinkle popcorn with Parmesan cheese; toss gently to coat. Stir in potato sticks, peanuts, and dried fruit. Makes about 12 cups.

Per 1 cup: 190 cal., 13 g fat (2 g sat. fat), 1 mg chol., 125 mg sodium, 16 g carbo., 2 g fiber, 6 g pro.

Banana-Raisin Trail Mix
Start to Finish: 10 min.

 2 cups raisins
 2 cups dried banana chips
 2 cups unsalted dry-roasted peanuts
 1 6-ounce package mixed dried fruit (cut up
     any large pieces)

1. In a storage container, combine all ingredients. Cover and shake to mix. Store at room temperature for up to 1 week. Makes about 7 cups.

Per ½ cup: 172 cal., 9 g fat (4 g sat. fat), 0 mg chol., 6 mg sodium, 22 g carbo., 1 g fiber, 3 g pro.

Rocky Road Popcorn
Start to Finish: 40 min.

     Nonstick cooking spray
12 ounces chocolate-flavor candy coating,
     chopped
 2 tablespoons peanut butter
 1 package (6- to 7-cup yield) plain microwave
     popcorn
 2 cups dry roasted peanuts
 1 cup crisp rice cereal
 1 cup tiny marshmallows

1. Line a large baking sheet with foil. Lightly coat foil with cooking spray; set aside. Pop popcorn according to package directions. Pour popcorn into a very large bowl; set aside.

2. In a medium saucepan, stir the candy coating and peanut butter over low heat until melted and smooth.

3. Add peanuts, cereal, and marshmallows to popcorn; stir to combine. Pour warm chocolate mixture over popcorn mixture; toss until well coated. Spread popcorn mixture on prepared baking sheet. Cool; break into clusters. Store in an airtight container at room temperature for up to 2 days. Makes about 12 cups.

Per 1 cup: 360 cal., 25 g fat (11 g sat. fat), 0 mg chol., 147 mg sodium, 30 g carbo., 3 g fiber, 8 g pro.

Cherry Caramel Corn
Prep: 10 min.   **Bake:** 15 min.

 3 tablespoons butter
¼ cup light-color corn syrup
 1 tablespoon molasses
½ teaspoon baking soda
15 cups popped popcorn
 1 cup dried tart red cherries

1. Preheat oven to 325°F. In a small saucepan, melt the butter over medium-low heat. Remove from heat; stir in corn syrup, molasses, and baking soda until baking soda is dissolved. Place popcorn in a large roasting pan; drizzle molasses mixture over popcorn, tossing to coat.

2. Bake for 15 minutes, stirring twice. Transfer to a very large bowl. Stir in cherries; cool. Serve the same day or freeze to store. Makes 20 servings.

Per serving: 74 cal., 2 g fat (1 g sat. fat), 5 mg chol., 49 mg sodium, 14 g carbo., 1 g fiber, 1 g pro.

Caramel-Coated Spiced Snack Mix

Prep: 15 min.   **Bake:** 30 min.

1	12-ounce box crispy corn and rice cereal (about 10 cups)
1½	cups mixed nuts
½	cup packed brown sugar
½	cup light-color corn syrup
½	cup butter
1	teaspoon ground cinnamon
½	teaspoon ground ginger
1½	cups chocolate-covered raisins
1½	cups semisweet or milk chocolate pieces

1. Preheat oven to 300°F. In a large roasting pan, stir together cereal and nuts; set aside.

2. In a small saucepan, stir together brown sugar, corn syrup, butter, cinnamon, and ginger. Stir over medium heat until butter is melted and mixture is smooth. Pour over cereal mixture; stir gently to coat.

3. Bake for 30 minutes, stirring twice. Spread cereal mixture on a large piece of buttered foil. Cool; break into pieces. Stir in chocolate-covered raisins and chocolate pieces. Store in an airtight container at room temperature for up to 1 week. Makes 16 cups.

Per ½ cup: 216 cal., 10 g fat (5 g sat. fat), 10 mg chol., 129 mg sodium, 30 g carbo., 1 g fiber, 2 g pro.

Snack mixes are so **versatile.** If there's an ingredient you don't like, swap it for something you do like.

Pretzel Bread Houses

Prep: 1 hr. **Bake:** 12 min. per batch

- 4 to 4½ cups all-purpose flour
- 1 package active dry yeast
- 1 tablespoon fennel seeds, crushed
- 1 tablespoon sugar
- 1 teaspoon salt
- 1½ cups warm water (120° to 130°F)
- 2 tablespoons cooking oil
- 1 egg white
- 1 tablespoons water
  Coarse sea salt
  Ball Park Mustard or Horseradish-Honey Mustard

1. In a large mixing bowl, stir together 1¾ cups of the flour, the yeast, fennel seeds, sugar, and 1 teaspoon salt. Add 1½ cups water and the oil. Beat with an electric mixer on low speed for 30 seconds, scraping sides of the bowl. Beat on high speed for 3 minutes. Using a wooden spoon, stir in as much remaining flour as you can.

2. Turn dough onto a lightly floured surface. Knead in enough remaining flour until dough is smooth and elastic (6 to 8 minutes). Shape dough into a ball. Divide in half. Cover and let stand 10 minutes. Preheat oven to 425°F. Lightly grease baking sheets; set aside.

3. Roll each dough half to a 13-inch square on a lightly floured surface. Using a 3½×3¼-inch house-shape cookie cutter, cut 12 houses from each square*. Arrange house cutouts on prepared baking sheets about 2 inches apart. In a small bowl, whisk together egg white and 1 tablespoon water. Brush each house with egg white mixture and sprinkle with coarse salt. Bake about 12 minutes or until golden. Transfer to a wire rack to cool. Serve with desired mustard. Makes 24 pretzels.

Ball Park Mustard: In a bowl, stir together one 8-ounce jar yellow mustard and ¼ cup packed brown sugar. Stir in ⅓ cup chopped peanuts just before serving.

Horseradish-Honey Mustard: In a bowl, stir together ¾ cup honey mustard and ¼ cup horseradish sauce.

*Gather dough scraps; shape into a ball. Cover and let rest 10 minutes. Roll and cut dough into more houses.

Per pretzel: 84 cal., 1 g fat (0 g sat. fat), 0 mg chol., 117 mg sodium, 15 g carbo., 1 g fiber, 2 g pro.

Crunchy Munchies

Prep: 20 min. **Bake:** 15 min.

- ¼ cup jalapeño pepper jelly
- 2 tablespoons butter
- ¼ teaspoon five-spice powder
- ¼ teaspoon salt
- ¼ teaspoon hot pepper sauce
- 2 cups whole cashews or dry roasted peanuts
- 1 cup dried banana chips
- 1 cup dried pineapple chunks, cut up
- 1 cup chopped dates
- 1 cup chow mein noodles

1. Preheat oven to 325°F. In a medium saucepan, combine jelly, butter, five-spice powder, salt, and hot pepper sauce. Heat and stir over low heat until jelly melts. Stir in remaining ingredients until well coated. Pour mixture into a large roasting pan. Bake for 15 to 20 minutes or until cashews are light brown, stirring once.

2. Spread cashew mixture on a large piece of foil to cool. Store in an airtight container at room temperature for up to 1 week. Makes 16 servings.

Per serving: 232 cal., 13 g fat (4 g sat. fat), 4 mg chol., 131 mg sodium, 29 g carbo., 2 g fiber, 4 g pro.

Peanut Poppers

Prep: 10 min.

- 4 cups popped popcorn (about 3 tablespoons unpopped)
- ½ cup peanuts
- ⅓ cup dried cranberries or raisins
- 1 tablespoon butter
- 1 tablespoon peanut butter

1. In a medium bowl, stir together popcorn, peanuts, and dried cranberries. Set aside.

2. In a small saucepan, combine butter and peanut butter. Heat and stir over medium heat until melted. Pour peanut butter mixture over popcorn mixture. Toss to coat. Serve within 6 hours of preparation. Makes 4½ cups.

Per ¾ cup serving: 146 cal., 10 g fat (2 g sat. fat), 5 mg chol., 67 mg sodium, 12 g carbo., 2 g fiber, 5 g pro.

Pretzels are natural snackers, and they come in all sorts of fun shapes.

Autumn Trail Mix

Autumn Trail Mix

Prep: 10 min. **Bake:** 10 min.

- 2 cups mixed nuts
- 2 cups small checker pretzels or other small pretzel twists
- 1 cup packed brown sugar
- ¼ cup water
- ½ to 1 teaspoon ground nutmeg
- 2 cups miniature chocolate chip cookies and/or bite-size rich round sandwich crackers with peanut butter filling

1. Preheat oven to 300°F. Line a baking sheet with foil; grease the foil. Set aside. In a large bowl, combine nuts and pretzels. Set aside.

2. In a medium skillet, combine brown sugar, water, and nutmeg. Heat and stir over medium heat until sugar dissolves. Bring to boiling; reduce heat and simmer about 5 minutes or until mixture is thickened and syrupy. Drizzle sugar mixture over nut mixture. Toss to coat. Spread on prepared baking sheet. Bake for 10 minutes; stir. Spread nut mixture on another piece of foil; let cool.

3. Break nut mixture into small clusters. Stir in cookies and/or crackers. Store in an airtight container at room temperature for up to 4 days. Makes about 8 cups.

Per ½ cup: 216 cal., 12 g fat (2 g sat. fat), 0 mg chol., 233 mg sodium, 26 g carbo., 2 g fiber, 4 g pro.

Pretzel Snack Mix

Prep: 5 min.

- 3 cups pretzel sticks
- 2 cups puffed corn cereal
- 2 cups honey graham cereal

1. In a large bowl, stir together pretzels and cereals. Store in an airtight container at room temperature for up to 3 days. Makes 6 cups.

Per ½ cup: 157 cal., 1 g fat (0 g sat. fat), 0 mg chol., 547 mg sodium, 33 g carbo., 1 g fiber, 1 g pro.

Chocolate Chip Sunflower Cookies

Prep: 20 min.   **Bake:** 9 min. per batch

- 1 18-ounce roll refrigerated chocolate chip cookie dough
- ½ cup flaked coconut
- ½ cup dry-roasted sunflower kernels

1. Preheat oven to 375°F. Place cookie dough and coconut in a large resealable plastic bag; knead to combine. Roll rounded teaspoons of dough into balls, then roll in sunflower kernels to coat. Place balls 2 inches apart on ungreased cookie sheets.

2. Bake for 9 to 11 minutes or until golden brown. Cool for 1 minute on cookie sheets. Transfer cookies to a wire rack; let cool. Makes about 2½ dozen cookies.

Per cookie: 101 cal., 5 g fat (2 g sat. fat), 2 mg chol., 66 mg sodium, 12 g carbo., 1 g fiber, 1 g pro.

Chocolate Chip Sunflower Cookies

Surprise Chocolate Bites

Prep: 30 min.   **Bake:** 10 min. per batch

- 1 18-ounce roll refrigerated sugar cookie dough
- ⅓ cup unsweetened cocoa powder
- ⅔ cup creamy peanut butter
- ⅔ cup powdered sugar
  Granulated sugar

1. Preheat oven to 350°F. Place cookie dough and cocoa in a large resealable plastic bag; knead to combine. In a bowl, stir together the peanut butter and powdered sugar until combined. With floured hands, roll the peanut butter mixture into thirty 1-inch balls.*

2. To shape cookies, take 1 tablespoon of the cookie dough and make an indentation in the center. Press a peanut butter ball into the indentation and form dough around ball to enclose it; roll ball gently in your hands to smooth it out. Repeat with remaining dough and peanut butter balls.

3. Place balls 2 inches apart on ungreased cookie sheets. Flatten the balls slightly with the bottom of a glass that has been dipped in granulated sugar. Bake for 10 to 12 minutes or until set. Transfer cookies to a wire rack; let cool. Makes 30 cookies.

*For easier handling, freeze the peanut butter balls for 30 minutes. Flatten the balls slightly to form disks, then press cookie dough around them.

Per cookie: 118 cal., 6 g fat (1 g sat. fat), 5 mg chol., 87 mg sodium, 15 g carbo., 0 g fiber, 2 g pro.

PB and Strawberry Pockets

Start to Finish: 15 min.

- 2 large white or whole wheat pita bread rounds, halved crosswise
- ½ cup chunky peanut butter
- ¼ cup raisins
- 1 cup sliced or chopped fresh strawberries
- 2 tablespoons dry-roasted sunflower kernels

1. Open pita bread halves to make pockets. In a small bowl, stir together peanut butter and raisins.

2. Spread peanut butter mixture inside pita pockets. Divide strawberries and sunflower kernels among pockets. Serve immediately, or wrap in plastic wrap and chill for up to 6 hours. Makes 4 servings.

Per serving: 333 cal., 18 g fat (3 g sat. fat), 0 mg chol., 318 mg sodium, 35 g carbo., 5 g fiber, 12 g pro.

{milk and cookies}

Milk and cookies are natural snack partners, and they give kids the energy they need to keep going through an active day. For an additional nutrition boost, try pairing cookies with soymilk (vanilla or chocolate), bottled or homemade smoothies, pure fruit juices, or even hot cocoa during those cold months.

Fruit and Chip Cookies

Prep: 25 min. **Bake:** 10 min. per batch

1	cup butter, softened
¾	cup packed brown sugar
½	cup granulated sugar
1	teaspoon baking soda
2	eggs
1	teaspoon vanilla
2	cups all-purpose flour
2	cups granola cereal
1	6-ounce package mixed dried fruit bits (1½ cups)
1	cup white baking pieces

1. Preheat oven to 350°F. In a mixing bowl, beat butter with an electric mixer on medium speed for 30 seconds. Add sugars and baking soda; beat until combined. Beat in eggs and vanilla. Beat in as much of the flour as you can with the mixer. Stir in any remaining flour and the granola. Stir in dried fruit bits and baking pieces.

2. Drop dough by rounded teaspoons 2 inches apart onto ungreased cookie sheets; flatten slightly. Bake about 10 minutes or until edges are golden. Cool on cookie sheets for 1 minute. Transfer to a wire rack; cool completely. Makes about 60 cookies.

Per cookie: 109 cal., 5 g fat (3 g sat. fat), 15 mg chol., 54 mg sodium, 15 g carbo., 1 g fiber, 2 g pro.

Tropical Treat

Double-Decker Fruit Stacks
Start to Finish: 20 min.

½ of an 8-ounce tub reduced-fat cream cheese (Neufchâtel), softened
½ teaspoon finely shredded orange peel
2 to 3 teaspoons fat-free milk
3 8-inch whole wheat or plain flour tortillas
1 medium apple, pear, and/or banana
¼ cup chopped almonds, pecans, or walnuts, toasted (optional)

1. In a small bowl, stir together cream cheese, orange peel, and enough milk to make spreading consistency; set aside. Spread cream cheese mixture on tortillas; set aside. If using apple or pear, core and thinly slice crosswise. If using banana, slice.

2. On 1 tortilla, arrange half of the fruit slices. If desired, sprinkle with half of the almonds. Top with another tortilla, cream cheese side up. Top with the remaining fruit slices and, if desired, almonds. Top with remaining tortilla, cream cheese side down. Cut into wedges. Makes 4 to 6 servings.

Per serving: 177 cal., 6 g fat (3 g sat. fat), 13 mg chol., 419 mg sodium, 26 g carbo., 2 g fiber, 6 g pro.

Fruit Salad with Banana Dip
Prep: 20 min.   **Chill:** up to 2 hr.

1 medium banana, sliced
½ cup low-fat lemon yogurt
1 tablespoon sugar
1 teaspoon lemon juice
4 cups cut-up fresh fruit, such as papaya, banana, strawberries, carambola (star fruit), cantaloupe melon, honeydew melon, mango, kiwifruit, and/or blueberries
Sliced bananas (optional)

1. In a blender, combine banana, yogurt, sugar, and lemon juice. Cover and blend until smooth. Transfer dip to a bowl. Cover and chill for up to 2 hours. To serve, arrange fruit on a platter. Serve with dip. If desired, garnish dip with additional banana slices. Makes 4 servings.

Per serving: 139 cal., 1 g fat (0 g sat. fat), 2 mg chol., 30 mg sodium, 32 g carbo., 3 g fiber, 2 g pro.

Tropical Treat
Start to Finish: 10 min.

1 single-serving container vanilla or banana pudding, applesauce, or vanilla yogurt
1 tablespoon tropical-blend dried fruit bits
1 tablespoon chopped almonds or macadamia nuts (optional)
1 teaspoon toasted coconut, toasted wheat germ, or granola cereal

1. In a small bowl, stir together the pudding, fruit bits, and, if desired, nuts. Top with toasted coconut. Makes 1 serving.

Per serving: 201 cal., 6 g fat (3 g sat. fat), 0 mg chol., 183 mg sodium, 33 g carbo., 1 g fiber, 2 g pro.

Frozen Yogurt Pops

Prep: 20 min. **Freeze:** overnight

- **2** cups low-fat vanilla yogurt
- **1** 12-ounce can frozen juice concentrate, thawed*
- **½** teaspoon vanilla

1. In a large bowl, combine yogurt, juice concentrate, and vanilla; divide among eight 4- to 6-ounce paper cups. Cover cups with foil. Make a small hole in the foil with a knife; insert wooden frozen-pop sticks through holes into cups. Freeze overnight or until firm. Makes 8 pops.

*For sweet, fruity pops, try grape, raspberry, or a fruit-blend juice concentrate. For milder pops or when using tart juices like orange or lemonade, make 6 pops using a 6-ounce can of fruit juice concentrate rather than a 12-ounce can. You can also make 2 or 3 different batches using different juices and swirl them together or layer them by freezing after each layer.

Per pop: 165 cal., 1 g fat (0 g sat. fat), 3 mg chol., 63 mg sodium, 36 g carbo., 0 g fiber, 3 g pro.

Tropical Fruit Pops

Prep: 15 min. **Freeze:** 4 hr.

- **1** cup guava nectar
- **1** cup pineapple juice
- **1** cup fresh pineapple chunks
- **1** cup coarsely chopped or sliced fresh fruit (strawberries, kiwifruit, papaya, melon)

1. In a blender, combine guava nectar, pineapple juice, and fresh pineapple chunks. Cover and blend until smooth. Divide chopped or sliced fruit among 12 frozen-pop molds or 4- to 6-ounce paper cups. Pour blended mixture over the fruit.

2. Add sticks and cover molds. Or cover each paper cup with foil. Make a small hole in the foil with a knife; insert a wooden frozen-pop stick through hole into cups. Freeze about 4 hours or until firm. Makes 12 pops.

Per pop: 34 cal., 0 g fat (0 g sat. fat), 0 mg chol., 1 mg sodium, 8 g carbo., 0 g fiber, 0 g pro.

Tutti-Fruity Slushes

Start to Finish: 15 min.

- **1** 12-ounce package frozen red raspberries or one 16-ounce package frozen unsweetened peach slices, thawed
- **1** cup apricot nectar
- **1** cup powdered sugar
  Ice cubes (4 to 4½ cups)
  Fresh raspberries (optional)

1. Press thawed raspberries, if using, through a fine-mesh sieve to remove seeds.

2. Transfer raspberry puree or the thawed peaches to a blender. Add apricot nectar and powdered sugar. Cover and blend until smooth.

3. Gradually add ice to mixture, blending until mixture is slushy. If desired, garnish with fresh raspberries. Makes 5 cups.

Per 1 cup: 160 cal., 0 g fat (0 g sat. fat), 0 mg chol., 2 mg sodium, 40 g carbo., 3 g fiber, 1 g pro.

Pretzel Pets

Pretzel Pets
Start to Finish: 15 min.

- ½ of an 8-ounce container whipped cream cheese
- 1 tablespoon honey
- 1 15-ounce can pear halves in light syrup, drained
  Small pretzel twists
  Pretzel sticks, broken
  Desired dried fruit, snipped as necessary

1. In a small bowl, stir together cream cheese and honey. Fill pear halves with cream cheese mixture. Top each with pretzels and fruit to create desired pet. Makes 5 servings.

Per serving: 200 cal., 7 g fat (4 g sat. fat), 22 mg chol., 391 mg sodium, 33 g carbo., 2 g fiber, 3 g pro.

Salami Kabobs
Prep: 35 min.   **Chill:** up to 2 hr.

- 6 ounces sliced salami
- 6 ounces mozzarella or provolone cheese, cubed
- 1½ cups cantaloupe and/or honeydew melon balls
- 1 cup purchased large pitted green olives and/or large pitted ripe olives
- ¾ cup cherry tomatoes

1. On six 6-inch bamboo skewers, alternately thread salami, cheese, and melon balls. On another six 6-inch skewers, alternately thread salami, cheese, olives, and cherry tomatoes. Place on a serving plate. Cover and chill for up to 2 hours before serving. Makes 12 kabobs.

Per kabob: 117 cal., 10 g fat (4 g sat. fat), 24 mg chol., 520 mg sodium, 2 g carbo., 0 g fiber, 5 g pro.

Fruit Gels
Prep: 15 min.   **Chill:** 2 hr.

- ¼ cup sugar
- 1 envelope (.25 ounce) unflavored gelatin
- 1 15.2-ounce bottle fruit juice blend (1¾ cups)
  Edible flowers (optional)

1. In a small saucepan, stir together sugar and gelatin. Stir in 1 cup of the juice. Cook and stir over medium heat until sugar and gelatin are dissolved. Remove from heat; stir in remaining juice.

2. Divide gelatin mixture among four 6-ounce cups or six 3- to 4-ounce glasses or small dishes. Refrigerate for 2 to 3 hours or until set. Garnish with edible flowers, if desired. Makes 6 servings.

Per serving: 73 cal., 0 g fat (0 g sat. fat), 0 mg chol., 4 mg sodium, 17 g carbo., 0 g fiber, 1 g pro.

Banana Tostadas
Start to Finish: 25 min.

- 2 7- to 8-inch multigrain or regular flour tortillas
  Light spreadable plain or flavored cream cheese
  Desired chopped fruit, such as bananas, strawberries, raspberries, kiwi, and/or blueberries
  Chopped nuts, such as toasted almonds, flavored sliced almonds, and/or toasted pecans (optional)

1. Preheat broiler. Cut tortillas into quarters or use desired-shape cutters. Broil 2 to 3 minutes or until toasted. Cool slightly. Spread cream cheese on wedges and top with desired fruit and nut toppings. Makes 4 servings.

Per serving: 133 cal., 4 g fat (2 g sat. fat), 8 mg chol., 236 mg sodium, 18 g carbo., 6 g fiber, 6 g pro.

Banana Tostadas

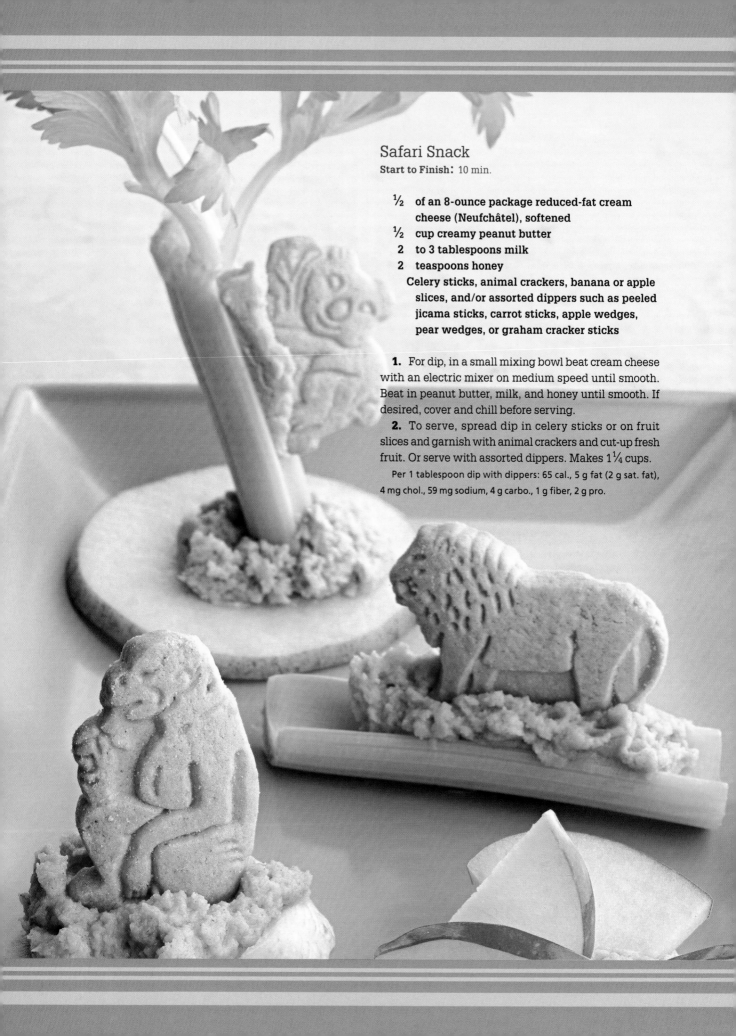

Safari Snack

Start to Finish: 10 min.

½ of an 8-ounce package reduced-fat cream
   cheese (Neufchâtel), softened
½ cup creamy peanut butter
2 to 3 tablespoons milk
2 teaspoons honey
   Celery sticks, animal crackers, banana or apple
   slices, and/or assorted dippers such as peeled
   jicama sticks, carrot sticks, apple wedges,
   pear wedges, or graham cracker sticks

1. For dip, in a small mixing bowl beat cream cheese
with an electric mixer on medium speed until smooth.
Beat in peanut butter, milk, and honey until smooth. If
desired, cover and chill before serving.

2. To serve, spread dip in celery sticks or on fruit
slices and garnish with animal crackers and cut-up fresh
fruit. Or serve with assorted dippers. Makes 1¼ cups.

Per 1 tablespoon dip with dippers: 65 cal., 5 g fat (2 g sat. fat),
4 mg chol., 59 mg sodium, 4 g carbo., 1 g fiber, 2 g pro.

Carrots with Dried-Fruit Dip

Prep: 15 min.

- 1 8-ounce tub cream cheese spread with honey and nuts or with brown sugar and cinnamon
- 2 to 3 teaspoons milk
- 1 cup dried tropical fruit bits, finely snipped
- 3 medium carrots, cut into sticks
- 3 stalks celery, cut into sticks

1. In a medium bowl, stir together cream cheese and milk until smooth. Stir in fruit bits. Serve dip with carrot and celery sticks. Makes 12 servings.

Per serving: 114 cal., 5 g fat (3 g sat. fat), 18 mg chol., 95 mg sodium, 15 g carbo., 1 g fiber, 1 g pro.

Veggie Mix with Ranch Dip

Start to Finish: 10 min.

- ½ of a medium red or yellow sweet pepper, cut into squares
- 1 stalk celery, cut into sticks
- 4 cherry tomatoes, halved
- ½ cup ranch salad dressing or cottage cheese
- ¼ cup coarsely shredded cucumber
- ⅛ teaspoon dried dill weed

1. In a medium bowl, combine pepper squares, celery, and cherry tomatoes. In a small bowl, stir together ranch dressing, cucumber, and dill. Serve dressing mixture as dip for vegetables. Makes 4 servings.

Per serving: 159 cal., 16 g fat (3 g sat. fat), 5 mg chol., 349 mg sodium, 4 g carbo., 1 g fiber, 0 g pro.

Veggies-on-the-Go

Start to Finish: 10 min.

- ¼ cup low-fat dill vegetable dip
  Finely shredded lemon peel
- ½ cup vegetable sticks* (carrots, zucchini, red sweet pepper, celery, jicama, blanched green beans)

1. In a small bowl, stir together vegetable dip and lemon peel to taste. Spoon dip into the bottom of a plastic cup. Insert vegetable sticks into dip in cup. Cover cup and tote with an ice pack. Makes 1 serving.

*Look for precut vegetable sticks in the produce aisle of your supermarket.

Per serving: 145 cal., 10 g fat (2 g sat. fat), 10 mg chol., 502 mg sodium, 10 g carbo., 2 g fiber, 1 g pro.

Kids will eat almost anything if they have a dip for it.

Carrots with Dried-Fruit Dip

Veggies-on-the-Go

15-minute desserts

Quick desserts don't have to come straight from a box or carton. **A homemade sauce** makes purchased cheesecake or ice cream special.

Cherry-Chocolate Sauce

Start to Finish: 15 min.

- ½ cup dried cherries
- 6 tablespoons butter
- ½ cup semisweet chocolate pieces
- 1½ cups powdered sugar
- ½ cup milk
- 1½ teaspoons vanilla
- Purchased cheesecake or ice cream

1. In a medium bowl, cover cherries with boiling water; let stand for 5 minutes. Drain well.

2. Meanwhile, in a medium saucepan, stir butter and chocolate pieces over medium-low heat until melted. Whisk in the powdered sugar, milk, and vanilla until smooth. Stir in the cherries. Spoon over cheesecake or ice cream. Store leftovers in a covered container in the refrigerator for up to 1 week. Makes 2 cups.

Per tablespoon sauce: 61 cal., 3 g fat (2 g sat. fat), 6 mg chol., 17 mg sodium, 9 g carbo., 0 g fiber, 0 g pro.

A Billow of Berries 'n' Brownies

A Billow of Berries 'n' Brownies
Start to Finish: 15 min.

- 2 cups fresh red raspberries
- 3 tablespoons sugar
- 1 teaspoon finely shredded orange peel
- 2 cups whipped cream
- 2 to 3 3-inch squares bakery brownies, cut into irregular chunks

1. Set aside ⅓ cup of the berries. In a medium bowl, combine the remaining berries, 2 tablespoons of the sugar, and the orange peel. Place the berry mixture in a 4- to 5-cup serving bowl or divide among 6 dessert dishes. Spoon whipped cream over raspberry mixture. Top the whipped cream with the brownie chunks and the reserved raspberries. Makes 6 servings.

Per serving: 327 cal., 27 g fat (15 g sat. fat), 95 mg chol., 85 mg sodium, 19 g carbo., 3 g fiber, 3 g pro.

Raspberry Waffle Stacks
Start to Finish: 15 min.

- 4 frozen square waffles
- 2 3.5-ounce (single-serving) containers lemon or vanilla pudding
- 1 cup fresh raspberries

1. Toast waffles as directed on package. Cut waffles in half. Place four halves on individual serving plates. Top evenly with pudding, reserving about 2 tablespoons of the pudding. Top pudding-covered waffles with raspberries. Cover with remaining waffle halves. Spoon remaining pudding on top of waffle stacks and garnish each with a raspberry. Makes 4 servings.

Per serving: 159 cal., 4 g fat (1 g sat. fat), 11 mg chol., 331 mg sodium, 28 g carbo., 3 g fiber, 2 g pro.

Fruit Whip
Start to Finish: 10 min.

- 2 peaches or mangoes, pitted and chopped
- ¼ cup cream cheese, softened
- 2 tablespoons white grape juice or orange juice
- 2 tablespoons chopped pistachios

1. Divide fruit between two bowls. In a small bowl, beat together cream cheese and juice. Spoon over peaches. Top with chopped pistachios. Makes 2 servings.

Per serving: 229 cal., 14 g fat (7 g sat. fat), 32 mg chol., 87 mg sodium, 24 g carbo., 4 g fiber, 5 g pro.

A **fast dessert** is as simple as jazzing up a convenience food from your grocer's bakery or freezer aisle.

Fruity Waffle Bowls
Start to Finish: 15 min.

- 1 4-serving-size package instant lemon or white chocolate pudding mix
- 1⅓ cups fat-free milk
- 1 cup fresh fruit (such as blueberries, sliced kiwifruits, sliced strawberries, sliced bananas, or raspberries)
- 4 waffle ice cream bowls or large waffle ice cream cones

  Fresh mint leaves (optional)

1. Prepare pudding according to package directions, except use the 1⅓ cups milk. Spoon fruit into waffle bowls or cones. Top with pudding. If desired, garnish with fresh mint. Makes 4 servings.

Per serving: 196 cal., 3 g fat (1 g sat. fat), 6 mg chol., 399 mg sodium, 40 g carbo., 1 g fiber, 3 g pro.

Tropical Fruit Shortcakes
Start to Finish: 15 min.

- 1 cup chopped papaya*
- 1 8-ounce can pineapple tidbits (juice pack), drained
- 2 kiwifruits, peeled and coarsely chopped
- 2 tablespoons honey
- ¼ cup orange juice
- 6 slices purchased pound cake or angel food cake, or 6 purchased shortcake cups
- 1½ cups frozen whipped dessert topping, thawed

  Toasted macadamia nuts or pecans (optional)

1. In a small bowl, stir together the papaya, pineapple, kiwifruits, and honey. Drizzle orange juice over the cake slices. Spoon fruit mixture over cake slices. Top with whipped topping and, if desired, sprinkle with nuts. Makes 6 servings.

* Look for jarred papaya in the refrigerated section of your supermarket's produce section.

Per serving: 428 cal., 19 g fat (12 g sat. fat), 115 mg chol., 163 mg sodium, 30 g carbo., 2 g fiber, 5 g pro.

Almond Poached Pears

Start to Finish: 15 min.

- 1   29-ounce can pear halves in syrup
- 2   tablespoons packed brown sugar
- ½   teaspoon ground nutmeg
- ½   teaspoon almond extract
- ⅓   cup sliced almonds, toasted, or purchased glazed sliced almonds (salad toppers)
  Vanilla yogurt or ice cream (optional)

1. Drain pear halves, reserving liquid; set pears aside. In a large skillet, stir together pear liquid, brown sugar, and nutmeg. Bring to boiling, stirring until sugar is dissolved. Add pears and almond extract, turning pears to coat. Remove from heat; cover. Set aside for 5 minutes.

2. Serve pears with some of the poaching liquid and sprinkle with almonds. If desired, serve with vanilla yogurt or ice cream. Makes 6 servings.

Per serving: 174 cal., 4 g fat (0 g sat. fat), 0 mg chol., 13 mg sodium, 33 g carbo., 2 g fiber, 2 g pro.

Fruit and Granola Parfaits

Start to Finish: 15 min.

- 1½   cups frozen vanilla or fruit-flavor yogurt or light ice cream
- ½   cup granola cereal
- 1   cup fruit, such as sliced bananas; peeled, sliced kiwifruit; sliced peaches or mangoes; and/or cut-up pineapple
- 6   tablespoons strawberry ice cream topping

- ¼   cup frozen light whipped dessert topping, thawed (optional)
- 2   maraschino cherries with stems (optional)

1. Place ¼ cup frozen yogurt in the bottom of each of 2 parfait glasses. Top each with 2 tablespoons granola, ¼ cup fruit, and 1 tablespoon strawberry topping. Repeat. Top each with ¼ cup frozen yogurt. Drizzle with remaining topping. If desired, top with whipped topping and garnish with cherries. Makes 2 servings.

Per serving: 375 cal., 9 g fat (4 g sat. fat), 15 mg chol., 138 mg sodium, 70 g carbo., 2 g fiber, 4 g pro.

Lemon Berry Parfaits

Start to Finish: 15 min.

- ½   cup whipping cream
- ½   teaspoon vanilla
- 2   teaspoons finely shredded lemon peel
- 1   cup sliced fresh strawberries
- 2   tablespoons sugar-free apricot preserves, melted

1. In a medium mixing bowl, beat whipping cream and vanilla with an electric mixer on high speed until soft peaks form (tips curl); fold in lemon peel.

2. In a small bowl toss together strawberries and preserves. Set aside about 12 of the preserves-coated berry slices. Divide the remaining berry mixture among four dessert dishes. Top each with whipped cream. Garnish with reserved berry slices.

Per serving: 121 cal., 11 g fat (7 g sat. fat), 41 mg chol., 12 mg sodium, 6 g carbo., 1 g fiber, 1 g pro.

Almond Poached Pears

Fruit and Granola Parfaits

Banana Split Trifles

Prep: 15 min. Freeze: up to 1 hr.

4   soft-style chocolate chip or oatmeal cookies, crumbled
2   bananas, cut into chunks
1   quart desired flavor ice cream
1   12-ounce jar hot fudge sauce or strawberry preserves
    Whipped cream

1. In each of four parfait glasses, layer cookies, bananas, scoops of ice cream, and sauce (you may not use all of the ice cream or sauce). Top with whipped cream and additional cookies. Cover; freeze for up to 1 hour. Makes 4 servings.

Per serving: 524 cal., 23 g fat (12 g sat. fat), 48 mg chol., 161 mg sodium, 73 g carbo., 3 g fiber, 6 g pro.

French-Toasted Angel Food Cake

Start to Finish: 20 min.

1   7- to 8-inch angel food cake
6   eggs, lightly beaten
1½ cups milk
3   tablespoons sugar
2   teaspoons vanilla
1   tablespoon butter
    Whipped cream or crème fraîche
    Maple syrup
    Cut-up fresh strawberries

1. Slice the cake into ten to twelve 1-inch-thick wedges. In a shallow dish, whisk together eggs, milk, sugar, and vanilla. Soak wedges in egg mixture for 1 minute per side. In a nonstick skillet or on a nonstick griddle, melt butter over medium heat. Cook 4 wedges at a time for 1 to 2 minutes per side or until golden brown. To serve, stand slices in cake formation. Top with whipped cream. Drizzle with maple syrup and garnish with strawberries. Makes 10 to 12 servings.

Per serving: 275 cal., 12 g fat (6 g sat. fat), 187 mg chol., 305 mg sodium, 33 g carbo., 1 g fiber, 8 g pro.

A plain angel food cake from the bakery is a **perfect start** to a classy dessert.

Easy Peach-Blueberry Crisp

Start to Finish: 15 min.

- 2 cups frozen unsweetened peach slices
- 2 tablespoons packed brown sugar
- 1 tablespoon water
- ½ teaspoon pumpkin pie spice
- ¼ cup fresh or frozen blueberries
- 8 shortbread cookies, coarsely crushed

1. In a medium saucepan, stir together peaches, brown sugar, water, and spice. Bring to boiling, stirring to combine; reduce heat. Simmer, uncovered, for 4 to 5 minutes or until thickened. Gently stir in blueberries. Remove from heat. Cover and let stand for 5 minutes. Spoon into four dessert dishes. Sprinkle with cookies. Makes 4 servings.

Per serving: 208 cal., 8 g fat (0 g sat. fat), 10 mg chol., 133 mg sodium, 35 g carbo., 2 g fiber, 4 g pro.

Whoopie Pies

Start to Finish: 15 min.

- ¼ cup butter, softened
- ½ of an 8-ounce package reduced-fat cream cheese (Neufchâtel), softened
- ½ of a 7-ounce jar marshmallow creme
- 12 purchased soft chocolate cookies

1. For filling, in a medium mixing bowl, beat butter and cream cheese with an electric mixer on medium to high speed until smooth and fluffy. Fold in marshmallow creme until combined. Spread filling evenly on the flat sides of half of the cookies. Top with remaining cookies, flat sides down, to make sandwiches. For firmer filling, wrap and chill whoopie pies for 2 hours before serving. Makes 6 sandwiches.

Per serving: 710 cal., 36 g fat (16 g sat. fat), 55 mg chol., 423 mg sodium, 90 g carbo., 1 g fiber, 6 g pro.

Chocolate-Drizzled Angel Food Cake

Start to Finish: 15 min.

- 1 7- to 8-inch angel food cake
- 2 tablespoons orange liqueur
- 2 tablespoons orange juice
- 6 ounces bittersweet or dark chocolate
- ½ cup butter
- 1½ cups powdered sugar
- ¼ cup whipping cream

1. Using a long wooden skewer, generously poke holes through the top of the cake all the way to the bottom. Stir together orange liqueur and orange juice. Drizzle orange mixture over cake. For the chocolate glaze, in a small saucepan, stir chocolate and butter over low heat until melted and smooth. Remove from heat. Whisk in powdered sugar and whipping cream. Spoon evenly over cake. Makes 10 to 12 servings.

Per serving: 436 cal., 18 g fat (11 g sat. fat), 33 mg chol., 440 mg sodium, 66 g carbo., 2 g fiber, 5 g pro.

Crunchy Pound Cake Slices

Can-Do Cannoli

Start to Finish: 15 min.

- ¾ cup ricotta cheese
- ¼ cup miniature semisweet chocolate pieces
- 1 tablespoon sugar
- ½ teaspoon vanilla
- ½ cup frozen light whipped dessert topping, thawed
- 6 purchased cannoli shells
  Miniature semisweet chocolate pieces (optional)
- ½ cup miniature semisweet chocolate pieces, melted (optional)

1. In a small bowl, stir together ricotta, the ¼ cup chocolate pieces, the sugar, and vanilla. Fold in whipped topping. Spoon mixture into a heavy plastic bag.

2. Snip off corner of bag; pipe filling into cannoli shells. If desired, sprinkle any exposed filling with additional chocolate pieces. If desired, drizzle with melted chocolate. Makes 6 servings.

Per serving: 231 cal., 15 g fat (5 g sat. fat), 16 mg chol., 37 mg sodium, 20 g carbo., 1 g fiber, 6 g pro.

Indoor S'mores

Start to Finish: 10 min.

- 4 graham crackers, quartered
- 4 teaspoons fudge ice cream topping
- 64 miniature marshmallows (about ¾ cup)
- 4 teaspoons strawberry jam

1. Place 8 graham cracker quarters on a microwave-safe plate. Spread ice cream topping evenly on crackers. Top evenly with marshmallows (about 8 each). Microwave on 100 percent power (high) for 30 seconds.

2. Spoon jam evenly over marshmallows and quickly top with remaining graham cracker quarters. Makes 8 s'mores.

Peanut Butter S'mores: Prepare as directed, except use chocolate graham cracker squares and substitute peanut butter for ice cream topping. If desired, omit jam.

Per s'more: 52 cal., 0 g fat (0 g sat. fat), 0 mg chol., 32 mg sodium, 12 g carbo., 0 g fiber, 0 g pro.

Crunchy Pound Cake Slices

Start to Finish: 15 min.

- 4 ½-inch slices purchased pound cake
- ¼ cup chocolate-hazelnut spread
- ¼ cup chopped nut topping for ice cream
- 1 pint caramel or cinnamon ice cream

1. Preheat broiler. Place the pound cake slices on a baking sheet. Broil 3 to 4 inches from the heat for 1 minute per side or until light brown. Cool slightly. Spread one side of each slice with 1 tablespoon chocolate-hazelnut spread. Sprinkle with nut topping. Transfer each slice to a dessert plate and serve with a scoop of ice cream. Makes 4 servings.

Per serving: 387 cal., 22 g fat (8 g sat. fat), 62 mg chol., 193 mg sodium, 42 g carbo., 1 g fiber, 7 g pro.

{whipped cream}

Frozen whipped topping is a great time-saver, but when you can, splurge on the real thing. Place 2 cups whipping cream, 2 tablespoons sugar, and ½ teaspoon vanilla in a chilled bowl. Beat with an electric mixer on medium speed until soft peaks form. For more flavor, add ½ teaspoon lemon or orange peel or ¼ teaspoon ground cinnamon or nutmeg.

Indoor S'mores

Chocolate Fondue

Chocolate Fondue

Prep: 15 min.

- 8 ounces semisweet chocolate, coarsely chopped
- 1 14-ounce can (1¼ cups) sweetened condensed milk
- ⅓ cup milk

  Assorted dippers, such as angel food or pound cake cubes, brownie squares, marshmallows, whole strawberries, banana slices, pineapple chunks, dried fruit, cookies, or melon pieces

1. In a heavy medium saucepan, melt chocolate over low heat, stirring constantly. Stir in sweetened condensed milk and milk; heat through. Transfer to a fondue pot; keep warm over a fondue burner.

2. Serve fondue sauce immediately with assorted dippers. Swirl pieces as you dip. If the fondue mixture thickens, stir in additional milk. Makes 8 servings.

Mocha Fondue: Prepare as above, except substitute ⅓ cup strong coffee for the milk.

Chocolate-Peanut Fondue: Prepare as above, except stir ½ cup creamy peanut butter in with the milk.

Per serving: 306 cal., 14 g fat (8 g sat. fat), 18 mg chol., 67 mg sodium, 44 g carbo., 2 g fiber, 6 g pro.

Quick Apple Crisp

Start to Finish: 15 min.

- 1 21-ounce can apple pie filling
- ¼ cup dried cranberries
- ¼ teaspoon ground ginger or cinnamon
- ¼ teaspoon vanilla
- 1 cup granola
- 1 pint vanilla ice cream

1. In a medium saucepan combine pie filling, dried cranberries, and ginger; heat through, stirring occasionally. Remove from heat; stir in vanilla. Spoon into bowls. Top individual servings with granola. Serve with ice cream. Makes 4 servings.

Per serving: 507 cal., 15 g fat (8 g sat. fat), 68 mg chol., 113 mg sodium, 88 g carbo., 6 g fiber, 9 g pro.

It's not as hard as it looks to make lacy sugar strands as a garnish.

Raspberries on a Citrus Cloud

Raspberries on a Citrus Cloud

Start to Finish: 15 min.

- 2 cups fresh red raspberries
- 4 teaspoons raspberry liqueur (optional)
- 1 8-ounce carton lemon-flavor yogurt
- ¼ of an 8-ounce container frozen fat-free whipped dessert topping, thawed
- 3 tablespoons sugar (optional)

1. Reserve ¼ cup raspberries. If desired, in a bowl toss remaining raspberries with liqueur.

2. In a small bowl, stir together yogurt and dessert topping. Spoon berry mixture into 4 dessert dishes. Spoon yogurt mixture over berries.

3. If desired, place sugar in a heavy saucepan. Heat over medium-high heat until sugar begins to melt, shaking pan occasionally. (Do not stir.) Once sugar starts to melt, reduce heat to low. Cook about 5 minutes more or until all the sugar is melted and golden, stirring occasionally. Remove pan from heat. Let stand for 1 minute. Dip a fork into melted sugar; let it run off the fork for several seconds before shaking it over desserts, allowing strands of melted sugar to fall over berries. If sugar starts to harden in the pan, return to heat, stirring until melted. Top with reserved berries. Makes 4 servings.

Per serving: 148 cal., 1 g fat (0 g sat. fat), 2 mg chol., 41 mg sodium, 32 g carbo., 3 g fiber, 3 g pro.

Cranberry Cheesecake Shake

Cranberry Cheesecake Shake
Start to Finish: 10 min.

> 1 3-ounce package cream cheese, softened
> 1 cup milk
> 2 cups vanilla ice cream
> ½ of a 16-ounce can jellied cranberry sauce
> 1 cup fresh cranberries
>   Sugared cranberries (optional)*

1. Place cream cheese and milk in a blender. Cover and blend until combined. Add ice cream, cranberry sauce, and the 1 cup cranberries. Cover and blend until nearly smooth, stopping to scrape down sides if necessary. Serve immediately. If desired, garnish with sugared cranberries. Makes four servings.

*Note: For sugared cranberries, freeze whole fresh cranberries; roll in sugar until coated.

Per serving: 385 cal., 21 g fat (13 g sat. fat), 73 mg chol., 163 mg sodium, 45 g carbo., 2 g fiber, 6 g pro.

Gooey Brownie Cups
Prep: 8 min. **Bake:** 7 min.

> 4 purchased unfrosted chocolate brownies, cut into irregular-size chunks
> 1 cup tiny marshmallows
> ¼ cup peanut butter-flavor pieces and/or milk chocolate pieces
> 2 tablespoons chopped cocktail peanuts
>   Chocolate or vanilla ice cream
>   Chocolate ice cream topping

1. Preheat oven to 350°F. In a large bowl, toss together brownie chunks, marshmallows, peanut-flavor pieces, and peanuts. Divide brownie mixture among 4 individual baking dishes.

2. Bake for 7 to 8 minutes or until warm and marshmallows are golden brown. Serve with ice cream and drizzle with ice cream topping. Makes 4 servings.

Per serving: 581 cal., 28 g fat (9 g sat. fat), 63 mg chol., 280 mg sodium, 78 g carbo., 3 g fiber, 9 g pro.

Ice cream and frozen yogurt are the ultimate for **quick desserts**. Top warm brownies, whip them into a shake, or just top a cone.

Fast and Fruity Banana Split Tarts

Start to Finish: 10 min.

- 1 8-ounce tub cream cheese with pineapple
- ¼ cup strawberry preserves
- 1 banana, thinly sliced
- 1 2.1-ounce package (15) miniature phyllo dough shells
- ⅓ cup chocolate ice cream topping

1. For filling, in a small mixing bowl, beat the cream cheese and preserves on medium speed of an electric mixer until light and fluffy. Spoon filling evenly into shells.

2. To serve, divide banana slices among shells. Drizzle with ice cream topping. Serve immediately. Makes 15 tarts.

Per tart: 115 cal., 6 g fat (3 g sat. fat), 13 mg chol., 63 mg sodium, 14 g carbo., 0 g fiber, 1 g pro.

Moo Juice

Start to Finish: 5 min.

- 1 pint vanilla, chocolate, or strawberry frozen yogurt or ice cream
- ½ to ¾ cup milk

1. Put the frozen yogurt and milk in a blender. Cover and blend until smooth. Pour shakes into tall glasses. Makes 2 large servings.

Candy Moo Juice: Prepare as above using either vanilla or chocolate yogurt or ice cream. Add 6 bite-size chocolate-covered peanut butter cups or one 1⅛-ounce bar chocolate-covered English toffee, broken up, to the blended mixture. Cover and blend just until the candy is coarsely chopped.

Cookie Moo Juice: Prepare as above using either vanilla or chocolate yogurt or ice cream. Add 4 chocolate sandwich cookies or chocolate-covered graham crackers to the blended mixture. Cover and blend just until the cookies are coarsely chopped.

Per serving: 168 cal., 6 g fat (4 g sat. fat), 12 mg chol., 73 mg sodium, 24 g carbo., 0 g fiber, 5 g pro.

Chocolate-Peppermint Malts

Start to Finish: 15 min.

- 3 cups chocolate milk
- 1 quart vanilla or chocolate ice cream
- ⅓ cup malted milk powder
- ½ teaspoon peppermint extract
   Coarsely crushed hard peppermint candies

1. In a blender, combine chocolate milk, half of the ice cream, the malted milk powder, and peppermint extract. Cover and blend until smooth.

2. Pour into 6 chilled tall glasses. Top each malt with a scoop of remaining ice cream. Sprinkle with crushed candy pieces. Makes 6 servings.

Per serving: 541 cal., 29 g fat (18 g sat. fat), 150 mg chol., 237 mg sodium, 58 g carbo., 1 g fiber, 12 g pro.

Rocky Road Malts

Banana Cream Pie-in-a-Glass
Start to Finish: 15 min.

- 2 medium bananas, cut up and frozen
- ⅔ cup milk
- ¼ cup French vanilla-flavor liquid coffee creamer
- 1½ cups French vanilla or vanilla ice cream
  Whipped cream
- 3 vanilla wafers

1. In a blender, combine bananas, milk, and creamer. Cover and blend until smooth. Add half of the ice cream at a time, blending until smooth after each addition. Divide among three glasses. Top each with whipped cream and a vanilla wafer. Makes 3 servings.

Per serving: 350 cal., 16 g fat (9 g sat. fat), 78 mg chol., 159 mg sodium, 48 g carbo., 2 g fiber, 6 g pro.

Drink Your Pumpkin Pie
Start to Finish: 10 min.

- 1 quart milk or vanilla soymilk
- 1 cup canned pumpkin
- ¼ cup sugar
- 1 teaspoon ground nutmeg
- 1 teaspoon vanilla
  Whipped cream (optional)

1. In a large saucepan, stir together milk, pumpkin, sugar, and nutmeg. Heat through (do not boil). Remove from heat; stir in vanilla. Ladle into mugs. If desired, top with a spoonful of whipped cream. Makes 6 servings.

Per serving: 133 cal., 3 g fat (2 g sat. fat), 13 mg chol., 69 mg sodium, 20 g carbo., 1 g fiber, 6 g pro.

Rocky Road Malts
Start to Finish: 10 min.

- 1 quart chocolate ice cream
- ⅓ to ½ cup milk
- ⅓ cup chocolate instant malted milk powder
- ¼ cup creamy peanut butter
  Marshmallow creme
  Coarsely chopped peanuts
  Miniature sandwich cookies

1. In a blender, combine half of the ice cream, ⅓ cup of the milk, the malted milk powder, and peanut butter. Cover and blend until smooth, stopping to scrape down sides if necessary. Add remaining ice cream; blend until smooth. If necessary, add additional milk until malts are of desired consistency.

2. To serve, spoon into four glasses. Top as desired with marshmallow creme, chopped peanuts, and miniature sandwich cookies. Makes 4 servings.

Per serving without topping: 493 cal., 24 g fat (11 g sat. fat), 47 mg chol., 252 mg sodium, 66 g carbo., 4 g fiber, 11 g pro.

Chocolate Mousse Shakes
Prep: 10 min. Stand: 5 min.

- 1½ cups fat-free milk
- 1 4-serving-size package instant chocolate pudding mix
- 3 tablespoons unsweetened cocoa powder
- 1 teaspoon vanilla
- 3 cups chocolate ice cream
  Sweetened Whipped Cream (optional)
  Shaved semisweet or milk chocolate

1. In a blender, combine milk, pudding mix, cocoa powder, and vanilla. Cover and blend for 1 minute. Gradually add the ice cream, blending until smooth after each addition.

2. Divide shake among four glasses. Let stand for 5 minutes for mixture to thicken slightly. Top with Sweetened Whipped Cream, if desired, and shaved chocolate. Makes 4 servings.

Sweetened Whipped Cream: In a small chilled mixing bowl, whisk ¼ cup whipping cream, 2 teaspoons sugar, and ¼ teaspoon vanilla until soft peaks form.

Per serving: 368 cal., 14 g fat (8 g sat. fat), 41 mg chol., 478 mg sodium, 56 g carbo., 2 g fiber, 8 g pro.

Maple-Glazed Bananas
Start to Finish: 15 min.

¼   cup butter
¼   cup packed brown sugar
¼   cup pure maple syrup or maple-flavor syrup
1   tablespoon lemon juice
½   teaspoon ground cinnamon
3   firm, ripe bananas, halved lengthwise and cut into 1-inch pieces
1   pint vanilla ice cream

1. In heavy medium skillet, melt butter over medium heat. Stir in brown sugar, maple syrup, lemon juice, and cinnamon. Bring to boiling; reduce heat. Simmer, uncovered, for 2 minutes. Add bananas; spoon some of the syrup mixture over bananas. Cook and stir for 1 to 2 minutes more or until heated through. Remove from heat.

2. Scoop ice cream into four dessert dishes. Spoon warm bananas and syrup over top. Makes 4 servings.

Per serving: 471 cal., 24 g fat (15 g sat. fat), 99 mg chol., 135 mg sodium, 64 g carbo., 2 g fiber, 4 g pro.

{ice cream toppers}

There are a variety of fresh and prepared items you can use to top ice cream for a fast dessert that can be customized to everyone's tastes. Sprinkle fresh berries (strawberries, blueberries, raspberries, boysenberries) directly on top or toss them with sugar first. Drizzle a variety of prepared ice cream toppings (hot fudge, caramel, butterscotch, strawberry) on top. Or try jams, peanut butter, lemon curd, or marshmallow creme.

Sparkling Sorbet Floats
Start to Finish: 10 min.

1   pint mango, peach, strawberry, or desired flavor frozen sorbet
  Desired flavor carbonated fruit juice,* chilled

1. Place two scoops of sorbet in each of four 6- to 8-ounce glasses. Fill each glass with carbonated fruit juice. Makes 4 servings.

*Make your own carbonated fruit juice by combining your favorite juice with club soda.

Per serving: 160 cal., 0 g fat (0 g sat. fat), 0 mg chol., 11 mg sodium, 41 g carbo., 1 g fiber, 0 g pro.

{recipe index}

101

174

16

continued on page 190

{index}

continued from page 189

160

Better Homes and Gardens®

Whether you're looking for timesaving recipes, a simple no-fuss meal, or a wide variety of options, Better Homes and Gardens® books have the answer.

A great way to experience the taste and variety of America's favorite cookbook brand.

Fast Fix Family Food has more than 200 family-approved, quick and easy recipes to please everyone in the family.

5-Ingredient Favorites is full of recipes for everything from appetizers to hearty main course meals—all with the flavor of home cooking.

365 Last-Minute Meals features 365 delicious, fast recipes that make it easy to answer the never-ending question "What's for dinner?" with a meal everyone will love.

ADT1019_0308